The Enemy
at Home

ALSO BY DINESH D'SOUZA

Letters to a Young Conservative

What's So Great About America

The Virtue of Prosperity

Ronald Reagan

The End of Racism

Illiberal Education

The Enemy at Home

*The Cultural Left and
Its Responsibility for 9/11*

Dinesh D'Souza

DOUBLEDAY
New York London Toronto Sydney Auckland

PUBLISHED BY DOUBLEDAY

Published in the United States by Doubleday, an imprint
of The Doubleday Broadway Publishing Group,
a division of Random House, Inc., New York.
www.doubleday.com

DOUBLEDAY and the portrayal of an anchor with a dolphin
are registered trademarks of Random House, Inc.

Book design by Nicola Ferguson

Library of Congress Cataloging-in-Publication Data

D'Souza, Dinesh, 1961–
The enemy at home : the cultural left and its responsibility for 9/11 / by Dinesh
D'Souza. — 1st ed.
p. cm.
Includes bibliographical references and index.
1. United States—Foreign relations—2001– 2. War on Terrorism, 2001—Moral
and ethical aspects. 3. Anti-Americanism—Islamic
countries. 4. Liberalism—United States. 5. United States—
Civilization—Foreign public opinion, Muslim. 6. United States—Moral
conditions—Foreign public opinion, Muslim. 7. Popular culture—Moral and
ethical aspects—United States. 8. United States—Relations—Islamic countries.
9. Islamic countries—Relations—United States. I. Title.
E902.D76 2007
973.931—dc22   2006019635

ISBN 978-0-385-51012-7

PRINTED IN THE UNITED STATES OF AMERICA

1   3   5   7   9   10   8   6   4   2

First Edition

For Jim and Gloria Brubaker

with love and appreciation

CONTENTS

ACKNOWLEDGMENTS

This book is the result of a four-year study of America and the West as seen through Muslim eyes. Numerous people in America, Europe, and the Muslim world have helped me with this project, and their names appear throughout this book. If others are nameless, it is because they assisted me while asking me not to use their names. I want to thank my editor, Adam Bellow, with whom I have worked so productively in the past and who has, more than anyone else, steered this book from its earliest conception to the finished product. I am grateful to my employer, the Hoover Institution, and its director, John Raisian, for providing me with the institutional support to do my work. The Rishwains, Bob and Karen, are my sponsors and friends, and I am proud to identify myself as the Rishwain Fellow at the Hoover Institution. I appreciate the long relationship I have had with my agent, Rafe Sagalyn, who negotiates my contracts and also provides valuable suggestions and advice. My research assistants, Michael Hirshman and Pratik Chougule, have proved more mature than their years, and have contributed not only the standard tasks but also substantive criticism and advice. I also wish to thank the following people: C. I. Anderson, Peter Baumbusch, Rob Brendle, Ralph Crump, Kenneth Dahlberg, David Dominguez, Robert Fayfield, Martin Fenton, Foster Friess, Ted Haggard, Mike Hogan, James D. Jameson, John Mackey, Jai Nagarkatti, Harvey Popell, Sam Reeves, William Reiling, Bruce Schooley, Peter Selden, Bob Serenbetz, and Dean Spatz. Finally, I am ever-conscious of the support that I get from my wife, Dixie. She and my daughter, Danielle, are a constant source of love, encouragement, and inspiration.

Shall we expect some transatlantic military giant to step over the ocean and crush us at a blow? Never! All the armies of Europe, Asia and Africa combined, with all the treasure of the earth (our own excepted) in their military chest, with a Bonaparte for a commander, could not by force take a drink from the Ohio, or make a track on the Blue Ridge, in a trial of a thousand years. At what point, then, is the approach of danger to be expected? I answer, if it ever reach us, it must spring up amongst us. It cannot come from abroad. If destruction be our lot, we must ourselves be its author and finisher. As a nation of freemen, we must live through all time, or die by suicide.

Abraham Lincoln

The Enemy
at Home

INTRODUCTION

In THIS BOOK I make a claim that will seem startling at the outset. The cultural left in this country is responsible for causing 9/11. The term "cultural left" does not refer to the Democratic Party. Nor does it refer to all liberals. It refers to the left wing of the Democratic Party—admittedly the most energetic group among Democrats, and the main source of the party's ideas. The cultural left also includes a few Republicans, notably those who adopt a left-wing stance on foreign policy and social issues. Some leading figures in this group are Hillary Clinton, Ted Kennedy, Nancy Pelosi, Barbara Boxer, George Soros, Michael Moore, Bill Moyers, and Noam Chomsky. Moreover, the cultural left includes organizations such as the American Civil Liberties Union, the National Organization for Women, People for the American Way, Planned Parenthood, Human Rights Watch, and moveon.org.

In faulting the cultural left, I am not making the absurd accusation that this group blew up the World Trade Center and the Pentagon. I am saying that the cultural left and its allies in Congress, the media, Hollywood, the nonprofit sector, and the universities are the primary cause of the volcano of anger toward America that is erupting from the Islamic world. The Muslims who carried out the 9/11 attacks were the product of this visceral rage—some of it based on legitimate concerns, some of it based on wrongful prejudice, but all of it fueled and encouraged by the cultural left. Thus without the cultural left, 9/11 would not have happened.

I realize that this is a strong charge, one that no one has made before. But it is a neglected aspect of the 9/11 debate, and it is critical to understanding the current controversy over the "war against terrorism." Here in America, the political right routinely accuses the left of being weak in its response to Islamic terrorism. For example, conservatives often allege that the left's desire to "understand" the roots of Islamic discontent dilutes American resolve in fighting the enemy. If this is true, then fortifying the left's resolve becomes the obvious solution. My argument is quite different. It is that the left is the primary reason for Islamic anti-Americanism as well as the anti-Americanism of other traditional cultures around the world. I intend to show that the left has actively fostered the intense hatred of America that has led to murderous attacks such as 9/11. If I am right, then no war against terrorism can be effectively fought using the left-wing premises that are now accepted doctrine among mainstream liberals and Democrats.

The left is responsible for 9/11 in the following ways. First, the cultural left has fostered a decadent American culture that angers and repulses traditional societies, especially those in the Islamic world that are being overwhelmed with this culture. In addition, the left is waging an aggressive global campaign to undermine the traditional patriarchal family and to promote secular values in non-Western cultures. This campaign has provoked a violent reaction from Muslims who believe that their most cherished beliefs and institutions are under assault. Further, the cultural left has routinely affirmed the most vicious prejudices about American foreign policy held by radical factions in the Muslim world, and then it has emboldened those factions to attack the United States with the firm conviction that "America deserves it" and that they can do so with relative impunity. Absent these conditions, Osama bin Laden would never have launched the 9/11 attacks, nor would the United States today be the target of Islamic radicals throughout the world. Thus when leading figures on the left say, "We made them do this to us," in a sense they are correct. They are not correct that *America* is to blame. But their statement is true in that *their* actions and *their* America are responsible for fostering Islamic anti-Americanism in general and 9/11 in particular.

We cannot understand any of this without rethinking 9/11. Only now, with some distance, are we in a position to understand 9/11 and its implications. So far, we have fundamentally misunderstood the enemy. Even more tragically, we have misunderstood ourselves. The mixed results in the war against terrorism, the stalemate in Iraq, the seemingly inexhaustible supply of suicide bombers bent on killing Americans, and the public anxiety about America's Middle East policy are all the tragic consequence of these errors.

Even so, the errors are understandable. September 11 was a deeply traumatic event. It produced two reactions: "One America" and "Us vs. Them." One America refers to the coming together of the American tribe, and such tribal unity is typically based on emotional displays of patriotism. The second reaction was Us vs. Them—a blind rage toward the enemy. The immediate desire was to annihilate, not understand, the attacker.

The early statements by the Bush administration reflected this unified belligerence. The terrorists are stateless outlaws. They are not Muslims. They are apostates to Islam. True Muslims must denounce them. They are fanatics. They are lunatics. They are suicidal maniacs who don't care about their lives. These themes were echoed across the political spectrum. Now, with reflection and more information, we can see that these statements are false. Specifically, the terrorists were not stateless outlaws. The Al Qaeda training camps were supported by the Taliban government in Afghanistan. As their diaries showed, the terrorists were deeply pious Muslims. Traditional Muslims were reluctant to denounce them as apostates to Islam because they were not apostates to Islam. Nor were they lunatics or even suicidal in the conventional sense. A typical suicide is someone who doesn't want to live. The terrorists wanted to live, but they were willing to die for a cause that they deemed higher. Not that they loved their life less, but they hated America more.

Once the initial shock subsided, so did the national unity it had produced. Soon a heated debate erupted in America about the meaning of 9/11 and the ongoing war against terrorism, a debate that quickly broke down into partisan camps: the left versus the right, the liberals versus the conservatives, Blue America versus Red America. In a moment of genuine indignation, left-wing activist Michael Moore conveyed how large a chasm separates the two Americas. Reacting to 9/11, Moore posted the following message on his Web site. "Many families have been devastated tonight. This is just not right. They did not deserve to die. If someone did this to get back at Bush then they did so by killing thousands of people who DID NOT VOTE for him! Boston, New York, D.C., and the planes' destination of California—these were places that voted AGAINST Bush!"[1] Moore's eruption, read with hindsight, seems slightly comic. It's hard to imagine bin Laden and his associates distinguishing between Bush supporters and Bush opponents for the purpose of launching attacks. The most striking aspect of Moore's statement, however, is its implication that Al Qaeda hit the wrong target: they should have hit Red America, not Blue America! However objectionable this may seem to many Americans, Moore's statement is important because of the connection it instinctively makes between two apparently disparate events: *(a)* the 9/11 attacks and *(b)* the internal divide between Red America and Blue America. I believe that the significance of this divide for understanding 9/11 and the war against terrorism has not been adequately appreciated.

On the other side of the spectrum, the right-wing preacher Jerry Falwell confirmed in equally strong terms his perception of the political divide, even while invoking God's wrath on the sinners in Blue America. "The Lord has protected us so wonderfully these past 225 years," Falwell said. He worried that something "has caused God to lift the veil of protection which has allowed no one to attack America on our soil." Falwell did not shrink from specifying: "The abortionists have got to bear some burden for this because God will not be mocked. I really believe that the pagans, and the abortionists,

and the feminists, and the gays and the lesbians who are actively trying to make that an alternative lifestyle, the ACLU, People for the
American Way, all of them who have tried to secularize America, I
point the finger in their face and say: You helped this happen." Unlike Moore, Falwell was fiercely denounced for his comments, and
he promptly apologized for them.[2]

These words are not insightful in the theological sense that Falwell intended. I cannot make sense of Falwell's suggestion that God
used 9/11 to punish America for its sins. If God was aiming for the
abortionists and the feminists and the homosexuals, it seems he
mostly killed stockbrokers and soldiers and janitors (some of whom
may have been homosexual, but few of whom, probably, had second
jobs as abortionists). The real issue raised by Falwell's comments is
entirely secular. What impact did the abortionists, the feminists, the
homosexual activists, and the secularists have on the Islamic radicals
who conspired to blow up the World Trade Center and the Pentagon? Unfortunately this crucial question got buried, and virtually no
one has raised it publicly.

Why is it so maddeningly difficult, even years after the fact, to
make sense of 9/11? One reason is that the very terms used by both
sides in the debate are misleading. Consider the very name of the
war America is fighting: a "war against terrorism." But America is no
more fighting a war against terrorism than during World War II it
was fighting a "war against kamikazism." No, during World War II
the United States was fighting the armies of imperial Japan. Kamikazism was simply the tactic or strategy used by the enemy. In the
same vein, America today is not fighting against "terrorism." There
are terrorist groups all over the world—the IRA in Northern Ireland,
the Tamil Tigers in Sri Lanka, the Maoist rebels in Nepal, the Revolutionary Armed Forces of Colombia (FARC), the Shining Path guerrillas in Peru. Is America at war with all these groups? Of course not.
The war is against a virulent species of Islamic radicalism. Terrorism
is merely the weapon of choice used by the enemy to intimidate and
kill us. In this sense bin Laden is not so much a terrorist as he is a
religious ideologue who has chosen terrorism as the most effective
way to achieve his goals.

* * *

IT'S TIME TO GO back to the drawing board, and the logical place to start is the debate over 9/11. On the left, scholars like Edward Said, Richard Falk, and Noam Chomsky have argued that 9/11 was the result of Islamic anger over American foreign policy. In this view, echoed by politicians like Ted Kennedy and liberal magazines like *The American Prospect,* the radical Muslims don't hate us because of who we are, they hate us because of what we've done to them. As leftist commentators never tire of pointing out, the West has a long history of colonialism and imperialism. Even today, they say, America one-sidedly supports Israel and props up dictatorial regimes (notably Pakistan, Egypt, and Saudi Arabia) in the Muslim world. The left-wing view can be summed up this way: they are justifiably furious at us because we are the bad guys.

The word in the previous sentence that deserves our most careful attention is "we." When the left says "we" it doesn't mean "we." The left's "we" is not intended as self-incrimination. This is why the conservative complaint about "liberal guilt" is so beside the point. Liberals do not consider themselves guilty in the slightest. When a leftist politician or blogger bemoans "how we overthrew Mossadegh in Iran" or expresses outrage at "what we did at Guantánamo Bay and Abu Ghraib," the speaker does not mean "what I and other people like me did." In formulations like this, "we" really means "you." The apparent confession is really a disguised form of accusation. The liberal's point is that Bush is guilty, conservatives are guilty, America is guilty. Specifically, the liberal is saying to the conservative, "Your America is responsible for this. Your America is greedy, selfish, imperialist. Your America extols the principles of democracy and human rights, but in practice backs savage dictators for the purpose of maintaining American access to Middle Eastern oil." Thus, without saying so directly, the left holds the right and its conduct of American foreign policy responsible for 9/11.

On the social and cultural front, the American left clearly does not approve of the way of life in Muslim countries, particularly those under the sway of Islamic fundamentalism. It is common to see left-wingers walking around with clothes featuring the swashbuckling visage of Che Guevara, but you will never see liberals and leftists wearing T-shirts displaying the raven's stare of Ayatollah Khomeini. Indeed, the left detests the social conservatism that is the hallmark of the whole swath of cultures stretching from the Middle East to China. Those cultures are viewed by many Western liberals as backward, hierarchical, patriarchal, and deeply oppressive. And of these cultures none seem to be more reactionary than Islamic culture. Indeed, the regimes supported by the Islamic fundamentalists are undoubtedly the most illiberal in the modern world. In Iran, for example, the ruling regime routinely imprisons its critics, who are dubbed "enemies of Islam." Public floggings have been used to make an example of women found guilty of fornication. Homosexuality is harshly punished in fundamentalist regimes. The Taliban, for instance, had a range of penalties. As one Taliban leader explained, "One group of scholars believes you should take these people to the top of the highest building in the city, and hurl them to their deaths. The other recommends that you dig a pit near a wall somewhere, put these people into it, and then topple the wall so they are buried alive."[3]

Even so, it is rare to see the illiberal practices of Muslim cultures aggressively denounced by American or European liberals. There are a few notable exceptions, such as Christopher Hitchens and Paul Berman. But in general liberals seem to condemn illiberal regimes only when they are allied with the United States. Nor do liberals seem eager to support American efforts to overthrow hostile, illiberal regimes. Berman, who supported Bush's invasion of Iraq, counts "maybe fifteen or twenty" liberals who shared his position on this issue.[4] If the case of Iraq is any indication, most liberals actively oppose American efforts to use military power to install regimes that are more pro-American and pro-Western and embody a more liberal set of values, such as self-government, minority rights, and religious tolerance. Indeed, the central thrust of the left's foreign policy is to prevent America from forcibly replacing illiberal regimes with more liberal ones. This is a genuine mystery.

Liberal resistance to American foreign policy cannot be explained as a consequence of pacifism or even a reluctance to use force. With the exception of a few fringe figures, the cultural left is not pacifist. Its elected representatives—the Clintons, Ted Kennedy, Nancy Pelosi, Barbara Boxer—frequently support the use of American force. For instance, President Clinton ordered systematic bombings in Bosnia and Kosovo during his terms in office. Clinton's airstrikes were warmly endorsed in speeches by liberal Democrats such as Boxer, Paul Wellstone, David Bonior, and Carl Levin. Cultural liberals routinely call for America to intervene, by force if necessary, in places like Haiti and Rwanda. So liberals are not in principle opposed to regime change or to American intervention.

How, then, can we explain the mystery of liberal opposition to American foreign policy acting to secure liberal principles abroad? Superficially, the left's position can be explained by its attachment to multiculturalism. In other words, liberal antagonism toward the beliefs and mores of traditional cultures is moderated by its conviction "Who are we to judge these cultures?" This concept of withholding judgment is a product of multiculturalism and cultural relativism, both of which are based on the theory that there are no universal standards to judge other cultures. Our standards apply only to us.

But again, this multicultural rhetoric is a smokescreen. Liberal activists mercilessly condemn other regimes and cultures when they are friendly toward the United States. In the past liberals showed no hesitation to condemn the Philippines under Marcos, Nicaragua under Somoza, and even Saddam Hussein's Iraq (as long as America was allied with Hussein during the 1980s). Today liberal congressmen and talk show hosts are quick to deride pro-American despots like Egypt's Mubarak and the Saudi royal family. As a practical matter, liberal multiculturalism inhibits liberal condemnation and liberal judgment only when the regime in question is a sworn enemy of the United States. The suspicion of treason, although distasteful, is inevitable. What else could account for this bizarre double standard? Why would so many liberals oppose American foreign policy actions even when they would advance liberal principles abroad?

Treason is not the problem. To see what is, let us consider two revealing exhibits. The first is a short article by a left-leaning writer,

Kristine Holmgren, that appeared shortly after 9/11. Holmgren wrote, "Even in my waking hours, I am afraid." Was she afraid of a second 9/11-style attack? Not at all. "Nor am I afraid of planes striking my home or my children dying in their beds." What, then, was the source of Holmgren's trepidation? "My fears are more practical," she explained. Here in America, Holmgren wrote, the forces of Christian fundamentalism are gaining strength. They are threatening abortion rights and civil liberties. "My local school district is so afraid of adolescent sexuality, drug use and music videos that they are willing to suspend civil rights to proselytize for Jesus Christ." Holmgren concludes on a grim note: "Fascism crept up on post–World War I Europe with the same soft, calm footsteps it is using these days in the United States."[5] Here in clear view is the cultural left's mind-set. Just two months after 9/11, with its memory still fresh in the national consciousness, Holmgren candidly confesses that she is less scared of bin Laden than she is of Christian activists on her school board. In her view, bin Laden might do episodic damage, but the Christians are on their way to establishing a fascist theocracy in America!

For my second exhibit I offer excerpts from Senator Robert Byrd's recent book *Losing America*. In an early chapter, Byrd faults President Bush for his repeated references to the Islamic radicals as evil. "Presidents must measure their words and look past such raw simplicities," Byrd opined. "The notion of 'evil' and 'evildoers' tends to set one faith against another and could be seen as a slur on the Islamic faith. Bush's draconian 'them' versus 'us,' 'good' and 'evil,' serves little purpose other than to divide and inflame."[6] On the face of it, this passage seems to suggest Byrd's high-minded objection to using crude terms like "good" and "evil" to describe the world we live in. Byrd's point is that even if those labels are superficially descriptive, we should avoid them because they create unnecessary hostility and division.

A little later on in Byrd's book, however, we find Byrd comparing President Bush to Hermann Goering and the Nazis. Byrd accuses Bush of "capitalizing on the war for political purposes—using the war as a tool to win elections," which is "an affront to the men and women we are sending to fight and die in a foreign land and without good reason." Moreover, Byrd charges Bush with "a political gambit to keep the American people fearful" through a strategy of "silencing opposition" and diverting people's attention toward the war on terror and away from "the country's festering problems."[7] Now, if these charges are true—if Bush has concocted an unnecessary war that causes the deaths of American citizens for no reason other than to benefit himself politically—then he deserves impeachment and everlasting disgrace. Indeed, in some ways Bush would be worse than Goering because at least Goering believed in a cause larger than himself.

By these accusations, Byrd forces us to revise our interpretation of his earlier words. He shows, by implication rather than outright suggestion, that he *agrees* with Bush that some people are fundamentally evil and they deserve to be treated as such. Only, in Byrd's analysis it is the Bush administration and its allies, rather than the Islamic radicals, who are the genuinely evil force in the world. Thus dividing and inflaming, which Byrd thinks a harsh and self-defeating strategy in dealing with Islamic fundamentalism, is precisely Byrd's strategy in dealing with the Bush administration.

These examples show the wrongheadedness of the insinuation of liberal treachery. Holmgren and Byrd don't hate America. What they hate is *conservative America*. The two are fiercely loyal to the American values that they cherish, and it is in the name of those values that they are ready to take on the Bush administration. The lesson of these examples is that the cultural left is unwilling to fight a serious and sustained battle against Islamic radicalism and fundamentalism because it is fighting a more threatening political battle against American conservatism and American fundamentalism. The left cannot support Bush's efforts to promote liberal democracy abroad because it is more important for the left to reverse the nation's conservative tide by defeating Bush and his socially conservatives allies at home. In other words, the left's war is not against bearded Muslims who wear long robes and carry rifles; it is against pudgy white men who wear suits and carry Bibles. While the left is certainly not comfortable with Islamic mullahs, it is vastly more terrified of

George Bush, Dick Cheney, Antonin Scalia, James Dobson, and Rush Limbaugh.

Why? From the vantage point of many liberals, *our* fundamentalists are as dangerous as *their* fundamentalists, and President Bush is no less a threat than bin Laden. Author Salman Rushdie, who should know something about this topic, asserts that "the religious fundamentalism of the United States is as alarming as anything in the much-feared world of Islam." Columnist Maureen Dowd accused the Bush administration of following the lead of Islamic fundamentalists in "replacing science with religion, and facts with faith," and creating in the process "jihad in America . . . a scary, paranoid, regressive reality." Author and illustrator Art Spiegelman asserts, "We're equally threatened by Al Qaeda and our own government." Pursuing the analogy between Islamic fundamentalists and the Bush administration, columnist Wendy Kaminer described 9/11 as a "faith-based initiative."[8]

But if the left sees Christian fundamentalism in the same way as Islamic fundamentalism, why doesn't it fight the two with equal resolution? If Bush is as bad as bin Laden, why not expend equal effort to get rid of both? In reality, the cultural left is more indignant over Bush's Christian fundamentalism than over bin Laden's Islamic fundamentalism. Activist Cindy Sheehan makes this clear when she alleges that "the biggest terrorist in the world is George W. Bush." Other leading figures on the left endorse the view that Bush and his supporters, not bin Laden and Al Qaeda, are the real problem. Social critic Edward Said, who spent most of his career warning of the dangers of overestimating the threat of Islamic extremism, warned in a recent book that "the vast number of Christian fanatics in the United States," who form "the core of George Bush's support," now represent "a menace to the world." Jonathan Raban writes, "The greatest military power in history has shackled its deadly hardware to the rhetoric of fundamentalist Christianity." Writer Jane Smiley finds the people who voted for Bush to be "predatory and resentful, amoral, avaricious, and arrogant. . . . They are full of original sin and have a taste for violence." Eric Alterman fumes in *The Nation*, "Extremist right-wingers enjoy a stranglehold on our political system."

Author Jonathan Schell insists that "Bush's abuses of presidential power are the most extensive in American history." Author Garry Wills alleges that the Bush administration "weaves together a chain of extremisms encircling the polity . . . forming a necklace to choke the large body of citizens." There is no indication that these liberal authorities regard Islamic fundamentalism with anything approaching this degree of alarm.[9]

The rhetoric of left-wing political leaders is equally revealing. In examining speeches by Ted Kennedy, Hillary Clinton, Nancy Pelosi, and Edward Markey, I am struck by what may be called "the indignation gap"—the vastly different level of emotion that the speakers employ in treating bin Laden and his allies as opposed to Bush and his allies. At first the speaker will offer a ritual condemnation of Osama bin Laden and Al Qaeda: "I am no fan of Osama Bin Laden." "We can agree that Bin Laden is not a very nice guy." Having gotten those qualifications out of the way, the left-wing politician will spend the rest of the speech lambasting the Bush conservatives with uncontrolled belligerence and ferocity. In recent addresses Senator Kennedy denounced "the rabid reactionary religious right" and maintained that "no president in America's history has done more damage to our country than George W. Bush." Senator Hillary Clinton accuses the Bush White House and the Republican Congress of "systematically weakening the democratic traditions and institutions on which this country was built. They are turning back the clock on the twentieth-century. There has never been an administration . . . more intent upon consolidating and abusing power. It's very hard to stop people who have no shame . . . who have never been acquainted with the truth." Congressman Edward Markey darkly warned, "They wish to wipe us out."[10]

The "us" that Markey is concerned about here is not Americans in general but specifically liberals and leftists. Here, then, is a revealing clue to the motives of the left. Many in this camp are more exercised by Bush than they are about bin Laden because, as they see it, Islamic fundamentalism threatens to impose illiberal values abroad while American fundamentalism of the Bush type threatens to impose illiberal values at home. As leading figures on the left see it, the Islamic extremists pose a danger to the freedom and lifestyle of *others*, while their American equivalents pose a danger to *us*. Thus, for the left, the enemy at home is far more consequential and frightening than the enemy abroad.

I WANT TO say more about these liberal fears, but first I want to say a word about the conservative, or right-wing, understanding of 9/11. It is a common belief on the right that many Muslims—perhaps most Muslims—hate America because of a deep religious and cultural divide between our civilization and theirs. In this view, popularized by scholars such as Bernard Lewis and Samuel Huntington, Western civilization stands for modern values such as prosperity, freedom, and democracy, which the Muslim world rejects. In this conservative view, Islamic radicals lash out at us because they blame us for problems of poverty and tyranny that are actually the fault of Muslims themselves. One variant of this position holds that the radical Muslims are simply envious of American wealth and power.

How, then, do conservatives think America should respond to Muslim antagonism? Some on the right, like Pat Buchanan, as well as some libertarians, argue that the best way for America to protect itself from Muslim rage is to withdraw from the Middle East—to retreat behind our own borders. But the majority on the right, led by the Bush administration, insists that America has no choice but to fight the Islamic radicals, because if we don't defeat them over there, they will bring the battle to us here. Most conservatives seem to agree with Bush that war is the best and only option. The general view on the right is that bin Laden and the Islamic radicals don't despise us for what we do, they despise us for who we are. As President Bush has said, on various occasions, "They hate us because of our freedom."

Is this really true? There is no evidence that Muslims—or even the Islamic fundamentalists—hate the West because the West is modern, or because the West embodies technology, prosperity, and democracy. There is a universal desire for prosperity in today's world, and the Islamic world is no exception. Moreover, Islamic fun-

damentalists are not opposed to technology; it is technology that enables them to build bombs and fly planes into buildings. Many Al
Qaeda operatives have scientific and technical (as opposed to religious) training. Even among Islamic fundamentalists, freedom is
rarely condemned, and the term is often used in a positive sense, as
in "Let us free ourselves from Western domination" or "Let us liberate Muslim land from Israeli occupation." Finally, there is widespread support for democracy in the Muslim world. While bin Laden
is an enemy of democracy, most of the organizations of radical Islam,
including Hamas, Hezbollah, and the Muslim Brotherhood, have become champions of democracy. The reason is quite simple: the Islamic radicals have seen that if their countries have free elections,
their group can win!

Shortly after the fall of Baghdad, graffiti began to appear on the
walls of the city and its environs. The following scrawl caught my attention. "Marriage of the same sex became legal in America. Is this,
with the mafia and drugs, what you want to bring to Iraq, America?
Is this the freedom you promised?" Even if the source of this statement is of little consequence, the content is revealing. It is not an objection to freedom, but to the kind of freedom associated with drug
legalization and homosexual marriage. As such, it is a vital clue to the
sources of Muslim rage. And here is a quote from a recent videotape
by Ayman al-Zawahiri, deputy of bin Laden and reputed mastermind
of the 9/11 attacks: "The freedom we want is not the freedom to use
women as a commodity to gain clients, win deals, or attract tourists;
it is not the freedom of AIDS and an industry of obscenities and homosexual marriages; it is not the freedom of Guantanamo and Abu
Ghraib."[11]

What these statements convey is that these Islamic radicals do not
hate America because of its wealth and power; they hate America
because of how Americans use that wealth and power. They do not
hate us for our freedom; they hate us because of what we do with
our freedom. The radical Muslims are convinced that America and
Europe have become sick, demented societies that destroy religious
belief, undermine traditional morality, dissolve the patriarchal family, and corrupt the innocence of children. The term that Islamic rad-

icals use to describe Western influence is *firangi*. The term means "Frankish" disease, and it refers to syphilis, a disease that Europeans first introduced to the Middle East.[12] Today Muslims use the term in a metaphorical sense, to describe the social and moral corruption produced by the virus of Westernization.

The Muslims who hate us the most are the ones who have encountered Western decadence, either in the West or in their own countries. The revealing aspect of the 9/11 terrorists is not that so many came from Saudi Arabia, but that so many of them, like the ringleader, Muhammad Atta, and his Hamburg group, had lived in and been exposed to the West. My point is that their hatred was not a product of ignorance but of familiarity; not of Wahhabi indoctrination but of firsthand observation.

But isn't it true, as many Americans believe, that American culture is broadly appealing around the world? Yes, and this is precisely why America and not Europe is the main target of the Islamic radicals. Decadence is arguably far worse in Europe than in America, and Europe has had its share of attacks, such as the Madrid train bombing of 2004 and the London subway bombing of 2005. But even in those cases the European targets were picked because of their governments' support for America. The Islamic radicals focus on America because they recognize that it is the leader of Western civilization or, as they sometimes put it, "the greatest power of the unbelievers." Bin Laden himself said in a 1998 interview, "What prompted us to address the American government is the fact that it is the head of the Western and crusading forces in their fight against Islam and against Muslims."[13] Moreover, Muslims realize that it is American culture and values that are penetrating the far corners of the globe, corroding ancient orthodoxies, and transforming customs and institutions. Many Americans, whatever their politics, generally regard such change as healthy and good. But this attitude is not shared in traditional societies, and it is virtually nonexistent in the Muslim world. America is feared and despised there not in spite of its cultural allure but because of it.

An anecdote will illustrate my point. Some time ago I saw an interview with a Muslim sheikh on a European TV channel. The interviewer told the sheikh, "I find it curious and hypocritical that you are so anti-American, considering that two of your relatives are living and studying in America." The sheikh replied, "But this is not hypocritical at all. I concede that American culture is appealing, especially to young people. If you put a young man into a hotel room and give him dozens of pornography tapes, he is likely to find those appealing as well. What America appeals to is everything that is low and disgusting in human nature."

There seems to be a growing belief in traditional cultures—a belief encouraged but by no means created by Islamic fundamentalism—that America is materially prosperous but culturally decadent. It is technologically sophisticated but morally depraved. As former Pakistani prime minister Benazir Bhutto puts it, "Within the Muslim world, there is a reaction against the sexual overtones that come across in American mass culture. America is viewed through this prism as an immoral society." In his book *The Crisis of Islam,* Bernard Lewis rehearses what he calls the "standard litany of American offenses recited in the lands of Islam" and ends with this one: "Yet the most powerful accusation of all is the degeneracy and debauchery of the American way of life."[14] As these observations suggest, what angers religious Muslims is not the American Constitution but the scandalous sexual mores they see in American movies and television. What disgusts them is not free elections but the sights of hundreds of homosexuals kissing one another and taking marriage vows. The person that horrifies them the most is not John Locke but Hillary Clinton.

In other cultures—China, Nigeria, India—there are similar concerns that American culture and values are destroying the moral basis of those traditional societies. This resistance is summed up in a slogan often used by Singapore's former prime minister Lee Kuan Yew: "Modernization Without Westernization."[15] What this means is that traditional cultures want prosperity and technology, but they don't want to become like America. The Islamic fundamentalists are the most extreme and politically mobilized segment of this global resistance. What distinguishes them is the depth of their repulsion and their willingness to fight and to die to eradicate American influence from their part of the world.

Their main motive is the belief that the fate of Islam is at stake. Bin Laden in one of his videos said that Islam faces the greatest threat it has faced since Muhammad.[16] How could he possibly think this? Not because of U.S. troops in Mecca. Not even because of Israel. The threat bin Laden is referring to is an infiltration of American values and mores into the life of Muslims, transforming their society and destroying their religious beliefs. Even the term "Great Satan," so commonly used to denounce America in the Muslim world, is better understood when we recall that in the traditional understanding, shared by Judaism, Christianity, and Islam, Satan is not a conqueror; he is a tempter. In one of its best-known verses, the Koran describes Satan as "the insidious one who whispers into the hearts of men."

THESE CONCERNS PROMPT a startling thought—are the radical Muslims right? Is America a threat to the traditional cultures of the world? Is American culture a worldwide destroyer of morals? Do American values undermine the traditional family and corrupt the innocence of children? Many Americans are likely to indignantly answer, "No." Conservatives are no less reluctant than liberals to admit that some radical Muslims may have valid objections to American society. Patriotism itself seems to demand an American response that highlights the horrors of Islamic behavior: "Look how your religion inspires terrorists to kill women and children!" "Look how you oppress women!" As broad judgments on Muslim society, these charges reflect a narrow and somewhat prejudiced view of Islamic culture. But even if the charges were true, they would hardly constitute a vindication of American culture.

We should not dismiss the Islamic or traditional critique so easily. In fact, as our own domestic and cultural debate shows, we know that many of the concerns raised by the radical Muslims are widely shared in our own society. Many conservative and religious Americans agree with the Islamic fundamentalists that American culture has become increasingly vulgar, trivial, and disgusting. I am referring not merely to the reality shows where contestants eat maggots, or the talk shows where guests reveal the humiliating details of their sex lives. I am referring also to "high culture," to liberal culture that offers itself as refined and sophisticated.

Here, for example, is a brief excerpt from Eve Ensler's *Vagina Monologues,* a play that won rave reviews and Hollywood accolades and is now routinely performed (according to its own publicity materials) in more than twenty countries, including China and Turkey. In the book version of the play—now sold in translation in Pakistan, India, and Egypt—Ensler offers what she terms "vagina occurrences": "Glenn Close gets 2,500 people to stand up and chant the word *cunt.* . . . There is now a Cunt Workshop at Wesleyan University. . . . Roseanne performs 'What Does Your Vagina Smell Like?' in her underwear for two thousand people. . . . Alanis Morissette and Audra McDonald sing the cunt piece."[17] And so on. If all of this makes many Americans uncomfortable and embarrassed—which may be part of Ensler's objective—one can only imagine how it is received in traditional cultures where the public recitation of such themes and language is considered a grotesque violation of manners and morals. Nor is Ensler an extreme example. If the garbage heap of American excess leaves many Americans feeling dirty and defiled at home, what gives America the right to dump it on the rest of the world?

The debate over popular culture points to a deeper issue. For the past quarter century we have been having a culture war in this country, which has, until now, been viewed as a debate with only domestic ramifications. I believe that it has momentous global consequences as well. When we debate hot-button issues like abortion, school prayer, divorce, and gay marriage, we are debating two radically different views of liberty and morality. Issues like divorce and family breakdown are important in themselves, yet they are ultimately symptoms of a great moral shift that has occurred in American society, one that continues to divide and polarize this country, and one that is at the root of the anti-Americanism of traditional cultures.

The shift can be described in this way. Some years ago I read Tom Brokaw's book *The Greatest Generation*, which describes the virtues of the World War II generation. I asked myself whether this was truly the "greatest" generation. Was it greater than the generation of the American founding? Greater than the Civil War generation? I don't think so. The significant thing about the World War II generation is that it was the *last* generation. Last in what way? It was the last generation to embrace an external code of traditional morality. Indeed, this generation's great failure is that it was unable to inculcate this moral code in its children. Thus the frugal, self-disciplined, deferred-gratification generation of World War II produced the spoiled children of the 1960s—the Clinton generation.

From the American founding until World War II, there was a widespread belief in this country that there is a moral order in the universe that makes claims on us. This belief was not unique to Americans. It was shared by Europeans since the very beginning of Western civilization, and it is held even today by all the traditional cultures of the world. The basic notion is that morality is external to us and is binding on us. In the past, Americans and Europeans, being for the most part Christian, might disagree with Hindus and Muslims about the exact source of this moral order, its precise content, or how a society should convert its moral beliefs into legal and social practice. But there was little doubt across the civilizations of the world about the existence of such an order. Moreover, laws and social norms typically reflected this moral consensus. During the first half of the twentieth century, the moral order generated some clear American social norms: *Go to church. Be faithful to your wife. Support your children. Go when your country calls.* And so on. The point is not that everyone lived up to the dictates of the moral code, but that it supplied a standard, accepted virtually throughout society, for how one should act.

What has changed in America since the 1960s is the erosion of belief in an external moral order. This is the most important political fact of the past half century. I am not saying that most Americans today reject morality. I am saying that there has been a great shift in the source of morality. Today there is no longer a moral consensus in American society. Many Americans locate morality not in a set of external commands but in the imperatives of their own heart. For them, morality is not "out there" but "in here." While many Americans continue to believe in the old morality, there is now a new morality in America, which may be called the morality of the inner self, the morality of self-fulfillment.

Here, at the deepest level, is the divide between conservatives and liberals, between Red America and Blue America. Conservatives believe in traditional morality. Liberals believe in personal autonomy and self-fulfillment. And liberals have been winning the culture war in the sense that they have been able to produce a massive transformation of American society and culture along the lines of their new moral code. My point is not that liberals would approve of all the grossness and sensuality of contemporary popular culture, but that the liberal promotion of autonomy, individuality, and self-fulfillment as moral ideals make it impossible to question or criticize or place limits on these cultural trends. In the moral code of self-fulfillment, "pushing the envelope," or testing the borders of sexual and moral tolerance, becomes a virtue, and fighting for traditional morality becomes a form of repression or vice.

To American liberals, the great social revolution of the past few decades—with its 1.5 million abortions a year, with one in two marriages ending in divorce, with homosexuality coming out of the closet and now seeking full social recognition and approval—is viewed through the prism of an expansion of civil liberties, "freedom of choice," and personal autonomy. Thus it is seen as a moral achievement. But viewed from the perspective of people in the traditional societies of the world, notably the Muslim world, these same trends appear nothing less than the shameless promotion of depravity. So it is not surprising to see pious Muslims react with horror at the prospect of this new American morality seeping into their part of the world. They fear that this new morality will destroy their religion and way of life—and they are quite right!

Osama bin Laden chose his words carefully when he said that 9/11 was an attempt to scorch "the head of the snake." In the view of the Islamic radicals, America is the embodiment of pagan depravity. According to bin Laden, this is why religious Muslims must stop fighting local battles and concentrate on destroying Satan's empire on earth. This is seen as nothing less than a divine mission. In bin Laden's words, 9/11 showed "America struck by Almighty God in its vital organs."[18] For the Islamic radicals, 9/11 was a message to America that said: Your America is a repulsive sewer. This sewer is now pouring itself into the rest of the world. We will fight to the death to keep it out of our part of the globe. In fact, we will fight in any way we can until every vestige of your sick, demented culture is eradicated from the holy ground of Islam. We may be poor and oppressed, but we would rather be poor and oppressed than become the immoral, perverted society that America has become. So get the hell out of the Middle East, because you represent the values of the Devil.

THUS WE HAVE the first way in which the cultural left is responsible for 9/11. The left has produced a moral shift in American society that has resulted in a deluge of gross depravity and immorality. This deluge threatens to engulf our society and is imposing itself on the rest of the globe. The Islamic radicals are now convinced that America represents the revival of pagan barbarism in the world, and 9/11 represents their ongoing battle with what they perceive to be the forces of Satan.

I have focused so far on American cultural depravity and its global impact. But there is a second way in which the cultural left has helped to produce 9/11. In the domain of foreign policy, the left has helped to produce the conditions that led to the destruction of the Pentagon and the World Trade Center. First, under Jimmy Carter, the liberals helped to get rid of the shah and to install the Khomeini regime in Iran. The pretext was the shah's human rights failings, but the result was the abdication of the shah and the triumph of Khomeini. The Khomeini revolution, which has proved the viability of Islamic theocracy in the modern age, was the match that lit the conflagration of radicalism and fundamentalism throughout the Muslim world. It is Khomeini's success that paved the road to 9/11.

During the Clinton administration, liberal foreign policy conveyed to bin Laden and his coconspirators a strong impression of American vacillation, weakness, and even cowardice. When Al Qaeda attacked and killed a handful of marines in Mogadishu in 1993, the Clinton administration withdrew American troops from Somalia. When Al Qaeda orchestrated the bombings of the American embassies in East Africa in 1998 and the attack on the USS *Cole* in 2000, President Clinton responded with desultory counterstrikes that did little harm to Al Qaeda. These American actions, bin Laden has confessed, emboldened him to strike directly at America on September 11, 2001.

Now that America is fighting back, seeking to uproot the terrorists and transform the political landscape in the Middle East, the left is fighting hard to prevent that campaign from succeeding. It does so not simply by resisting at every stage whatever actions are proposed and implemented to win the war, but, just as important, by unceasingly fueling the hatred of American foreign policy among Muslims. It is a common belief among Muslims, for example, that the main reason America consistently sides with Israel is that Americans hate Muslims. A Muslim lawyer I interviewed in Tunis puts the matter this way: "I keep hearing," he says, "that countries base their foreign policy on self-interest. The self-interest of America is in obtaining access to oil, and we are the ones who have all the oil. The Israelis don't have any oil. So why is America always on the side of Israel and against the Muslims? Please don't tell me it's because Israel is America's only friend in the Middle East. After all, Israel is one of the main reasons why so many Muslims are America's enemy. So I am forced to conclude that there is only one reason why America acts against its self-interest and backs Israel. The reason is that Americans hate Muslims. America is violently opposed to Islam. So the Christians are making allies with the Jews to get rid of Islam."

This is a relatively articulate expression of one of the central themes of fundamentalist propaganda. The argument is that America is a bigoted nation that wants to take over Muslim countries and steal their oil. In reality this claim is absurd. Americans do not hate Muslims, and America does not want to occupy the Muslim world or seize its natural resources. America supports Israel for complex reasons of history, common ideology, and the domestic political influence of Jewish Americans. So this Islamic perception of American foreign policy is utterly wrong. But it is routinely confirmed by the American left. The writings of leading leftists affirm that, yes, America is a racist power that wants to conquer and plunder non-Western peoples. Political scientist Anne Norton writes that anti-Muslim bigotry is now "the unacknowledged cornerstone of American foreign policy." Legal scholar Mari Matsuda insists that "the history of hating Arabs as a race runs strong in the United States," where Arabs are "reviled even more than blacks." Rashid Khalidi contends that America's actions are based on "wildly inaccurate and often racist stereotypes about Arabs, Islam, and the Middle East." Writing in the Egyptian newspaper *Al-Ahram*, Edward Said claims that "for decades in America there has been a cultural war against the Arabs and Islam" and that America's Middle East policy is based on blind hatred for stereotypical "sheikhs and camel jockeys."[19] By confirming Muslims in their worst prejudices, the American left has strengthened their conviction that America is evil and deserves to be destroyed.

To repeat—because this is a point on which I do not wish to be misunderstood—I am in no sense suggesting that the left is disloyal to America. To say this is to confuse the success of the Bush administration, or even of American foreign policy, with the interest of the country as a whole. As we saw earlier with Senator Byrd, the left has its own view of what's good for America, and it is fiercely loyal to that ideal. So disloyalty is not the issue. The issue is why the left is so passive, reluctant, and even oppositional in its stance in the American war on terrorism. My answer is that the cultural left opposes the war against the radical Muslims because it wants them to succeed in defeating President Bush in particular and American foreign policy in general. Far from seeking to destroy the movement that bin Laden and the Islamic radicals represent, the American left is secretly allied with that movement to undermine the Bush administration and American foreign policy. The left would like nothing better than to see America in general, and President Bush in particular, forced out of Iraq. Although such an outcome would plunge

Iraq into further chaos and represent a catastrophic loss for American foreign policy, it would represent a huge win for the cultural left, in fact the left's greatest foreign policy victory since the Vietnam War.

The notion that the American left seeks victory for Islamic radicals in Iraq may at first glance seem implausible. One person who does not think so, however, is bin Laden. In his October 30, 2004, videotaped message, apparently timed to precede the presidential election, bin Laden drew liberally from themes in Michael Moore's *Fahrenheit 9/11* to condemn the Bush administration. Bin Laden denounced Bush for election rigging in Florida, for going to war to enrich oil companies and contractors like Halliburton, for curtailing civil liberties under the Patriot Act, and for reading stories to schoolchildren while the World Trade Center burned.[20] Apart from the rhetorical flourishes of "Praise be to Allah," bin Laden sounds exactly like Michael Moore. And why not? In opposing President Bush and American foreign policy, they are both on the same side.

Moreover, several leading figures on the left are very candid about what they are fighting for. Moore writes, "The Iraqis who have risen up against the occupation are not 'insurgents' or 'terrorists' or 'the enemy.' They are the Revolution, the Minutemen, and their numbers will grow—and they will win." Author James Carroll commends the insurgents for exemplifying "the simple stubbornness of human beings who refuse to be told what to think and feel." Writing in salon.com, Joe Conason calls on Bush to enter into a "negotiated settlement" with the Iraqi insurgents, an outcome Conason concedes would be a "defeat for the United States and a perceived victory for Al Qaeda and its allies." Gwynne Dyer states in a recent book, "The United States needs to lose the war in Iraq as soon as possible. Even more urgently, the whole world needs the United States to lose the war in Iraq." Activist Arundhati Roy declares on behalf of the left, "We must consider ourselves at war."[21] What she means is that the left is fighting a political battle not against Al Qaeda or Islamic fundamentalism but rather against the Bush administration.

In placing the cultural left and the Islamic fundamentalists on the same side, I am not trying to score a partisan or even an ideological point. In fact, if the political left and the Islamic fundamentalists are in the same foreign policy camp, then by the same token the political right and the Islamic fundamentalists are on the same wavelength on social issues. The left is allied with some radical Muslims in opposition to American foreign policy, and the right is allied with an even larger group of Muslims in their opposition to American social and cultural depravity. This is the essential new framework I propose for understanding American foreign policy and American social issues. I conclude by spelling out the implications of these alignments for American conservatives.

In a way, conservatives are in the best position to understand why traditional cultures fear and hate America. That's because conservatives share many of the moral concerns of traditional people. The right should not be deaf to complaints about the dissolution of religious and family ties, because it worries about those things in this country. The right understands the implications of the erosion of traditional morality, because it has seen the consequences of that erosion in the United States. Thus the right can play an important mediating role in helping America and the traditional cultures of Asia, Africa, and Latin America to understand one another better.

But so far the right has kept its blinders on since 9/11. The isolationist right labors under the illusion that America can retreat behind its borders and fight a one-front battle against the cultural left at home. As a practical matter, this is foolish. Islamic hatred of America will not go away if American troops come home, because this hatred is not based on the presence of American troops abroad. Hasty withdrawals from Afghanistan or Iraq will further embolden bin Laden and his allies and make the United States less, not more, safe.

The right's myopia, however, is not confined to the Buchanan and libertarian wings. Mainstream conservatives (including the Bush administration) understand better the military need to take the war to the enemy, and also appreciate that there is a political battle to be fought against the left at home. But most conservatives do not see how these two battles are related to each other. Moreover, the Bush administration is wrong to see the war against Islamic radicalism as a purely military operation. The military component is indispensable, but it is not sufficient to achieve victory. The reason the war seems endless is that the ranks of the enemy continue to grow. It is simply not possible to kill all the terrorists, because the engine of Islamic rage is powerful enough to keep generating more of them. The only way to win the war is to create a wedge between Islamic radicals and traditional Muslims, and to support traditional Islam against radical Islam.

To date, the Bush administration has made no serious attempt to articulate the moral case for American foreign policy to Muslims (or to anyone else). Many conservatives compound the problem by defending American decadence against the foreigners who hate and fear it. Shortly after 9/11, the Bush administration began consulting Hollywood executives and Madison Avenue executives to market "brand America" abroad. To this day the administration persists with this foolishness. Strangely enough what the administration is promoting are liberal solutions—separation of church and state, feminism, and the idea of the working woman—together with the debased values of American popular culture. Of course these "solutions" only compound the problem. They further alienate traditional Muslims and push them toward the fundamentalist camp. So the liberals are correct that U.S. policy is "creating more terrorists"—but not for the reasons they think.

The Bush administration and the conservatives must stop uncritically promoting American popular culture, because it is producing a blowback of Muslim rage. With a few exceptions, the right should not bother to defend American movies, music, and television. From the point of view of traditional values, they are indefensible. Moreover, why should the right stand up for the left's debased values? Why should *our* people defend *their* America? Rather, American conservatives should join the Muslims and others in condemning the global moral degeneracy that is produced by liberal values.

American foreign policy should stand up for liberal values, but not for the liberal values associated with the cultural left. Rather, it must work to promote classical liberal ideas abroad. As conservatives, we should export our America. That means introducing in places like Iraq the principles of self-government, majority rule, minority rights, free enterprise, and religious toleration. There are also healthy aspects of American culture that we can be proud to share with the rest of the world. But we must stop exporting the cultural left's America. That means we should stop insisting on radical secularism, stop promoting the feminist conception of the family, stop trying to promote abortion and "sex education," and we should try to halt the export of the vulgar and corrupting elements of our popular culture. When we cannot do these things, we should apologize to the rest of the world and make it clear that we too find a good deal in this culture to be embarrassing and disgusting.

There is no "clash of civilizations" between Islam and the West. But there are two clashes of civilizations that are shaping the world today. The first is a clash between liberal and conservative values within America. The second is a clash between traditional Islam and radical Islam, a clash within Islamic society. So, realize it or not, American conservatives are fighting a two-front war. The first is a war against Islamic radicalism and fundamentalism. The second is a political struggle against the left and its pernicious political and moral influence in America and around the globe. My conclusion is that the two wars are intimately connected. In fact, we cannot win the first war without also winning the second war.

ONE

Illusions on the Right

*What Conservatives "Know" About 9/11,
and Why It's Wrong*

THE REASON AMERICA'S "war on terrorism" is imperiled is that there is no clear sense of who the enemy is. Is Al Qaeda the problem? A network of terrorist groups operating through the Al Qaeda "franchise"? State-sponsored terrorism? Weapons of mass destruction in the hands of hostile states? Or is Islamic fundamentalism to blame, since it appears to be the incubator of terrorism? Or is the West facing a very old enemy, Islam itself?

Not only is the identity of the enemy obscure; many Americans also have no idea why these people are so murderously hostile to the United States. Five years after 9/11, most people still have little sense of what would cause a bunch of men to want to blow themselves up in order to smash the Pentagon and topple the World Trade Center. The *9/11 Commission Report,* for all its length and lucidity, only describes how the grisly event occurred but gives no coherent explanation for why it occurred.

Americans—including the U.S. government—also seem confused about what is the overall objective of the enemy. Terror for its own sake? U.S. troops out of Mecca? The destruction of the state of Israel?

Islamic control of the Middle East? World domination? Moreover, since the enemy's goals are unknown, it is virtually impossible to figure out its strategy; about all that seems known is that terrorism is one of its components. Without reliable knowledge of what the enemy wants and how it intends to achieve its goal, it seems virtually impossible to have an effective counterstrategy, either at home or abroad. In addition, America's people and leaders are deeply divided about whether this is a war with an end point, over what would constitute "success," and over whether success is even possible in this new kind of war.

No nation ever won a war under these conditions. Therefore, the crisis of the war against terrorism is primarily an intellectual crisis, a crisis of understanding. To fight this war better it is necessary to understand it better. Therefore let us return to the beginning, to the cataclysmic attack that launched this new war for a new century.

Approximately five years after 9/11, we know a great deal about that nightmarish event. Many Americans actually saw it happen. If you were watching television the morning of September 11, 2001, you would have had your programming interrupted shortly before 9 A.M. That's when the first plane hit the North Tower of the World Trade Center. Word spread rapidly, and millions of Americans were riveted to their TV sets when, a few minutes later, a second plane flew directly into the South Tower. The sight of the slow-motion collapse of these two landmarks of the New York skyline, with chaos everywhere and people running for their lives, will long remain etched on the national psyche. One of the most gruesome symbols of 9/11 was the sight of people jumping out of windows, preferring to fall to their deaths rather than be roasted alive in the fiery inferno. Soon Americans discovered that a third plane had slammed into the northwest side of the Pentagon, and a fourth, headed for an unknown destination, had crashed in a field in Pennsylvania. As the magnitude of the disaster slowly registered, Americans saw heroic scenes of firefighters trying to rescue survivors, and poignant portraits of desperate New Yorkers trying to locate family members, hanging on to the slender hope that they had made it out of the burning buildings alive. Here is a typical plea, taken from a collection of recordings from the 9/11 archive: "If anyone has any idea, or if they've seen him or know where he is, call us. He's got two little babies. Two little babies."

It was the worst day in American history, worse than Pearl Harbor, worse even than Gettysburg. Those were military catastrophes, one of them off American shores, in which soldiers killed soldiers. By contrast, 9/11 was an attack on the American mainland; it was an attack on the core institutions of America, and it took nearly three thousand lives, the vast majority of them civilians. The Cold War lasted for decades, cost hundreds of billions of dollars, and confronted Americans with the prospect of nuclear annihilation, but fewer Americans were killed over the entire duration of the Cold War than perished on a single day in September 2001. What made 9/11 even more sobering was the recognition that its perpetrators intended to blow up the White House or the Capitol—the apparent destination of the fourth plane—and they meant to kill a lot more people. Nearly fifty thousand people worked in the World Trade Center, and the death toll from 9/11 could have been much higher.

Today, with the perspective of hindsight, and thanks to the detailed government investigation that culminated in *The 9/11 Commission Report*, we have a lot of information about 9/11. We know a great deal about what happened and how it happened. We know that the original plan, proposed by Khalid Sheikh Mohammed, called for the hijacking of ten planes to be crashed into targets on both coasts.[1] (Bin Laden settled for the final plan that was executed on September 11.) We can follow the movements of the terrorists in the period leading up to 9/11. We have a detailed account of what they did that day: where and when they boarded the planes, when they spoke to one another, what they carried with them, and what they left behind in their rooms. The report has a moment-by-moment description of the climactic denouement. We can read heartbreaking transcripts of passengers calling family members to say "I love you," and, "Good-bye." We can hear what flight attendant Madeline Sweeney said as she saw American Airlines flight 11 zoom over the Hudson River toward the World Trade Center. "I see water and buildings," Sweeney told her ground supervisor. "Oh my God, oh my God!"

What *The 9/11 Commission Report* does not tell us, however, is why it happened.[2] On the subject of why the terrorists and their sponsors did what they did, the report is largely silent. This failure to comprehend the motives and goals of the enemy greatly limits the value of the report. Moreover, the report's discussion of the vital question of whether 9/11 could have been prevented suffers from an air of unreality. The report concludes that 9/11 could have been averted had America done this and that and the other—if only America had better control of its borders, if only the agencies of government were restructured to permit better sharing of intelligence, if only there were more systematic checks on airlines and other modes of transportation, and if only America had eliminated the Al Qaeda training camps and their support structures.

This conclusion is a fallacy. Call it the fallacy of retroactive insight. The characteristic feature of 9/11 was that it was a *surprise* attack designed to take advantage of an existing vulnerability in America's defenses. After the attack, it is easy to say that we should have taken the measures that would have prevented the attack. But imagine the uproar if a newly elected President Bush had ordered massive air strikes on Afghanistan prior to September 11. Imagine if someone, prior to 9/11, proposed restructuring the government at the cost of hundreds of billions of dollars, restricting the freedom and convenience of Americans through extensive security checks and measures like the Patriot Act, and ousting the Taliban through military force. Such a person would have been dismissed as a paranoid and a crackpot, akin to someone today who called for America to take drastic measures to stop the Chinese from invading Florida.

In this sense, I do not believe 9/11 could have been prevented.

BUT WHY DID they do it? The terrorists didn't leave an explanatory note, and the question of their motives has haunted America ever since the fateful attacks. At first 9/11 generated a spectacular moment of national unity, in which Americans came together to grieve over the terrible loss of life, acknowledge a new sense of shared vulnerability, and cherish the heroism of the police officers and firefighters. From the far ends of the world came words of sympathy and solidarity. Even the French commiserated, and *Le Monde* ran a banner headline proclaiming, "We are all Americans."

At the same time, however, Americans were startled by the reaction to 9/11 from certain quarters of the Muslim world. "Allah has answered our prayers" declared the Palestinian weekly *Al-Risala* in its September 13, 2001, issue. The Egyptian newspaper *Al-Maydan* noted that when the news broke that the towers were hit, "Millions of us shouted in joy." There were celebrations in Lebanon, Syria, Pakistan, and Jordan. Even in London, some Muslims rejoiced and Sheikh Omar Bakri Mohammed preached a sermon in his mosque calling September 11 "a towering day in history" and hailing the "magnificent 19" for what they did.[3] In many parts of the Muslim world, Osama bin Laden became an instant sensation for having hit America where it hurt. Americans who hoped that these reactions were grotesquely aberrant, and expected them to be strongly repudiated by the rest of the Muslim world, found these hopes disappointed.

Wracked with grief over 9/11, and furious at this bloody assault on civilian life, American leaders and opinion makers responded with instinctive and sputtering contempt toward their attackers. Several TV commentators and talk radio hosts proclaimed the 9/11 attackers "insane." Columnist Thomas Friedman declared that Osama bin Laden was simply "a psychopath." Another theory was that 9/11 was pointless, what scholar-activist Edward Said termed "a terror mission without message, senseless destruction." Historian Stanley Hoffman, not previously known for his expertise in Koranic interpretation, noted that the bin Laden crew were acting "on so peculiar an interpretation of the Koran that there is very little one can do to rebut it." President Bush took up this theme on September 20, 2001, charging that the 9/11 attackers "blaspheme the name of Allah. The terrorists are traitors to their own faith, trying, in effect, to hijack Islam itself." Columnist Barbara Ehrenreich suggested that 9/11 was an uprising on the part of the wretched of the earth, seeking to remedy "the vast global inequalities in which terrorism is ultimately rooted." Writing in *The New Yorker*, Hendrik Hertzberg and David Remnick announced, "This is a conflict that pits all of civilized society against a comparatively small, essentially stateless band of murderous outlaws."[4]

It is easy to sneer, with the benefit of hindsight, at these outlandish theories. But there was a good deal of evidence even at the time they were uttered that they were wrong. Clearly the terrorists were not insane, or they could never have pulled off the most successful terrorist attack in history. By all accounts 9/11 required a degree of imagination, precision, and coordination of which insane people simply are not capable. At the meager cost of $500,000, and armed only with box cutters, the 9/11 hijackers managed to inflict heavy casualties, cause hundreds of billions of dollars of damage, and transform the way of life of the world's most powerful nation.[5] Since bin Laden was one of the richest men in the world, his deputy Ayman al-Zawahiri a physician from one of the most prominent families in Egypt, and most of the 9/11 hijackers from educated middle-class backgrounds, 9/11 was hardly a poor man's uprising; one might almost call it "terrorism of the rich." By all accounts bin Laden and Zawahiri are deeply pious Muslims, and the diaries left behind by the 9/11 hijackers show them to be equally sincere and devout.[6] There are many people in the Muslim world who disagree with bin Laden and the perpetrators of 9/11, but few Muslim clergy consider them to be apostates or betrayers of Islam. Moreover, it was clear from the beginning that lots of Muslims supported and rejoiced in 9/11, and that far from being stateless outlaws, bin Laden and his men enjoyed the sponsorship and support of at least one Islamic regime, the Taliban government of Afghanistan.

These errors are not surprising. The mood in the immediate aftermath of 9/11 was disturbed and intemperate. Many Americans expressed the view that they didn't care why America was hated; they just wanted to find the people who planned and carried out the 9/11 attacks, and to obliterate them. No wonder that many senseless things were said in this truculent frame of mind. What is surprising is that for a time there was moral and ideological unity in America of a kind not seen since World War II. Suddenly the old divisions in America—over race, over taxes, over the Clinton legacy, over the 2000 election and the Supreme Court decision that put Bush in office—evaporated. The whole nation felt itself under attack by a common enemy. One powerful symbol of this unity was the sight of the entire U.S. Congress, conservative Republicans joined by liberal Democrats, singing "God Bless America" in front of the nation's Capitol. Despite their previous disagreements, the Democrats in Congress pledged to support President Bush in a unified national response to 9/11.

Even old ideological adversaries began to speak the same political language. A few days after the attacks, the *New York Times* declared that bin Laden and the hijackers "acted out of hatred for the values cherished in the West such as freedom, tolerance, prosperity, religious pluralism, and universal suffrage."[7] I am not concerned at this point with the veracity of the *Times*'s statement. I am struck, however, that a major newspaper that can be relied on to condemn President Bush here sounded exactly like him. Thus 9/11 produced something that Americans once took for granted but now experienced as a novelty. One America. One America united against its enemies.

But this moment of national unity was brief. It lasted as long as the impact of 9/11 was fresh. But as soon as that emotional wound began to heal, the moral and ideological unity disappeared and a furious debate broke out over the meaning of 9/11. This debate has only intensified the division in the country, revealing the division to be bigger than 9/11, bigger even than foreign policy. Ultimately 9/11 has exposed a deep chasm in the American soul over the meaning of America itself.

I WANT TO begin by discussing the mainstream conservative view of 9/11 that formed the basis for the Bush administration's war against terrorism. This view is sometimes called the "neoconservative" approach, although I believe it is wrongly labeled as such.

Some neoconservative strategists may have helped to devise it, but ultimately it is President Bush who adopted it and it is the Bush position that enjoys general support on the right and in the Republican Party. I recognize of course that there are dissident factions on the right, primarily the Buchanan wing of the "old right" and the libertarian critics. I will address their views later. Here I outline the central principles of Bush's conservative understanding of 9/11.

Terrorism is the problem. The first premise is that there is a new kind of warfare in today's world that is substantively different from earlier types of war. The new type of war is terrorism, reflecting what President Bush called "the very worst of human nature." What makes the new kind of war especially dangerous is that it targets civilians rather than military targets. Consequently terrorism is immoral in itself. As Bush told the United Nations General Assembly on November 10, 2001, "There is no such thing as a good terrorist. No national aspirations, no remembered wrong, can ever justify the deliberate murder of the innocent."[8] Conservatives recognize that the main perpetrators of terrorism are not nation states but independent groups like Al Qaeda, Islamic Jihad, Hezbollah, and Hamas that operate across formal boundaries. Since terrorist groups often collaborate with one another, there is an international network of terrorism that poses a threat to America, to Europe, to Israel, indeed to civilization itself. "This is civilization's fight," President Bush told a Joint Session of Congress on September 20, 2001. "Every nation now has a decision to make. Either you are with us or you are with the terrorists." Bush pledged that America would lead a "war against terrorism" to eradicate the threat posed by this international network of terrorist groups.

They hate us for our freedom. A second key notion in Bush's conservative understanding is that America stands for freedom and it is freedom that the terrorists envy and despise. "America was targeted for attack," President Bush said in his first televised address after 9/11, "because we're the brightest beacon for freedom and opportunity in the world." In his speech to Congress a few days later, Bush explained the motives of bin Laden and the 9/11 attackers: "They hate what we see right here in this chamber—a democratically elected government. They hate our freedoms—our freedom of religion, our freedom of speech, our freedom to vote and assemble and disagree with each other." One line of conservative analysis holds that many in the Muslim world lack the blessings of freedom and blame America for the self-inflicted problems of their own society. Author Victor Davis Hanson writes, "Rather than looking to itself— by emancipating women, holding free elections, opening markets, drafting constitutions, outlawing polygamy, curbing fundamentalism, insisting on secular education, and ending tribalism—the Islamic world has more often cursed others."[9]

This is World War IV against a new evil empire. The Cold War was, in fact, World War III. Now the West is engaged in World War IV, and the enemy, although different, bears a close resemblance to Nazis and Communists. Conservative commentators like Norman Podhoretz and Daniel Pipes have sounded this theme, and the Bush administration has echoed it. The new adversary is, in President Bush's view, "the heir of all the murderous ideologies of the twentieth century." Here, then, is another possible explanation for why the terrorists hate freedom: like the Nazis and the Soviets before them, they are partisans of despotism and totalitarianism. Conservatives often describe the enemy as "Islamo-fascism" or, as the *American Enterprise* recently called it, "Bolshevism in a headdress." Recalling Reagan's "evil empire" description of Soviet communism, Bush discovered in nations like Iraq and Iran an "axis of evil" in the modern world.[10] The remedy, naturally, is to defeat Islamic totalitarianism and leave it on the ash heap of history, to bring about what Richard Perle and David Frum termed (in the title of their book) "an end to evil."

The "radicals" and "extremists" are our true enemy. The Islamic world is divided into "extremists" and "moderates." As conservatives like Francis Fukuyama and Daniel Pipes insist, the extremists are the ones who are against modernity. Scorning science, capitalism, and democracy, they seek to impose Islamic law across the Middle East, if not on the whole world. One version of this argument is that extremism springs out of an especially virulent religious fanaticism deriving from the Wahhabi strain in contemporary Islam. No wonder, writes Fox News anchor John Gibson, that so many of the 9/11 hijackers came from Saudi Arabia, where Wahhabi Islam is officially practiced and promoted by the Saudi royal family. Others on the right maintain that power, rather than religion, is the true motivation of the extremists. The power-hungry mullahs achieve their goals by conning and manipulating young people through incentives such as the promise of an eternity in paradise attended by seventy-two virgins. Now we see why the 9/11 hijackers went so willingly to their deaths! Conservatives disagree about the degree of support enjoyed by the extremists. Bush, however, seems convinced that they are a tiny minority who "practice a fringe form of Islam." Bush argues that the majority of Muslims in the world are moderates who follow "the peaceful teachings of Islam" and embrace "progress and pluralism, tolerance and freedom."[11]

Force is a necessary response. Since the terrorists oppose us for who we are, not for what we do, there is no appeasing them. As British prime minister Tony Blair said shortly after 9/11, "There is no compromise possible with such people, no meeting of minds, no point of understanding with such terror."[12] The only solution is to attack the Al Qaeda training camps, and to destroy the wider network of international terrorist groups. Islamic Jihad, Hamas, Hezbollah—they should all renounce violence, or face annihilation. Even more, the war against terrorism means toppling and transforming regimes that support terrorists. The magnitude of the task suggests a long war, perhaps an unending war. While America should seek international support for this enterprise, allying with countries like Russia and Israel that are also fighting terrorism, there are cases like Iraq where America should be willing to fight the battle by itself.

Liberals simply don't understand the threat. Conservatives both inside and outside the Bush administration seem puzzled that liberals, who regularly profess their allegiance to the values of liberalism and democracy, seem unenthusiastic about fighting a two-fisted war against terrorism. The reason for this, conservatives surmise, is that liberals are reflexively anti-American, or that liberals simply don't comprehend the threat. In his writings, David Horowitz has hammered unceasingly on the gullibility of liberals, and on their alleged hatred of their own country. A few right-wingers have gone even further, suggesting that liberals are traitors. Most conservatives do not share this view. Conservatives generally agree, however, that liberals are dangerously naïve in placing their hopes for peace in unending mutual dialogue, or in the procedures of the United Nations. Liberals seem to think that if America leaves the Muslims alone, the Muslims will leave America alone. Finally, liberals don't understand the need for comprehensive programs of homeland security such as are provided for by the Patriot Act. In this analysis, liberals are so concerned with protecting our civil liberty that they are unwittingly jeopardizing our security.

The goal is a liberal, democratic Middle East. The Bush administration is resolved that, with or without a national consensus, the war against terrorism must go on. Terrorism is seen as arising out of the dysfunctional culture of the Middle East, a culture that the Islamic radicals exploit. Therefore the ultimate answer is for the West to take up what Daniel Pipes terms the "burden of bringing Islam into harmony with modernity." The Bush administration has adopted the view that America should work to advance the two institutions that the Islamic radicals fear most, namely liberalism and democracy. In his Second Inaugural Address, delivered on January 20, 2005, Bush declared the promotion of liberal democracy the centerpiece of American foreign policy. Every nation, Bush said, must have either "oppression, which is always wrong," or "freedom, which is eternally right." Bush also insisted that "the best hope for peace in our world is the expansion of freedom in the entire world." Therefore, he concluded, "America's vital interests and our deepest beliefs are now one."[13]

Bush is convinced that it is especially important for America to promote freedom and democracy in the Muslim world. In some cases, this was to be accomplished through the use of force. In others, Bush and his allies intend to use diplomacy, economic sanctions, and other forms of pressure or persuasion. Some conservatives even seek to compel American allies like Saudi Arabia to move away from Wahhabi extremism toward liberal democracy. Liberal democracy is the best remedy for terrorism, in this view, because when Muslims discover the benefits of self-government and freedom they will not be attracted to extremist groups that promote suicide bombings and violence. When that happens, Bush said in 2005, "The flow of violent radicalism to the rest of the world will slow, and eventually end."[14] As prosecuted by the Bush administration, America's long-term strategy is to undermine support for extremists by converting Muslims into liberals, and autocratic states into democratic states. The conservative hope is that if this strategy shows signs of working, the vast majority of Americans will unite behind the project to promote liberal democracy abroad.

THERE ARE ELEMENTS of truth in the conservative account, but it contains serious flaws that have inhibited understanding and helped produce a confused policy that has failed to win broad public support. Here I examine three of these flaws, although others will emerge in the course of this book. If the war against terrorism is lost, it will be because the Bush administration and its conservative allies never really understood what they were up against, and therefore never carried out the strategy necessary to defeat the adversary.

First, *terrorism is not the enemy.* In the previous chapter I noted that terrorism is not an adversary; terrorism is a tactic that is sometimes used by the adversary. Even Al Qaeda should not be understood exclusively as a terror group or franchise. Primarily it is a combat training enterprise whose training camps in Afghanistan, the Sudan, Yemen, and elsewhere were used to develop paramilitary fighters. Several of Al Qaeda's attacks, such as the bombing of the U.S.S. *Cole,* were clearly aimed at military targets and can hardly be called "terrorism" in any meaningful sense. Even on 9/11, bin Laden's goal was not to kill civilians per se but to strike out at the symbols of America's economy (World Trade Center), America's government (the White House or the Capitol), and America's military (the Pentagon). Although 9/11 is routinely described as a terrorist attack, can anyone seriously maintain that the Pentagon was not a military target? Yes, there were civilians on the planes but the purpose of hijacking planes was not to kill the civilians on board but to use the winged juggernauts as flaming projectiles to destroy the intended symbolic targets. Whether those who happened to be in the World Trade Center and the Pentagon happened to be civilian or military seems incidental to the planners. Moreover, would 9/11 have been less an act of war had the World Trade Center been unoccupied at the time of the attacks?

I do not deny that bin Laden wanted to kill noncombatants. We saw him on the videotape rejoice over the large number of civilian deaths. Undoubtedly he would have been even more delighted had thirty thousand rather than three thousand perished in those attacks. So I am not objecting to the characterization of 9/11 as terrorism. I am simply drawing attention to the wider scope of Al Qaeda, and to the fact that terrorism is simply one feature of its declared war against America. This is also true of the insurgency in Iraq. While it is quite willing to kill civilians, mostly Shia, the insurgents would prefer to kill American soldiers. Their strategy is not terrorism for its own sake but to make Iraq ungovernable and to push the country toward civil war. The objective is to topple the elected government, and drive America out of Iraq.

A further problem with the notion of a war against terrorism is that it provides a misleading framework for understanding the post-9/11 world. In particular, this framework has encouraged the Bush administration and many conservatives to describe as "terrorist" causes that cannot be dismissed in this way, and thus to make enemies of people who pose no real danger to the United States. Since 9/11, whenever there is trouble in the world—the Bali bombing, the conflict between the Israelis and the Palestinians, the Madrid bombing, the Chechen uprising, the Kashmir conflict, the London bombing—the Bush administration recalls 9/11 and cries out, "Terrorism!" Now some of these episodes—the Bali bombing, the Madrid bombing, and the London bombing—are terrorism in the classic sense. But there is a crucial distinction between those cases, on the one hand, and the conflicts in Palestine, Chechnya, and Kashmir, on the other. These latter cases involve wars of self-determination, disputes over legitimate title to land and rule. In these situations it is preposterous to dismiss the merits of one side's claims by simply chanting "terrorism." No one can deny the horror of Palestinian and Chechen attacks on civilians, but these have to be measured against the state-sponsored terror on the other side: the bulldozing of Palestinian homes, the shooting of stone-throwing teenagers, the obliteration of the Chechen capital of Grozny (involving innumerable civilian casualties) by Russian troops. The issue here is not merely one of moral symmetry, or the need to assess the culpability of both sides. It is that the Bush administration is making deadly foes of groups that have no reason to seek to harm America, until they discover that America is taking sides against them.

A second problem with the Bush administration's understanding of 9/11 is that contrary to what the many on the right claim, *the Islamic radicals are not against modernity, science, or democracy.* Although conservatives like to emphasize the fact that fifteen of the nineteen 9/11 hijackers came from Saudi Arabia—home of Wahhabi Islam—this is the least important fact about those men. They could just as easily have come from Pakistan, Egypt, Somalia, or any of a dozen other Muslim countries. Many of Al Qaeda's top leaders are Egyptian. Some of bin Laden's closest advisers are Pakistani. The U.S. military did a country-by-country breakdown of the three hundred or so foreign nationals captured in Iraq during the summer of 2005. Of that group, 78 were Egyptian, 66 Syrian, and 41 from the Sudan. Only 32 were Saudis. The rest came from Jordan, Iran, Tunisia, Algeria, and the West Bank.[15] Moreover, as other terrorist operations show, Al Qaeda and its allies are also capable of recruiting terrorists born in the West.

This may come as news to some conservatives, but Wahhabi Islam is not a breeding ground of Islamic radicalism. It is a breeding ground of Islamic obedience. The essence of the Wahhabi doctrine is doctrinal and social conservatism. The Muslim legal scholar Khaled Abou El Fadl terms Wahhabism "distinctively inward-looking" with an "obsession with orthodoxy and correct ritualistic practice."[16] When Muhammad al-Wahhab formed his fateful alliance with the tribal chief Muhammad bin Saud, the basis of their pact was that bin Saud would enforce al-Wahhab's conservative social doctrines in exchange for which al-Wahhab would preach that the people had a religious duty to obey their rulers. Thus bin Laden's jihad against the Saudi royal family and its American supporters represents a radical break with the Wahhabi doctrine. The important point here is not the conservative misreading of Wahhabi theology—a minor error—but the conservative failure to see what really distinguishes the 9/11 terrorists, their sponsors, and their intellectual leaders. The relevant characteristic is not their "backward" origins but their exposure to the "progressive" culture of America and to the West.

Almost without exception, the major figures of Islamic radicalism and fundamentalism are Western born, Western trained, or lived in the West. A good example is Khalid Sheikh Mohammed, one of the chief architects of 9/11, who studied in America in the 1980s at two different colleges in North Carolina. Radicals like Mohammed typically do not have religious backgrounds but have been trained in science and engineering. Bin Laden studied civil engineering, Mohammed mechanical engineering, Zawahiri medicine, and Muhammad Atta urban planning. It was in Germany, not in his native country of Egypt, that Atta reportedly joined the bin Laden cause. The pattern extends far beyond 9/11. Ramzi Yusuf, the mastermind of the 1993 World Trade Center bombing, is an electronics engineer who graduated from the Swansea Institute in South Wales. The man who beheaded journalist Daniel Pearl in Pakistan was born in England and studied at the London School of Economics. The shoe bomber Richard Reid was also British born. Zacarias Moussaoui, who got a life sentence for plotting terrorist attacks in America, is a native of France. Jose Padilla, who trained at an Al Qaeda facility and was also implicated in terrorist plots, was born and radicalized in the United States. The perpetrators of the 2005 London subway bombings were native-born British Muslims. So were most of the subjects in the foiled 2006 plot to blow up several airliners over the Atlantic ocean.

Modern forms of media and communications are vital to the spread of Muslim fundamentalist ideas. The Iranian revolution was the first electronically driven revolution in history, and it was made possible by the cassette, the means by which Khomeini's incendiary sermons were heard throughout the country. Al Jazeera uses the latest techniques of TV sensationalism to publicize the cause of bin

Laden and Al Qaeda. Bin Laden could never have functioned so effectively out of Afghanistan without an operating network of satellite phones. Al Qaeda communicates with its followers—and with the world—by videotapes and Web sites.

The 9/11 attacks themselves showed all the hallmarks of modernity: not simply the use of the paraphernalia of modern technology to blow up the symbols of American modernity, but the entire stage management of 9/11, a special kind of "reality show" using martyrdom as a form of advertising and real people in the explosion scenes. It was TV that gave 9/11 its emotional impact. In the same manner, the beheadings of Americans and American "collaborators" in Iraq are routinely videotaped and broadcast over the Internet: such propaganda is vital to the grisly enterprise. Without media, these forms of terrorism would be much less terrifying.

Not only do Islamic radicals like science and technology—if only to further their purposes—they are also supporters of commerce and capitalism. Historically, of the three Mediterranean religions—Judaism, Christianity, and Islam—Islam is the most favorable to trade. The Prophet Muhammad was, after all, a trader. Although Islam, like Christianity, condemns usury, unlike Christianity it has always looked favorably on profit and commercial activity. Islamic fundamentalists are generally procapitalist, and some have adopted the very latest business models. The *9/11 Commission Report* terms Khalid Sheikh Mohammed a "terrorist entrepreneur" and the French scholar Gilles Kepel describes Al Qaeda as a kind of terrorist "franchise" that does not orchestrate attacks so much as fund "start-up" groups whose business plans it finds promising.[17]

Finally, *many Muslim radicals and fundamentalists have become supporters of democracy.* To be sure, bin Laden and Al Qaeda are outspoken critics of democracy. Abu Musab al-Zarqawi, Al Qaeda's former head of operations in Iraq, frequently railed against "this evil principle of democracy." The main reason he opposed Iraqi democracy was that his group, the Sunnis, are in the minority. (For the same reason, the Iraqi Shia, led by the ayatollah Ali al-Sistani, have become avid proponents of democracy. They are the majority group, and they realize that democracy means that they win.) Just as predictable, the ruling mullahs of Iran, who don't wish to risk their power in free elections, reject the idea.

But as Noah Feldman writes, the major organizations of radical Islam are "the loudest voices calling for greater democracy . . . in nearly every Muslim country." Once again, this is not because Islamic radicals have been reading John Stuart Mill or the *Federalist Papers*. Rather, Islamic radicals support democracy as a means to gain political power. In the early 1990s in Algeria, the Islamic Salvation Front (FIS) enjoyed stunning electoral success, routing the National Liberation Front (FLN) that had led the fight for the country's independence. One of the group's leaders, Abbasi Madani, made it clear that his support for democracy was tactical. "Yes, the way is the elections. There is no other way at the present moment. All other ways have been obstructed by Allah."[18] So alarming was the prospect of this fundamentalist group taking power that the ruling party nullified the election result, plunging the country into civil war.

Islamic radicals could hardly have missed the significance of their recent successes in Egypt and the Palestinian territories. In Egypt's 2005 parliamentary election, the Muslim Brotherhood won five times as many seats as it previously held, making itself the leading opposition to the Mubarak regime. No wonder that Mohammed Mahdi Akef, head of the group, speaks favorably about democracy. As he said recently, "The ballot box has the final say. We don't believe in any other means of taking power." In the 2006 Palestinian elections, Hamas routed the candidates of the late Yasser Arafat's Fatah Party. Sheikh Nayef Rajoub says that Hamas has learned that the way to take over the government is to play "the democracy game."[19] All of this places the Bush administration in an awkward situation.

Are Bush and his conservative allies sincere in calling for democracy in the Muslim world? Consider the risk they are taking. Quite possibly free elections would result in every pro-American ruler, including all America's major allies (Musharraf in Pakistan, Mubarak in Egypt, King Abdullah in Jordan, and the royal family in Saudi Arabia), being ejected from power. Fareed Zakaria writes, "Across the Arab world elections held tomorrow would probably bring to power regimes that are more intolerant, reactionary, anti-Western, and anti-Semitic, than the dictatorships currently in place."[20]

Imagine a free election six months from now in Saudi Arabia. The Saudi royal family is voted out. Islamic radicals of the bin Laden stripe are elected by an overwhelming margin. They are now in control of Islam's holy sites, as well as the oil fields of Saudi Arabia. Backed by the Saudi people, they announce their willingness to use their newfound power to wage more effective jihad against the United States. Would the United States be willing to live with this outcome? Of course not. Nor should it. So for the United States to let the Saudi people decide on their rulers is to risk an outcome that could be, from the American point of view, catastrophic. For this reason, I think it is highly doubtful that either President Bush or his conservative supporters would hazard a Saudi election that might bring Islamic radicals and Al Qaeda supporters to power. Contrary to President Bush's naïve assertion, America's ideals and its interests are not identical.

It's time for Bush and the conservatives to rethink 9/11.

TWO

Reluctant Warriors

9/11 and the Liberal Paradox

LET US TURN now to the liberal and left-wing understanding of 9/11. If the Bush administration's conservatism is characterized by a relentless "war against terrorism," the left's position is characterized by an equally determined "war against the war against terrorism." The goal of left-wing agitation is to convince the Democratic Party as a whole to oppose the war. It is also to sway public opinion against the Bush administration so that the conduct of the war itself becomes untenable. The left has made substantial progress on both fronts.

Unified liberal opposition to the war against terrorism has emerged gradually since 9/11, gaining momentum with each passing year. A few days after 9/11, Congress voted pretty much unanimously to give President Bush the authority to use military force to respond to the terrorist attack. Only a minority of liberals—and very few Democrats in Congress—opposed the American invasion of Afghanistan to oust the Taliban. Many more liberals opposed the invasion of Iraq, although a few supported it. Democrats in the House and Senate were divided over the October 2002 Iraq War Resolution.

Most Democrats voted against it, but the margins were fairly close. Over time, however, the current of liberal opposition has grown stronger and more confident. Now there is a virtual liberal consensus, encompassing most congressional Democrats and the Democratic leadership, against Bush's war on terrorism. Explaining this process in a recent interview, liberal senator Barbara Boxer explained, "We were so hit by 9/11 . . . that we didn't get our legs back. It took a while. But now the Democratic Party is back."[1]

As we have seen, conservatives frequently characterize liberal opposition to American foreign policy, and in particular to the war against terrorism, as uninformed, weak, and anti-American. I believe it is none of those things. From the last chapter it should be clear that conservatives are not particularly knowledgeable about the nature, the goals, or the strategy of the enemy. Liberals are at least as well informed as conservatives on these subjects. The charge of timidity or weakness is equally misplaced. It assumes that liberals and leftists want to fight this war but simply lack the courage. This assumption is wrong. Liberals and leftists have loudly insisted that they are against the main thrust of Bush's war. Most liberals agree with John Kerry's position, articulated during the 2004 presidential campaign, that the Iraq war is the wrong war in the wrong place at the wrong time. Conservatives can hardly be surprised that liberals are timid about fighting a war that most of them don't want to fight in the first place.

Indeed liberal resolve is largely invested in opposing the war. Conservatives who persist in thinking that liberals are weaklings who lack political backbone should consider the tenacity that liberals show in fighting conservatism. Look at the implacable determination that liberals showed in keeping Robert Bork off the Supreme Court. Try outlawing abortion and see if the liberals react weakly or timidly! Liberals are not bashful in fighting for causes in which they believe.

Nor is the campaign against the war on terrorism a form of anti-Americanism. Liberals are understandably outraged when conservatives make this charge. "Liberals like me love America," says liberal radio host Al Franken. "We just love America in a different way."

Michael Moore fumes, "I am the most patriotic American. I'm the person who . . . believes in the actual real principles of this country."[2] Putting aside for a moment what these "actual real principles" might be, I think that Franken and Moore are sincere. They aren't against America, they are simply against the Bush administration's foreign policy. Opposing a president's foreign policy—or even American foreign policy in general—doesn't make you anti-American.

Liberals aren't anti-American for fighting against conservative foreign policy any more than conservatives are anti-American for fighting against liberal social policy. Robert Bork thinks America is "slouching towards Gomorrah," but this view doesn't make him anti-American. Right-wing pundit Pat Buchanan thinks America has become a "cultural wasteland and a moral sewer that are not worth living in and not worth fighting for."[3] He may be wrong, but his patriotism is not in doubt. The right-wing accusation of anti-Americanism is invalid because it confuses liberal opposition to specific government policies and specific features of America with opposition to the country.

True, liberals sometimes sound anti-American because they use a generalized America-bashing rhetoric that you won't hear on the right. One liberal professor, Robert Jensen, said on the day after 9/11, "We must say goodbye to patriotism because the world cannot survive indefinitely the patriotism of Americans." Even after the collapse of the World Trade Center, a prominent liberal columinist, Katha Pollitt, refused to let her daughter fly the American flag outside their New York apartment window. Her reason? "The flag stands for jingoism and vengeance and war."[4] Don't these sentiments qualify as anti-American? Actually, no. What liberals are condemning is conservative values and the way that they have traditionally been marshaled to advance goals that liberals abhor. When liberals speak loosely and condemn "America" they always intend their condemnation to apply to *conservative* America. They are not condemning the abolitionist Frederick Douglass, the slave rebel Nat Turner, the suffragette movement, the New Deal, the welfare state, rallies against the Vietnam War, the Stonewall riots, the "nuclear freeze" movement, the sexual revolution, separation of church and state, the Supreme

Court's decision in *Roe v. Wade*, or the Massachusetts high court's decision to legalize homosexual marriage.

Comedian Janeane Garofalo recently said, "When I see the American flag, I go: Oh, my God, you're insulting me. When I see a gay parade on Christopher Street in New York, with naked men and women on a float cheering, 'We're here, we're queer!' that's what makes my heart swell. Not the flag, but a gay naked man or woman burning the flag. I get choked up with pride." Behind Garofalo's over-the-top rhetoric there is a serious point. Liberals may reject one America, but they support the other America. This other America represents the "American way" that TV producer Norman Lear had in mind when he founded the activist group People for the American Way. This other America represents what Michael Moore considers "the actual real principles" of the country.

Let us now turn to the liberal understanding of the war against terrorism as it has developed since 9/11. My purpose here is not to rehearse every argument, canvass every recommendation. Rather, it is to capture the general contours of liberal thought. I recognize, of course, that liberalism is a spectrum. There is a fairly wide range from moderate Democrats to the far left. Here I focus not on elected officials but on scholars and writers because they tend to provide the clearest, most coherent expression of the liberal mind. My goal is to convey the views of the liberal mainstream, while also taking note of what influential figures on the left flank have to say.

America's history of oppression is partly to blame. In the liberal view, 9/11 was a tragic but understandable response to a long history of Western—and specifically American—conquest and oppression. In a November 2001 speech at Georgetown University, former president Bill Clinton traced the roots of 9/11 to "the first Crusade, when the Christian soldiers took Jerusalem . . . and proceeded to kill every woman and child who was Muslim." Clinton added, "That story is still being told today in the Middle East and we are still paying for it." Clinton also invoked America's history of owning slaves and dispossessing native Indians to make the point that America has terrorized others in the past and therefore should not be surprised when it is terrorized in return.[5]

As the slogan has it, what goes around comes around. The official liberal term for this is "blowback," which refers to the hot fumes of rage that America's policies produce in the non-Western world. Left-wing icon Noam Chomsky writes, "During the past several hundred years the U.S. annihilated the indigenous population, conquered half of Mexico, conquered Hawaii and the Philippines, and in the past half-century particularly, extended its force throughout much of the world. The number of victims is colossal." In Chomsky's view, "the U.S. itself is a leading terrorist state" and 9/11 was simply a form of payback. "For the first time, the guns have been directed the other way."[6]

Chomsky is a somewhat extreme example, but what one detects in his analysis is a certain relish in 9/11, the satisfaction of witnessing a kind of rough justice. We can detect a similar sense of vindication in the analysis of author and activist Arundhati Roy: "The September 11 attacks were a monstrous calling card . . . signed by the ghosts of the victims of America's old wars: the millions killed in Korea, Vietnam, and Cambodia, the thousands killed when Israel invaded Lebanon in 1982, the tens of thousands of Iraqis killed in Operation Desert Storm, the thousands of Palestinians who have died fighting Israel's occupation of the West Bank, and the millions who died, in Yugoslavia, Somalia, Haiti, Chile, Nicaragua, El Salvador, the Dominican Republic, and Panama at the hands of dictators whom the American government supported . . . and supplied with arms."[7]

They hate us because of the destructive effects of current American foreign policy. Quite apart from what America has done in the past, many liberals argue that America's policies today are increasing the volume of anti-Americanism in the Muslim world and thus making 9/11 attacks more likely. "The United States is hated across the Islamic world because of specific U.S. government policies and actions," Michael Scheuer writes. The same note is struck by Richard Falk, a professor of international law. "Why do they hate us?" Falk asks. He proceeds to inform us that Muslim animus is directed against "the U.S. government, its policies and ties with oppressive forces in the region, its decade-long sanctions imposed on the Iraqi people, its refusal to normalize relations with Iran, and above all, its underwriting of the Israeli occupation of Palestinian territories and support for Israeli brutality directed against the Palestinians."[8]

The "oppressive forces" that Falk refers to are the undemocratic regimes that America supports in countries like Pakistan, Egypt, and Saudi Arabia. In the liberal view, Muslims suffer under these despotic regimes and the radical Muslims are able to increase their popular support by positioning themselves against these tyrannical rulers and their American backers. Many liberals note that America has long been allied with tyrants. Between the 1960s and the 1980s, America supported Somoza in Nicaragua, the shah of Iran, Marcos in the Philippines, Pinochet in Chile, and many other vicious and unsavory characters. Liberals blame the United States for orchestrating the 1953 coup that led to the restoration of the shah of Iran and the overthrow of the country's elected prime minister, Mohammed Mossadegh. No wonder, liberals note, that the Iranian people are furious with America and supported the Khomeini revolution. For liberals these are the fruits of an unprincipled, shortsighted American foreign policy that never seems to learn from its mistakes.

Bush's war against terrorism is a pretext for American imperialism. As liberals see it, the war in Afghanistan was one thing. That came right after 9/11, and was perhaps necessary to get rid of the Taliban-sponsored terrorist camps. But then Bush announced his intention to use force to remove Saddam Hussein as dictator of Iraq. Although Bush's stated reason was to eliminate the threat of Hussein's weapons of mass destruction, from the beginning many on the left found this more of a pretext for the war. As critics see it, reversing a long history of deterrence and defensive war, Bush proposed a preemptive attack on Iraq even though Iraq had not attacked the United States. Acutely conscious of this, the Bush administration whipped up the emotions of 9/11 in order to build American public support for the war, insinuating a connection between Iraq and 9/11, although there was never any connection at all. As Senator Ted Kennedy put it, the Iraq issue from the beginning "distracted us from the real threat of Al Qaeda in Afghanistan and elsewhere."[9]

When prominent European allies, notably France and Germany,

came out against the war, and when the United Nations refused to sanction it, Bush went ahead anyway, invading Iraq and later capturing Hussein. Liberals triumphantly note that no weapons of mass destruction were found. This in the liberal mind has confirmed a suspicion first raised by Bush's most extreme critics: Bush lied! Even mainstream Democrats like John Kerry now routinely assert that the Iraq war was "rooted in deceit and justified by continuing deception."[10] So thoroughgoing is Bush's dishonesty, according to his critics, that very little the president now says can be believed. His claims may be discounted, if not discredited, from the moment they are raised.

As many liberal magazines and blogs have suggested, Bush seems to have resolved to invade Iraq even before 9/11. His real reason? Imperial domination. Social critic Cornel West charges that the Bush administration has used 9/11 as an "occasion to launch an imperial vision of the United States dominating the world." In his book *Resurrecting Empire*, Rashid Khalidi faults America with "stepping into the boots of the former colonial rulers . . . as an occupying power." Columnist Maureen Dowd writes that after 9/11 Bush and his allies took the "opportunity . . . to reduce the rest of the world to subservience." With imperial power comes control of the Iraqi oil fields and, of course, lucrative government contracts for Bush's defense buddies and campaign contributors. *New York Times* columnist Bob Herbert adds, "There are billions of dollars to be made in Iraq and the gold rush is already under way."[11]

However America seems to be doing in Iraq at a given time, liberals tend to emphasize the negative and take genuine relish in the failures of American foreign policy. Many liberals are not impressed that America captured Saddam Hussein, killed Zarqawi, and held free elections. None of these "successes," they point out, seems to have stabilized the country. Instead, American troops continue to face a powerful insurgency, manned by skilled bomb makers and a seemingly unending stream of suicide bombers. In addition, there is the problem of sectarian strife, propelling Iraq toward civil war. As liberal philanthropist George Soros views it, "We find ourselves in a quagmire that is in some ways reminiscent of Vietnam." So, as liberals see it, in the name of "fighting terrorism" Bush and the conservatives have embroiled the country in a self-defeating war that has rent the fabric of Iraqi society and proven to be a fertile breeding ground for anti-Americanism. A "godsend for terrorists," Stanley Hoffman says. Herbert calls the Iraq situation "a gift-wrapped, gilt-edged recruiting tool for Al Qaeda."[12] It is only a matter of time, some liberals warn, before a newly replenished terrorist movement visits another catastrophe on American soil.

The war against terrorism has provided a dangerous excuse for human rights abuses and social controls. This liberal indictment can be summed up in a few phrases. The Patriot Act. Guantánamo Bay. Abu Ghraib. Domestic spying. Haditha. Liberals recognize that after 9/11, some things had to change. But from the beginning liberals insisted that if we fight the enemies of freedom by restricting freedom in America, we become more like the terrorists. The Patriot Act, many liberals insist, goes too far. Author Gore Vidal warns, "The Patriot Act makes it possible for government agents to break into anyone's home when they are away, conduct a search and keep the citizen indefinitely from finding out that a warrant was issued. They can oblige librarians to tell them what books anyone has withdrawn. If the librarian refuses, he or she can be criminally charged." By the count of the late Edward Said, "The Patriot Act . . . suppressed or abrogated or abridged whole sections of the First, Fourth, Fifth, and Eighth Amendments."[13]

Nor did liberals have to wait long for their theoretical fears to materialize. For many liberals, the Abu Ghraib scandal demonstrated the naked abuse of power: captives being stripped, humiliated, and forced to perform sex acts in the name of interrogation. Similarly, in the liberal view, Guantánamo Bay—where hundreds of prisoners are held without charge, without access to lawyers, and indefinitely at the whim of the U.S. government—reveals the abuses of basic constitutional liberty that occur when the Bush administration is given unchecked power. Historian Arthur Schlesinger Jr. calls the Guantánamo Bay camps a "national disgrace." Amnesty International termed the camps "the gulag of our time."[14]

Liberal groups routinely produce evidence that the U.S. military is engaged in the wanton killing of civilians, as at Haditha, or in various forms of torture that allegedly violate the Geneva Convention and international human rights codes. Some torture techniques are highlighted by human rights advocate Mark Danner: "heat and light and dietary manipulation . . . sleep and sensory deprivation . . . water-boarding, in which a prisoner is stripped, shackled, and submerged in water until he begins to lose consciousness, and other forms of near-suffocation."[15] Then there were reports of the U.S. government secretly taping conversations between American citizens and terrorist suspects abroad. Not only did the secret surveillance seem a clear violation of American law, but in the liberal view it also jeopardized the privacy rights of all Americans. Many liberals were outraged when the Bush administration asserted its right to perform such surveillance and insisted that it would continue doing so.

For liberals, all of this adds up to a truly frightening situation. Let's recall that many liberals have never considered Bush a legitimate president. He lost the popular vote in 2000 and was installed in power by the Supreme Court. By becoming a war president Bush was able to dispel liberal opposition and even to win reelection by a margin of several million votes. Many liberals openly allege that Bush used the war on terrorism to consolidate his political position. Even more infuriating for liberals, the war against terrorism gives the Bush administration virtually unlimited power that it can use to undermine liberal principles and to threaten liberals in their own country. "We will all be under surveillance," warns columnist Wendy Kaminer. "We are all suspects now." Anthony Lewis alleges that never before has the threat to civil liberties been greater because in previous cases of wartime repression, the repression ended when the war ended. "But it's hard to envisage an end to the current war. . . . So repressive measures may go on indefinitely."[16]

The deeper problem is the global danger posed by religious fundamentalism. Liberals argue that 9/11 was a horrible illustration of the damage that can be wrought by a phenomenon that is rising throughout the world—religious fundamentalism. And if Islamic fundamentalism produced a terrible tragedy that cost three thousand American lives, liberals fear that the fundamentalism of Bush and his political allies is producing the horrible results—the gratuitous invasions and mass killings, the abuses of power and use of torture, the suspensions of domestic civil liberties—that are justified in the name of a phony war against terrorism.

Many liberals profess to see little meaningful difference between Islamic fundamentalists and American religious and social conservatives. Richard Falk writes, "The Great Terror War has so far been conducted as a collision of absolutes, a meeting ground of opposed fundamentalisms." Social critic Edward Said found in both Islamic and Christian fundamentalism the same traits of "magical thinking" and "lying religious claptrap" leading to "bloody solutions." Political scientist Benjamin Barber warns of "an American jihad being waged by the radical right. These Christian soldiers bring to their ardent campaign . . . all the purifying hatred of the zealots in Tehran and Cairo."[17]

In the liberal view, both Islamic fundamentalists and Christian fundamentalists are implacably opposed to basic civil liberties, to women's rights and homosexual rights, and to separation of church and state. These are the people who "talk to God" and invoke his name to justify their punitive agenda. Both can become violent and dangerous when they do not get their way. It is impossible to argue with such people, who are fundamentally irrational and fanatical. The only viable solution is to defeat and marginalize these extremists.

How to fight the war against the war against terrorism. In Iraq the liberal solution is obvious: America should get out before more lives are lost. Some liberals recognize that a U.S. withdrawal would mean a stunning victory for the insurgents—a fulfillment of their objectives. This prospect does not deter the liberal leadership in Congress, and of the activist wing of the Democratic Party, because of their conviction that America is losing Iraq in any case.

Simply by occupying Iraq and staying there, many liberals say, America is strengthening the insurgency. A central premise here is that the war against terrorism is producing more terrorists. Congressman John Murtha has said many times that the Iraqi people don't want America there. In Murtha's view, America should leave before the situation deteriorates even further. Each liberal has his own timetable. Columnist Nicholas Kristof wants "every last soldier" home by the end of 2007. Columnist Robert Scheer advocates immediate withdrawal: "It is time we called a halt to our mindless messing in other people's lives."[18] Turn the place over to the Iraqis, or to the United Nations—the people who should have handled it in the first place.

Although most liberals are opposed to the Iraq war, they are not opposed to American action to fight terrorism or to bring the perpetrators of 9/11 to justice. Liberals emphasize that they support a targeted and focused campaign to capture or kill "the people who did 9/11." This means going after bin Laden and his chief lieutenants, and it means rooting out Al Qaeda. It means taking reasonable steps to prevent terrorists from launching further attacks. But liberals firmly believe that the Patriot Act will have to be drastically revised. They insist that Guantánamo Bay should be dismantled and the prisoners moved into a different program where their legal rights are upheld. Liberals want no more domestic surveillance without proper court warrants.

Most of all, liberals do not want to invade any more countries. They don't even want to hear about it. The ongoing rhetoric of "war" makes them uncomfortable. As these liberals see it, we are not in a state of war and we need a new way to think about how to fight terrorism. Instead of a war, author James Carroll contends that America should pursue "an unprecedented, swift, sure, and massive campaign of law enforcement." Robert Reich, a cabinet secretary in the Clinton administration, agrees: "Fighting international terrorism is not like fighting a war. It's more like controlling crime." Philanthropist George Soros echoes these sentiments: "Crimes require police work, not military action."[19]

Liberals do consider themselves to be at war, but it is more in the nature of a political battle. The enemy is religious fundamentalism in general, and the fundamentalism of the Bush administration and its supporters in particular. Liberals like Reich call for the forces of "reason" (by which he means liberals) to unite against the nefarious influence of both Islamic fundamentalism and the fundamentalism espoused by President Bush and his Christian allies. But the practical thrust of the liberal political campaign is at home. With an intensity that we have not seen on the left since the 1960s, liberals are agitating to evict conservatives from the corridors of power. This, for them, is not just a matter of partisan politics. Many liberals believe that the fate of their deepest beliefs, of liberalism itself, is at stake.

TAKEN AS A whole, the liberal critique of the war against terrorism is a powerful indictment, one that the Bush administration has not adequately answered. I will examine each of the central liberal themes in this book. Here I just want to raise a single paradox. Usually when liberals are confronted with a problem, such as poverty or racism or violence, they are not content to merely tackle its surface symptoms. Typically liberals demand that the problem be attacked at the level of "root causes." Only by getting to the bottom of it, only by confronting the reason behind it, do liberals expect to correctly diagnose a problem and remedy it. When there is a real social evil, such as poverty, liberals have not hesitated to declare a "war on poverty" to try and eliminate it.

But this approach is the very opposite of the one that liberals adopt when it comes to fighting Islamic radicalism and terrorism. Liberals know as well as anyone else that the crisis of 9/11 was not a simple matter of a group of bad guys planning an especially serious crime: catch the bad guys and the problem goes away. Liberals are fully aware that 9/11 was only the latest and most successful of a string of attacks against American lives and American interests. There have now been numerous terrorist attacks in other Western countries, as well as in Muslim countries friendly to the United States.

Many liberals also recognize that Al Qaeda's terror network draws its support from the community of Islamic radicals and fundamentalists. The radicals are in control of one country, Iran, that seems resolved to develop a nuclear capability. Everywhere else in the Muslim world, even in relatively moderate or secular countries, Islamic fundamentalism has made political gains. Every year there are hundreds of thousands of young Muslims who emerge from madrassas and mosques imbued with an animus toward America and the West. Even in the West, Islamic radicalism has been implicated in murders, such as the fatal stabbing of Theo van Gogh, and bombings, of the kind we saw in Madrid and London.

Moreover, this rising tide of Islamic fundamentalism, and the violence it breeds, is the product of the most illiberal ideology in the world today. Soviet communism, for all its repressive practices, at least identified ideologically with liberal goals such as equality and social justice. By contrast, Islamic fundamentalism has no affinity with liberalism at all. Christopher Hitchens notes that what Muslim fundamentalists hate about America "is not what Western liberals don't like and can't defend . . . but what they do like and must defend."[20] As liberals have seen in Afghanistan, Iran, and elsewhere, when Islamic fundamentalists are in power, they imprison dissidents, flog emancipated women, stone adulterers and homosexuals, and pronounce death sentences on blasphemers. Michael Moore himself pointed out that the chief target of 9/11, the World Trade Center, was in liberal New York.

One might expect American liberals to want to eradicate not just "the guys who did 9/11" (the actual perpetrators, liberals do not need reminding, are already dead) but the illiberal ideology of Islamic fundamentalism and the reactionary regimes that support Islamic terrorism. That ideology, those regimes, are the root cause behind 9/11. If there is anything that stimulates liberals to go to war, this should be it. But, if anything, liberals have mobilized against America's war to fight Islamic radicalism. It is possible, of course, for liberals (and even conservatives) to oppose this feature or that feature of Bush's war on terror. There are reasonable arguments to be made against Bush's invasion of Iraq, or how America is managing the intricate situation there. It is even possible for liberals to want to fight a very different kind of war, with a very different strategy, but with the same goal of defeating Islamic radicalism and terrorism.

The mystery is that liberals seem to oppose virtually every aspect of Bush's war, both on the domestic and the foreign front, without offering any comprehensive strategy of their own. Rather, liberals seem increasingly united in a political effort to restrict the scope of the fight against the foreign foe that has inflicted unprecedented harm on the United States. Opposition to Bush's war on terrorism is now a central feature of American liberalism. We are left with a profound paradox: today on the world scene, it is conservatives who are fighting to undermine illiberal forces and secure liberal values in the Muslim world. American fundamentalists are the ones who are most eager to go after Islamic fundamentalists, and American liberals are the ones who are most eager to stop them.

AS WE CAN see from this chapter and the previous one, there is a fundamental divide in America over foreign policy. Author Jonathan Franzen writes, "One half of the country believes that Bush is crusading against the Evil One while the other half believes that Bush is the Evil One." And this is only part of the chasm that has opened up between liberals and conservatives. The real divide is over the meaning of America itself. Recognizing this, Bill Moyers said in a recent speech, "Yes, there's a fight going on against terrorists around the globe, but just as certainly there's a fight going on here at home, to decide the kind of country this will be during and after the war on terrorism." Democratic pollster Stanley Greenberg concurs. "The country is now divided both politically and culturally with distinct and counterpoised views about government, values, the family, and the best way of life."[21] In some ways, of course, it has always been so. But today the differences are deeper, perhaps deeper than the country has seen in a century and a half, and the nature of the divide is new as well.

The depth of the divide can be seen in the vehemence that attends contemporary debate. Nicholson Baker writes a political tract, barely disguised as a novel, about a man who wants to kill President Bush. Philip Roth offers his attempt at social criticism with his book *The Plot Against America,* described by reviewer James Wolcott as "a cautionary tale about how easily the country could slide into fascism." Liberal columnists like Jonathan Chait confess to "Bush hatred," which Chait defines as "a deep and personal loathing for Bush." Democratic Party chairman Howard Dean describes the Republicans as "a white Christian party."[22] This is the political equivalent of a Republican leader describing the Democrats as the party of blacks, homosexuals, and atheists. The issue here is not whether these descriptions are accurate. It is the sharp decline in civility that such characterizations reveal.

Even sober voices have succumbed to the new stridency. In the months leading up to the 2004 election, liberal jurist Guido Calabresi gave a speech before the American Constitution Society in New York in which he said that Bush had ascended to the presidency through a kind of legal coup. Referring to the Supreme Court's decision to declare Bush the winner of the 2000 election, Calabresi said, "Somebody came to power as a result of the illegitimate acts of a legitimate institution." Then he added, "That is exactly what happened when Mussolini was put in by the king of Italy."[23]

Minor in itself, this episode is revealing because Calabresi is not a reckless man of the left. He is the former dean of the Yale Law School and now a federal judge. He is a widely respected and thoughtful liberal. The immoderation of his remarks shows the degree to which political campaigns have become exercises in character assassination. It is also an indicator of how civility has virtually disappeared from American politics. The "vital center" is largely gone, and now there is only the angry left and the angry right. The titles of recent books convey this anger: *Treason, Lies and the Lying Liars Who Tell Them, The Vast Left Wing Conspiracy,* and so on.

While some see the acrimony of contemporary politics as a mark of a general deterioration of American culture, I think it is also an indication of an erosion of shared values between liberals and conservatives. No longer do the two sides have the same goals and merely disagree about how to get there. In that situation the parties can easily see the benefits of civility and compromise. Now, however, liberals and conservatives seem to inhabit two different moral universes. They have different and sometimes irreconcilable objectives. In many cases, what one side considers good and desirable, the other side considers destructive and dangerous. In some ways the two groups want to live in very different countries.

Since liberalism and conservatism are the guiding principles of the Democratic and Republican Parties, the two major parties have become strange to each other in a way that America has not seen since 1860, when one faction saw slavery as a "positive good" and the other saw it as an entrenched evil. Now, as then, the two sides have difficulty recognizing each other as legitimate, as fully American, as possessing the same moral decency that we all take for granted in ourselves. The vicious liberal attacks on Bush, which parallel the vicious conservative attacks on Clinton, are a way of saying, "We have difficulty recognizing you as human beings who inhabit the same moral planet that we do. Consequently we see you as usurpers and moral reprobates who should be hounded and driven from the corridors of power by any means necessary."

The new moral divide has confused many observers because traditionally American politics has been divided along economic lines. In previous decades politics was very simple: wealthier people voted Republican and poorer people voted Democrat. Historically, the only clear exception to this voting pattern was Jews. As Irving Kristol once noted, Jews are the only group that earns like Episcopalians and votes like Puerto Ricans. But now the political ground has shifted, and in voting habits most of America has "gone Jewish." Indeed no group today, with the exception of African Americans, can be counted on to vote its economic self-interest.

The liberal political scientist Thomas Frank noticed this, and is greatly disturbed by it. During the 2000 and 2004 presidential elections, Frank saw what we all saw: the Democrats won the Northeastern states and the West Coast, plus a couple of Midwestern states, and the Republicans won the rest of the country. The significance of this was not lost on Frank. The richest states in the country were now voting Democratic, and the poorest states were voting Republican. Frank was especially perturbed to find out that in his home state of Kansas, all the poorest counties voted overwhelmingly for Bush. Frank concluded that a nefarious scheme was afoot: crafty Republican strategists were using religious and moral demagoguery to hoodwink poor people into voting against their economic interests![24]

Unfortunately Frank's one-eyed analysis prevented him from seeing the other side of the equation: if right-wing demagogues were conning the poor into a senseless alliance with Republicans, it would seem to follow that left-wing demagogues were bamboozling the rich into equally irrational support for Democrats. Frank never considered the possibility that neither group was being misled; rather, Americans at all economic levels are now voting on the basis of something other than, and perhaps more important than, their pocketbooks. This is not to say that economic issues are irrelevant. The pocketbook still counts, and poorer people are still on average more likely to be Democrats, and richer people to be Republicans. But economic class is no longer a good predictor of political preference. It has ceased to be the animating issue in American politics.

IN ORDER TO chart the moral and ideological divide in today's America, let's begin with a brief look at the results of the two previous presidential elections. I'm not sure if you noticed, but in the last two presidential elections every place in America with good restaurants voted for Al Gore and John Kerry. The political divide seems to reflect a culinary divide, or more broadly a cultural divide. Political pundits refer to this as the red state–blue state divide. This classification has its limits. Certainly many red states went narrowly for Bush and obviously contain a substantial minority of blue voters, and the reverse is true of the blue states that went for the Democratic candidate. If you look more closely at the electoral map, however, you will see a more illuminating distinction: in both presidential elections, virtually all the big cities went for Gore and Kerry, and virtually all the rural areas and small towns went for Bush. Viewed this way, liberal Democrats are the party of the urban lifestyle, and conservative Republicans are the party of the small-town lifestyle.

Even this analysis is incomplete, because there are some small-town liberals and big-city conservatives. There are NASCAR leftists and latte-sipping right-wingers. Liberal columnist Molly Ivins claims that she is a pickup-driving, beer-drinking, rodeo-watching liberal. These examples show that our cultural markers are not entirely accurate. To get to the real difference, one has to dig deeper. Political scientist Morris Fiorina, a colleague of mine at the Hoover Institution, disagrees with this approach. Pointing out the obvious flaws of the red America–blue America framework, he challenges the notion that there is any deep divide in American politics. His argument is that it is the political parties and the political activists, not the American people, who are bitterly divided. Fiorina draws on opinion poll data to make his case that the American people retain many shared values, even on controversial issues like abortion and homosexuality, and that political and cultural divisions, where they exist, are not as stark as some people think.[25]

I disagree with Fiorina on two counts. First, if the major parties and the political leadership of the country are deeply divided, then the nation is deeply divided, and the views of the "American people" don't enter into it at all. Abraham Lincoln once said that America is ruled by "public opinion," but by this he did not mean the opinion of the American public. The opinion of the American people counts— but only on Election Day. So how is America ruled? By elected leaders, yes, but what shapes the parameters of their choices? Public opinion. Here "public opinion" refers to the views of the minority of Americans who actively participate in political debate and shape the way that major issues are decided. Are you a member of this political elite? If you subscribe to the *Atlantic Monthly*, call in to the Rush Limbaugh radio show, contribute to moveon.org, write letters to your local newspaper, subscribe to the Focus on the Family newsletter, attend political conventions, or read political blogs on the Internet, you are part of the influential group of Americans that make "public opinion." If you don't know who Dick Cheney is, couldn't locate the Middle East on a map, and don't vote if it's raining outside, then you are not part of American "public opinion," and thank God for it!

When Fiorina concedes that American political parties and their most active supporters are further apart than ever before, he is conceding far more than he recognizes. Traditionally, the two parties were more like political clubs. The Republicans were a kind of Rotary Club and the Democrats a kind of Kiwanis Club. Both parties were ideologically diverse. For example, the Democratic Party was the party of civil rights—and of the Southern segregationists. (Bull Connor was not a Republican.) But in the past few decades the Democratic Party has become a liberal party and the Republican Party a conservative party. The moral divide in American politics is now expressed in the organized preferences of the two major parties.

My second criticism is that Fiorina's own data show profound differences between liberals and conservatives on both foreign policy and social and moral issues. Fiorina's data is corroborated by a study of the ideological and partisan divide in American politics conducted by the Pew Research Center. According to the Pew study, most Republicans and conservatives support the Iraq war, while most Democrats and liberals oppose it. There is an equally significant divide between conservatives and liberals on moral issues. While a substantial majority of conservatives think "government should do more to protect morality in society," nearly 90 percent of liberals think "the government is getting too involved in the issue of morality." Republicans and conservatives rank strengthening the country's moral values and protecting the homeland from terrorism as their highest priorities. By contrast, the Pew study found, "Just 2 percent of Kerry voters volunteer any topic related to moral values, and even fewer mention terrorism" as priorities they consider central.[26]

Fiorina downplays these differences by stressing areas of agreement among most Americans. We all know that Americans agree on certain things. For example, Americans agree that when there is a natural disaster, like hurricane Katrina, the federal government should help. Americans also agree that homosexuals are human beings who should be treated with tolerance and decency. Americans generally believe that abortion should be permitted under certain circumstances. Americans overwhelmingly believe that people of different religious faiths, or no faith, should be free to follow their convictions without government interference.

All of this is true, but largely irrelevant to politics. Politics focuses on those issues on which people disagree. At one time "the family" was not a political issue because there was widespread social agree-ment about it. Now the family is a source of heated debate—because the two sides strongly disagree on what a family is and on which "family values" American society should actively promote. Similarly, religion has become a major political issue because liberals and con-servatives now have very different views of what role religion should play in public life.

Religion and family are now at the center of the moral divide in contemporary America. This can be seen not just from the intensity of public debate over the two issues, but also from the actual voting behavior of the American people. After the 2004 election, there was a moment of liberal panic when commentators saw that nearly 25 percent of Americans said they voted on the basis of "moral values." Many of these commentators expressed relief when further analysis showed that Americans cast their ballots on the basis of a whole host of important issues, including unemployment, free trade, Iraq, and homeland security. If we look again at the election results, however, we find two extremely powerful predictors of the electoral choices of the American people.

The first is religious practice. Election results showed that reli-gious Americans were vastly more likely to vote for Bush, and non-religious or secular Americans were vastly more likely to vote for Bush's opponent. Bush overwhelmingly won the evangelical Chris-tian vote, but he also won heavily among churchgoing Catholics and Orthodox Jews. In the 2000 election, two out of three regular churchgoers voted for Bush and three out of four secular voters went for Gore. Four years later the same pattern was evident: Bush won the votes of practicing Catholics and Protestants by 25 percent-age points, while Kerry won the nonreligious vote by a stunning 40 point margin.[27]

The second reliable predictor of American voting behavior is fam-ily status. Married people, especially married people with children, were far more likely to vote for Bush. This pattern, which was evi-dent in the 2000 election, became even more pronounced in 2004. Married voters that year favored Bush over Kerry by 15 percentage points, while unmarried voters preferred Kerry by a margin of 18 points.[28] Former Clinton pollster Dick Morris points out that the "marriage gap" is far more significant than the "gender gap," and it shows some interesting contours. Taking note of group voting trends, Morris observes, "If a woman is divorced, she is almost certain to be a Democrat. If she's single, she is likely to lean Democratic. If she's married, she's likely to lean Republican. If she's married with children, she's safely in the Republican camp." The point here is not that Americans vote based on their religious affiliation or family status but that being religious, married, and a parent shapes the moral compass through which people see the whole range of political issues, from gay marriage to the war against terrorism. Religion and family are not the "issue" but the lens through which the issues are perceived.

In subsequent chapters we will see the significance of this new chasm that has transformed the nature of the national debate. Until now this divide has been reflected in the "culture war," which has been understood as a domestic or internal argument over the values and priorities of American society. I intend to show that this culture war is profoundly connected with the other great issue in American politics—the battle between America and the forces of radical Islam that are bent on destroying America. I will demonstrate that the two battles are part of the same struggle, a struggle not just over whether "America" or "American values" are good for us and the world, but over *which* America and *whose* American values are good for us and the world. But first we must look inside the Muslim world in order to understand the mind of our foreign enemy.

THREE

America Through Muslim Eyes

Why Foreign Policy Is Not the Main Problem

It is supremely difficult for Westerners—especially Americans—to understand the Muslim world. One reason, of course, is the embarrassingly poor level of knowledge that many Americans have of other cultures. The writer Salman Rushdie gives the example of his sister, who was asked on several occasions in California where she came from. When she said, "Pakistan," most people had no idea what she meant. One American said, "Oh, yes, Pakestine!" and immediately started talking about his Jewish friends.[1]

Such ignorance is sometimes reflected at official levels. In 1949, on the occasion of Thanksgiving, President Truman decided to present the president of Turkey with a gift that he considered especially appropriate: a turkey. The turkey, when it arrived in Istanbul, caused bewilderment and extensive speculation. The reason is that the bird that is known in English as a "turkey" is known in Turkish as a *hindi*—the Indian bird. Historians tell us that the Europeans first encountered the bird in the Americas, and having seen nothing like it, they named it after the most exotic place they could think of, which was Turkey. The Turks, in their turn, named the bird after the most exotic place *they* could think of, which was India. President Truman apparently never discovered his mistake, which fortunately was a harmless one.[2]

More recent, and potentially more harmful, is former New York mayor Ed Koch's statement that "the supporters of fundamentalist Islam are fanatics who are prepared to die to kill those who observe a religion other than Islam."[3] If Koch is right, it would seem to follow that the West must prepare to fight and if necessary kill a substantial segment of the world's Muslim population because Islamic fundamentalists simply cannot coexist with people of other religions. Yet historically Muslims of all types have coexisted with other religions and even permitted them within the Islamic empire. In the days of the Islamic caliphate that bin Laden nostalgically invokes, innumerable Jews and Christians lived and practiced their religion under Abbasid, Mughal, and Ottoman rule. No one in the Muslim world—not even Al Qaeda—has called for the murder of everyone in the world who observes a faith other than Islam.

Equally remarkable is columnist and former presidential candidate Patrick Buchanan's insistence that a written constitution is unlikely to work in Iraq because "Islamic men are not people of parchment."[4] This is being written of a people who have been living by parchment—not just the Koran but an elaborate system of written laws and codes—since the eighth century (when Buchanan's Irish ancestors could not even write their names).

The deeper problem, even for Americans who take the trouble to learn something about the Muslim world, is ethnocentrism. Although it is liberals—usually of the academic type—who like to complain about ethnocentrism, the problem affects Americans across the political spectrum. In fact, as we will see, it is especially egregious among liberals. Ethnocentrism simply means that we see others through the lens of our preexisting, homegrown prejudices. Regarding our own ways and values as normative and right, we are quick to find the customs and beliefs of others to be strange and ridiculous. We simply don't know why foreigners do what they do, and so we make sweeping inferences about them that are unjust and wrong. In some cases, we simply project our assumptions and values onto other cultures, presuming that their motives and goals must be identical with what ours would have been in a given situation.

Ethnocentrism is a universal tendency. Students who take courses in multiculturalism have heard a great deal about Western ethnocentrism, and indeed Western historical writing offers many examples of it. For hundreds of years Europeans referred to Muslims as "Mohammedans" because they erroneously presumed that Muhammad occupies the same position in Islam that Christ does in Christianity. There is also a tradition in the West, more characteristic of the modern than the Christian era, of viewing the East as mysterious, exotic, and inferior—a tendency that Edward Said called "Orientalism."[5] What Said ignores, however, is the equally long tradition in Muslim historiography of viewing the West as unmysterious, unexotic, but no less inferior. Said's work illustrates an unfortunate tendency in Western multicultural scholarship to deplore the sins of Western culture while ignoring or justifying the same (or greater) offenses in non-Western cultures.

The point here is that other cultures—not only Islamic culture but also Hindu culture and Chinese culture—also give striking displays of ethnocentrism. When Jesuit missionaries first arrived in China and showed the Chinese the new maps they had made of the known world, the officials of the Chinese court declared that the maps had to be wrong since they did not show China at the center of the globe. The Jesuits obligingly redrew their maps placing China at the center and the emperor and his courtiers were satisfied.

The Chinese may appear from this example to be amusingly unsophisticated, yet we all adopt a reference point that privileges our own position in space and time. When we speak of the "Middle East," for example, we are using a geographical term of Western origin. From the point of view of Western observers, the "East" began where Europe ended, and the middle region of the then-known East was conveniently called the Middle East. So, too, the term "Middle Ages" is based on a Western division of time into ancient, medieval, and modern. Obviously the people who lived in the Middle Ages didn't know they lived in the Middle Ages.

Moreover, terms such as "Middle Ages" or "Dark Ages" do not

have the same connotation outside Western civilization that they do within it. Recently historian Joseph Ellis accused Islamic fundamentalists of trying to take Muslims back to the "Dark Ages."[6] Apparently Ellis doesn't know—or simply forgot—that the Dark Ages were not dark in the Muslim world. In fact, the period between 700 A.D. and 1500 A.D. was the golden age of Islamic civilization. From the point of view of Muslim historians, the Islamic world was civilization itself and beyond Islam's borders were only barbarians.

This Islamic perception may strike us as arrogant, but historian Bernard Lewis writes that this arrogance was "not without justification." China during this period had a rich, powerful, and sophisticated civilization, but it remained regional, confined to one group of people and one part of the world. By contrast, Islam was the first universal civilization, stretching across three continents and encompassing an astonishing diversity of white, black, yellow, and brown people. Lewis notes that "Islam represented the greatest military power on earth. It was the foremost economic power in the world. It had achieved the highest level so far in human history in the arts and sciences of civilization."[7]

As historian Albert Hourani shows in *A History of the Arab Peoples,* the great culture of Islam radiated outward from its great cities: Damascus, Baghdad, Cairo, Nishapur, Granada, and Istanbul. This was at a time when London and Paris were small towns. The intellectual heritage of Greece and Rome, largely lost to Europe, was preserved, debated, and enriched by Islamic thinkers of the caliber of Ibn Rushd (Averroes), Ibn Sina (Avicenna), al-Farabi, al-Ghazali, al-Biruni, and al-Kindi.[8] Western historians commonly identify the "Dark Ages" as a low point of European history, so they define "progress" as moving onward and upward, away from the past. By contrast, many Muslim historians see their history as one of precipitous decline from the glorious era, and they do not hesitate to identify "progress" with moving back to the days when the Muslim civilization was at its summit.

Ethnocentrism is not only a problem in understanding history; it also inhibits us from understanding contemporary events, such as those leading up to 9/11. For example, it is an article of faith, at least among conservatives, that the West won the Cold War against what Reagan justly termed the "evil empire." But bin Laden strenuously disputes the premise. His view, echoed by other radical Muslims, is that by pushing the Soviet Union out of Afghanistan, the Muslims began the process that resulted in the Soviet collapse. Bin Laden thinks *he* won the Cold War. In making such a claim, he is not entirely delusional: the Soviets were driven out of Afghanistan by a combination of American technology, American and Muslim money, and the indefatigable fighting zeal of the Muslims who called themselves the "Arab Afghans." What matters here is not whether bin Laden is right or wrong, but that he is convinced of having won a great victory over godless communism, and this belief emboldened him to attack the United States.

To some degree ethnocentrism is unavoidable, because human beings have no alternative to viewing the world through some background set of assumptions and beliefs. If ethnocentrism cannot be completely overcome, however, the scope of its errors can be reduced and minimized. The way to do this is to turn assumptions into questions. We should always be aware of the blinders that ethnocentrism places on our minds. We should listen open-mindedly to what the Muslims have to say, trying to understand them as they understand themselves. We should try to make sense even of the people and practices that seem most outlandish to us, such as Muslims who seek divine rule in the modern world or Muslim men who marry multiple wives.

Equally important, we should try and see ourselves as they see us. In doing this we should recognize that they, too, are viewing us somewhat ethnocentrically, through the lens of their assumptions and beliefs. Even so, we should carefully consider what our critics and enemies say, even when what they say is harsh. We cannot content ourselves with goofball expressions of innocence, such as President Bush's profession of disbelief that there are people in other parts of the world who hate America. "I'm amazed that there's such misunderstanding of what our country is about that people would hate us. . . . Like most Americans, I just can't believe it. Because I know how good we are."[9] Painful though it may be to admit, some of what the critics or even enemies say about America and the West is not necessarily based on misunderstanding. Some of their charges may be true. In that case we will have to figure out how to respond to their justified complaints.

Contrary to the multicultural mantra, true understanding does not involve a suspension of judgment about other cultures, or a double standard that routinely condemns Western culture and exalts non-Western cultures. Rather, it involves a willingness to critically and open-mindedly evaluate other cultures as well as our own culture. In some cases, this involves a quest for an independent or universal standard of evaluation to assess others as well as ourselves. Although sometimes challenging, these efforts are indispensable to helping us comprehend better why the Muslims do what they do, so that we can more intelligently resolve what we should do about them.

THE WESTERN EFFORT to understand the Islamic world is never more difficult than when Muslims do things like blow themselves up while flying planes into buildings—actions no sane Westerner would even contemplate. Yet we must try to understand the suicide bomber, not only because of 9/11, but also because the Iraqi insurgency seems capable of recruiting a virtually inexhaustible supply of suicide bombers. Already there have been hundreds of suicide bombings in Iraq, and one report shows that suicide plays a role in two out of every three insurgent attacks.[10] The issue here isn't "terrorism" because terrorism is defined as an attack on civilians whereas many of the suicide attacks are launched against military targets. Whether the target is military or civilian, suicide missions are now the primary weapon of choice used by the enemy in this war, and so far they constitute a strategy that the West can neither comprehend nor effectively resist. Why would someone willingly seek death? How do you defend against an attacker who is ready to die?

If we listen carefully to the bombers—those who leave records or seek to explain their actions—we discover they speak a strange language. In the last hours before he piloted United Airlines flight 93, which crashed in Pennsylvania on 9/11, Ziad Jarrah wrote a final letter to his wife, Aysel Sengun. "I did not escape from you," he said, "but I did what I was supposed to. You should be very proud of me. It's an honor, and you will see the results, and everybody will be happy. I want you to remain very strong as I knew you. . . . Keep your head high. The victors never have their heads down!" Or consider the videotaped statement of London bomber Mohammad Sidique Khan, released through Al Jazeera: "I and thousands like me are forsaking everything for what we believe. Our driving motivation doesn't come from tangible commodities that this world has to offer. . . . Our words are dead until we give them life with our blood." A Palestinian volunteer for suicide bombing told journalist Nasra Hassan that his selection for a death mission was "the happiest day of my life." The only fear he felt, he confessed, was that something might go wrong and he might be prevented from successfully completing his mission. "The power of the spirit pulls us upward," he added, "while the power of material things pulls us downward."[11]

Such statements are not restricted to suicide bombers but are also made by Islamic radicals who go to fight for Islam in faraway countries or commit murder in the name of their religious cause. One Iranian who fought in the Iran-Iraq war says he envies his comrades who were killed. "I dream of martyrdom," he told author Elaine Sciolino. "I am waiting for it to happen. To prepare myself, I have eliminated all personal relationships. I have no attachment to my wife or son, only to God." Recently Muhammad Bouyeri, the twenty-seven-year-old Moroccan who slashed the throat of Theo van Gogh, a descendant of the family of painter Vincent van Gogh, was tried for homicide in a court in Amsterdam. The prosecutor, Frits van Straelen, told the court that Bouyeri had perpetrated a "hate crime." He said, "The accused preaches a message of hate and violence. He preaches that anyone who thinks differently can be killed." But, speaking in a calm voice, the defendant challenged this view. "I acted out of conviction and not out of hate," he said. "If I am ever released, I would do exactly the same thing again." Facing Theo van Gogh's mother, Bouyeri said, "I don't feel your pain. I don't know what it's like to lose a child that was brought into this world with so much pain. I hope that you will derive some comfort from the maximum sentence."[12]

Almost as disturbing as the suicide bombings and murderous attacks themselves are the celebrations and justifications offered by Islamic radicals. On September 11, 2001, Hamas issued an "Open Letter to America," which ended, "We stand in line and beg Allah to give you to drink from the cup of humiliation—and behold, heaven has answered." While terrorist actions like 9/11 inspire Muslim jubilation, few Muslims seem interested in publicly condemning suicide missions and the murder of innocents. Even the condemnations appear to assume a defensive mode. Listen to the words of Eyad al-Sarraj, a prominent physician in Gaza who is generally liberal and pro-American in a part of the world where those qualities are a rarity: "Martyrs are at the level of prophets. They are untouchable. I can denounce suicide bombings, which I have many times, but not the martyrs themselves, because they are like saints. The martyr sacrifices himself for the nation. If you want to be a part of this culture, you have to understand this. I don't believe in religion myself, but I cannot say that martyrs are wrong. If you do that, you will discredit yourself completely."[13]

Some Western analysts, baffled and dismayed, have tried to interpret suicide bombings and murder attacks as the desperate actions of losers who can't get a girl in this life and so strap bombs on their chest in the hope of getting seventy-two virgins in paradise.[14] Or maybe the suicide bombers simply hope to cash in on the few thousand dollars that their sponsors typically contribute to the families of the martyrs. In one or two cases, such as the pathetic "shoe bomber" Richard Reid, this description rings true, but as a generalization it seems dubious. After all, there are plenty of losers in America: how many of them could be persuaded to blow themselves up for a little money and the prospect of six dozen virgins in heaven? Even losers are smart enough to say, "First show me the virgins."

Moreover, it is not just the bombers we need to understand but the culture that produces large numbers of them. Even if many of the bombers are pathological or deluded, we need to figure out the system that finds such men and directs them to lethal political ends. In other words, we need to understand the motivation not merely of the compliant bombers but also of the powerful men who recruit them, train them, and then send them out to kill and be killed. Even more broadly, we require a better grasp of the tidal wave of resentment toward the United States that is coming from the Islamic world. This hatred is so strong that a 2005 Zogby survey showed Muslims would rather have China, instead of the United States, as the world's superpower. The suicide bombers are only the most extreme expression of an anti-American animus that seems widely shared among Muslims.

AMERICAN LIBERALS HAVE a confident explanation for suicide bombers and insurgents: they are striking back against America and Europe for the West's long and continuing history of oppression, conquest, occupation, and exploitation. In understanding Islamic radicalism, many liberals focus on the sins of Western history and American foreign policy. It is illuminating to consider some of the main outlines of this analysis.

They're very upset at us for the Crusades. In an earlier chapter I quoted Bill Clinton's argument that Muslims are still exchanging horror stories about the Crusades. Clinton's view is passionately advocated in James Carroll's recent book *Crusade*, which portrays the Crusades as a horrific act of Western aggression that still shapes the military thinking of America's leaders and inspires outrage in the Muslim world. "The Crusades were a set of world historic crimes," Carroll writes. "That trail of violence scars the earth and human memory even to this day—especially in the places where the crusaders wreaked their havoc."[15] President Bush himself seems unnerved by the term. Having once described the American response to Al Qaeda as a "Crusade," Bush promptly apologized for using this scary word. The best thing going for Clinton's and Carroll's argument is that bin Laden frequently describes Americans and Europeans as "Crusaders."

Is it reasonable to think that Muslims today are genuinely outraged about events that occurred a thousand years ago? It's true that Muslims have a good general knowledge of their history. It's possible that they have extremely long memories. But precisely for these reasons, we can be sure that the argument advanced by Clinton and Carroll is wrong. Let us remember that before the rise of Islam, the region we call the Middle East was predominantly Christian. There were Zoroastrians in Persia, polytheists in Arabia, and Jews in Palestine, but most of the people in what we now call Iraq, Syria, Jordan, and Egypt were Christian. The sacred places in Christianity—where Christ was born, lived, and died—are in that region. Inspired by Islam's call to jihad, Muhammad's armies conquered Jerusalem and the entire Middle East, then pushed south into Africa, east into Asia, and north into Europe. They conquered parts of Italy and most of Spain, invaded the Balkans, and were preparing for a final incursion that would bring all of Europe under the rule of Islam. So serious was the Islamic threat that Edward Gibbon speculated that if the West had not fought back, "Perhaps the Koran would now be taught in the schools of Oxford, and her pulpits might demonstrate to a circumcised people the sanctity and truth of the Revelation of Mahomet."[16]

More than two hundred years after Islamic armies conquered the Middle East and forced their way into Europe, the Christians finally did strike back. Rallied by the pope and the ruling dynasties of Europe, the Christians attempted in the eleventh century to recover the heartland of Christianity and to repel the irredentist forces of Islam. These efforts are now called "the Crusades." (The term is an invention of modern scholarship; it was unknown to the Christians and Muslims who fought in those battles.) The First Crusade was a modest success. The Christians captured Jerusalem in 1099. Then the Muslims regrouped and routed the Crusaders, and Saladin reconquered Jerusalem in 1187. Subsequent Crusades were failures, and Jerusalem remained under Muslim rule.

The Crusades were important to Europe because they represented a fight to capture Christianity's holiest site and also because they were part of a battle for the survival of Europe. The Crusades are also seen as a precursor to Europe's voyages of exploration and conquest, which inaugurated the modern era. By contrast, the Crusades have never been important to the Muslim world. Muslims were already in control of their own holy sites in Mecca and Medina. Not once did the Crusaders threaten the heartland of Islam. From the point of view of Muslim historians, those battles were seen as minor disruptions on the periphery of the Islamic empire. The Abbasid caliphs, based in Baghdad, were far more concerned with rival Islamic dynasties, such as the Fatimid dynasty in Egypt.

In summary, the Crusades were a belated, clumsy, and defensive reaction against a much longer, more relentless, and more successful Muslim assault against Christendom. Liberal scholars like Carroll view the Crusades as a clear example of the pointless and harmful effects of "holy war." Christendom, in their view, was simply not worth defending in this way. The striking aspect of the liberal critique is that it stresses the horrors of the Crusades while virtually ignoring the Islamic jihad to which the Crusades were a response. Even if liberals detest the Crusades, however, there is no good reason for many of today's Muslims to care about them, and there is no evidence that they think about the subject at all. So why does bin Laden still invoke the term? As we will see in later chapters, bin Laden uses the term "Crusaders" to mean something entirely different from the knights who rode with Richard the Lion Heart. Some liberals will continue to cite those medieval Christian campaigns to discredit the war against terrorism, but their argument that contemporary Islamic radicals are legitimately incensed about the Crusades is without merit.

They're angry about colonialism. Many on the cultural left, like Edward Said, attribute Muslim rage to the still-fresh wounds of Western conquest and subjugation. Said laments the plight of "the ravaged colonial peoples who for centuries endured summary injustice, unending economic oppression, distortion of their social and intimate lives, and a recourseless submission that was the function of unchanging European superiority."[17] But if the Islamic radicals are smoldering over Western colonialism, why would they launch their attacks now, a half century after colonialism ended and the Europeans went home? Let's recall that European colonialism in the Middle East was relatively brief, and with the exception of the French in Algeria, the Europeans didn't rule directly but through surrogates. After World War I, the British and the French established a series of protectorates and mandates in countries like Egypt, Tunisia, Libya, Morocco, and the Sudan. The French effectively controlled Lebanon and Syria, and the British were the de facto rulers in Transjordan and Iraq. Naturally many Muslims disliked European dominance, but if today's Muslims are so angry about their countries being ruled indirectly for decades, why aren't the Asian Indians even more incensed about being ruled directly for centuries? Yet there is a lot of anti-Western sentiment in the Muslim world and very little of it in India.

In addition, the radical Muslims know that Islam had its own empires. When the Muslims were strong they conquered other nations; when the Muslims became weak other nations dominated them. There are no grounds here for shock and outrage. Of course the Muslims fought to oust their colonial occupiers, and sometimes they were successful, as in Algeria. But even without wars of independence the Europeans gave the Muslims the rest of their countries back, while Islam has never voluntarily returned the territories that over the centuries it seized by force.

Moreover America—the focal point of the anger of radical Muslims—has virtually no history of colonialism in the Middle East. If the Filipinos or American Indians were launching suicide bombers in New York, their actions could perhaps be attributed to a reaction against colonial subjugation. But until the Bush administration ordered the invasion of Afghanistan and Iraq in the aftermath of 9/11, America had never occupied a Muslim country. This was not for lack of opportunity. After World War II, America could quite easily have colonized the entire Middle East, but never even considered doing so.

America's record is one of opposing British and French colonial initiatives, and of encouraging the European colonial powers to withdraw from the Middle East. Liberal scholar Rashid Khalidi admits, "For many years after World War II the United States continued to be seen by people in the Middle East as a potential ally against the old colonial powers, and indeed played such a role in Libya in 1950–51, during the Suez War of 1956, and the Algerian War of Liberation from France in 1954–62."[18] So Muslim anti-Americanism has to be explained by factors other than colonial occupation in the Middle East, since prior to 9/11 America has no record of colonial occupation in the Middle East.

They're resentful because America continues to support unelected dictators in the Middle East. This is a very peculiar argument for liberals to make. How can Islamic radicals be upset that America supports tyrannical regimes in the Middle East when, except for Israel, there are no other kinds of regimes in the Middle East? True, America has historically supported despotic rulers like the shah of Iran, and even now America is allied with dictators in Pakistan, Egypt, and Saudi Arabia. If you read bin Laden's statements, however, you see that his objection is not that America supports unelected rulers, but that America supports the *wrong kind* of unelected rulers. Bin Laden is not a democrat, and he could hardly fault America for ignoring principles of free elections and self-government that bin Laden himself does not believe in. Rather, bin Laden's objection is that America supports the tyranny of the infidel while he himself supports the tyranny of the believers.

It is a staple of liberal commentary that America in the early 1950s overthrew the elected government of Mohammed Mossadegh in Iran and restored the hated shah, which supposedly set off a reverberating current of Islamic disillusionment. Actually Mossadegh was not elected by the Iranian people, but rather, chosen by the parliament and appointed by the shah. Shortly after assuming power Mossadegh clashed with the shah, and in the ensuing power struggle he dissolved parliament and suspended civil liberties. In this battle between two despots, the Eisenhower administration approved U.S. participation in a plan to oust Mossadegh and restore the shah to full power. It may have been a mistake for America to get involved, but the idea that Mossadegh was some kind of elected democrat is spurious. In any event, far from being perturbed at Mossadegh's departure, the Muslim fundamentalists were delighted by it. The ayatollah Khomeini hated Mossadegh, whom he denounced as a socialist and an infidel. When Mossadegh fell, Khomeini preached a sermon thanking Allah for getting rid of an enemy of Islam. Iranian textbooks today portray Mossadegh as a betrayer of Muslims. The point is that America's role in Mossadegh's fall has nothing to do with why Islamic radicals today hate America.

There are unelected despots in the Middle East, and Muslim fundamentalists do oppose them. They are opposed, however, not because they are tyrannical or undemocratic but because they are perceived to be working against Islam. Liberal scholars often commit the ethnocentric fallacy of attributing to Muslims their own parochial complaints about American foreign policy.

They're outraged because America's foreign policy is based on selfishness and oil interests. This argument reflects liberal ethnocentrism at its comic best. Only a liberal could denounce his country for pursuing its own interests. Elsewhere in the world, and emphatically in the Muslim world, nations are expected to act in their self-interest. Shortly after 9/11 the Pakistani leader Pervez Musharraf was asked, "You used to support the Taliban. Now you are against them. Why?" His answer was brief. "Our national self-interest has changed." Next question? Muslims, being realists, expect America to pursue its interests in the Middle East, including of course its interest in Middle Eastern oil. Islamic radicals who despise President Bush sometimes point out that American action is based not on high ideals but on economic and political interests. This criticism, however, is intended to unmask American self-righteousness and hypocrisy. It is not a denial that America has every right to pursue its interests, in the same manner that every other country in the world unhesitatingly does.

What puzzles and frustrates Muslims is that they see America acting *against* self-interest in repeatedly and unbendingly allying with the state of Israel. Muslims of all stripes profess amazement that a country would make enemies of people who have oil in order to make friends with people who have nothing. "It would be one thing if these Jews had the same ancestry as Americans or if they practiced the same religion as you do," one Muslim lawyer complained to me. "You have nothing in common with them. Yet you risk American lives and give them billions of dollars and endanger your position in the whole Arab world on their account. You refused to reexamine your support for Israel even when faced with an oil embargo that severely injured your economy. Why do you give up so much for the Jews? What are the Jews giving you in return?" The man said he wished America would act more selfishly and less idealistically. "We understand your interests," he said. "We don't understand your ideals." It is this sort of thinking that leads to theories of Jewish conspiracy that abound in the Muslim world.

They're angry because American actions have killed so many Muslims. Actually America has actively fought on the side of Muslims in several recent conflicts. During the 1970s the United States supported the Afghan mujahedin and their Arab allies in driving the Soviet Union from Afghanistan. In 1991 the United States assembled an international coalition of countries, including many Muslim countries, in order to drive Saddam Hussein out of Kuwait and restore the sovereignty of that small Muslim country. Later in the decade, President Clinton ordered American bombings and intervention to save Muslim lives in Bosnia and Kosovo. True, many Muslims hold America accountable for Israel's military actions in Lebanon and in the Palestinian territories. And Muslims frequently deplore the civilian lives lost in the American invasions of Afghanistan and Iraq. These deaths, however, are small in number compared with the devastation that other invading armies, including Muslim armies, have wrought through the centuries right down to the present day.

For instance, when the Mongols stormed through Iran and Iraq—already having laid waste in China, India, and Russia—they massacred all the men in sight, enslaved the women and children, and looted, pillaged, and burned. Muslim histories record the devastation that ensued when the Mongols in 1258 killed the last Abbasid caliph and sacked Baghdad. Compared to the Mongols, the American invaders of the early twenty-first century seem like amateurs, jeopardizing their own soldiers in Afghanistan and Iraq to minimize civilian casualties, even distributing food to Afghan families in the course of getting rid of the Taliban. Muslims are fully aware that when the Mongols sped across Muslim lands they did not seek to ameliorate the sufferings of Muslim families by handing out bowls of Mongolian beef.

Moreover Muslims have demonstrated their own skills at invasion, conquest, and killing. Recall that Constantinople used to be a Christian city, the capital of the Byzantine Empire. When Mehmet the Conqueror captured Constantinople in 1453, he rode his horse into Hagia Sophia and proclaimed that the cathedral would henceforth become a mosque. Mehmet then gave his soldiers permission to loot the city for three days.[19] In Iraq, by contrast, the American soldiers who put up an American flag were ordered to take it down and put up the Iraqi flag instead. No mosques were converted into churches. The only looting that followed Saddam Hussein's ouster in Iraq was carried out by Iraqis, while many American liberals blamed the American government for permitting it to occur.

More recent Muslim wars, such as the Iran-Iraq war, have also produced unbelievable horrors and casualty lists. Over the eight-year period of the Iran-Iraq war, for instance, between five hundred thousand and 1 million Muslims were killed. Several hundred thousand Muslims have been killed by the Sudanese regime as the result of civil strife in Darfur. All of the conflicts involving Israel and the Muslims, including the Palestinian struggle and all the Arab-Israeli wars, have not come close to this level of slaughter. Despite the vaunted power of American "shock and awe" technology, America simply cannot keep pace with the mass killings that Muslim nations have inflicted on one another. Islamic radicals know all this, which is why one cannot find in their literature the kind of indignation over America's killing of Muslim civilians that one routinely finds in liberal magazines, radio shows, and Web sites. Liberal apoplexy over American actions appears to be sustained mainly by omitting any historical context and by ignoring how Muslim nations themselves have acted, both against Christians and against one another.

They're outraged about America's treatment of Muslim prisoners at Guantánamo Bay and Abu Ghraib: Historian Bernard Lewis has pointed out that compared to prisons throughout the Arab world, Guantánamo Bay and Abu Ghraib are like Disneyland. Certainly in terms of cleanliness, food, and amenities, America's prisons are comparable to the accommodations in midlevel Middle Eastern hotels. Many on the left, no doubt, will protest such comparisons. In the liberal view, Muslim prisoners—even if they are not American citizens—are entitled to their basic rights, such as the right to a lawyer, a right to know the charges against them, a right to a speedy trial, and so on. But Islamic radicals of the Al Qaeda stripe are unaccustomed to these rights in their own countries. They can hardly expect from America any treatment other than what they would mete out to American prisoners that fall into their captivity. Their own methods for dealing with American captives include torture and decapitation.

Consequently it is doubtful that Muslim fighters and insurgents are outraged about being tortured—they expect to be tortured. If Muslim fundamentalists are enraged by American abuses at Guantánamo Bay and Abu Ghraib, it has to be for reasons other than legal deprivation or even torture. When I raised this point in a recent speech a liberal professor angrily responded, "What infuriates them is that America holds itself to a higher standard!" My answer was: Why should Muslims care whether America lives up to its standards or not? It makes no sense for a Muslim to say, "Yes, America's prisons are probably some of the best places in the world for Muslims to be held captive, but we continue to be outraged at America because America's high standards demand even more lenient treatment." For radical Muslims to say this would be to concede America's moral superiority—something they will never admit, and do not believe in.

My conclusion is that the main reasons that liberal scholars and activists give to explain the antagonism of the Islamic radicals toward America are fallacious.

THE PROBLEM OF ethnocentrism—and the distortions it produces—is not restricted to liberals. Let us now consider some errors

generated by conservative ethnocentrism. In particular, I want to re-
fute the notion, popular on the right, that radical Islam can be understood as the latest incarnation of totalitarian movements that the
West has seen before, such as the Nazis and the communists. Since
Islamic radicalism seems to have succeeded those movements in
threatening the West, some conservatives seek to understand the
new war on terrorism in the light of previous great wars that the
West has fought. As we saw in an earlier chapter, conservatives commonly refer to the Islamic radicals and fundamentalists as "Islamo-
fascists" or robed Bolsheviks, and some even try and explain their
philosophy as a variation of fascism or Nazism. While there is an ideological kinship between fascism and the secular Baath movements
in Syria and Iraq, there is no connection—there is not even a simi-
larity—between twentieth-century Western fascism and contemporary Islamic fundamentalism.

Nor can Islamic radicalism and fundamentalism be helpfully understood by invoking the analogy of the Cold War. Norman Podhoretz and others have dubbed the contemporary conflict "World
War IV," and there is no harm in this, if you want to place the great
wars of our time in historical sequence or to highlight the global
scope of the conflict. But if the Cold War constituted World War III,
it represented a very different kind of battle from the one against Islamic radicalism. The Soviets had a mammoth arsenal of nuclear
weapons and could threaten nuclear Armageddon. The Muslim radicals are undoubtedly trying to get their hands on a nuclear bomb,
but clearly they are not even close to posing a doomsday threat.

Even so, the Islamic radicals have something that the Soviet communists, particularly toward the end, did not have—true believers.
By the time the Berlin Wall fell, the only place to find true-believing
Marxists was in the humanities and social science departments of
elite universities in the United States, Canada, and Europe. There
seemed to be scarcely any left in the Soviet Union. By contrast, Islam today is teeming with true-believing radicals who are willing to
give their lives to destroy America and the West. Moreover, Nazism
and communism were movements within Western civilization that
could easily be understood in Western terms. Their language was

familiar, and their goals fully understandable within the Western conceptual framework. One might not agree with Marxist goals such as state ownership of property, the rule of the working class, or the global proletarian revolution, but there was little doubt about what such concepts meant. Marx was, after all, a "dead white male" who was educated in the Western intellectual canon.

By contrast, we need to move outside the familiar orbit of Western civilization in order to understand Islamic radicalism. Recall that for all the fanaticism produced by the Nazis and the communists, neither movement produced a single suicide bomber. The Japanese during World War II produced suicide bombers—the kamikazes— but the kamikazes were combat soldiers, military men. The Japanese never sought to persuade civilians, such as students and immigrants and mothers of two, to destroy themselves in murderous attacks against civilian targets. Clearly something new is going on. And while suicide attacks and murder missions are not restricted to the Muslim world, most of them either occur in the Muslim world or are perpetrated by Muslims.

The common element between Nazism and communism is that both were ideologies rooted in atheism. Significantly, many in the West spoke of "godless communism." The distinguishing feature of Islamic radicalism is that it is Islamic. This is easily overlooked in the West for a reason given by historian Bernard Lewis: "Most Muslim countries are still profoundly Muslim in a way and in a sense that most Christian countries are no longer Christian."[20] Consequently the danger of ethnocentric blinders is particularly severe when Western observers—especially secular Western observers—seek to understand a religious culture such as that of Islam. The intense religiosity of that culture, not simply at its point of historical origin but even today, generates surprise and even incomprehension among many Americans and Europeans. Even when Muslims insist they are acting out of religious conviction, these Westerners refuse to believe it, and attribute Muslim behavior to some other "genuine" motive.

At the sentencing trial of Ramzi Yusuf, who was convicted of conspiring in 1993 to blow up the World Trade Center, Judge Kevin

Duffy declared that the defendant "cared little or nothing for Islam." Addressing Yusuf, Duffy informed him, "Your God is not Allah. Your god is death."[21] For all his self-assurance, Duffy was speaking the purest nonsense. Unfortunately, proclamations of this sort are quite common and are issued not only by indignant judges but also by scholars and policy makers.

My broader point is that no real understanding of Islamic culture is possible that refuses to take Islam seriously. The reason is that even now across the Muslim world, many centuries after the death of Muhammad, Islam retains the force of its original revelation. In that world, unity based on shared religious identity is expected in the sphere of international relations. Despite their differences, Muslim governments throughout the Middle East have constructed a complex apparatus of consultation, cooperation, and common action. They routinely articulate a "Muslim position" on various policy questions. To see how odd this is, imagine if someone suggested that the Protestant nations of Germany, Holland, and the United States unite as a "Protestant coalition," or that the Catholic countries of southern Europe and South America form a "Catholic league," or that the Buddhist countries of Eastern and Southern Asia unify as a "Buddhist bloc." The nations in question would regard such suggestions as absurd. Yet Muslim countries find such joint action to be not only sensible but in some sense religiously mandated.

Moreover, Islamic identity is even stronger in domestic than in international issues. Lewis writes, "In no Christian country at the present time can religious leaders command the degree of religious belief and the extent of religious participation by their followers that are usual in Muslim lands. Christian leaders do not exercise or even claim the kind of political role that in Muslim lands is not only common but is widely accepted as proper." Unlike many Christians, who have multiple identities only one of which is that they happen to be Christian, Muslims typically regard their religion as central to both private and public identity, and consider all other affiliations as secondary or derivative. As we will see, Islamic radicalism draws from these deep wells of piety. Lewis writes that even today, across an entire civilization, "Islam is the most powerful rallying-cry, and it is for Islam, more than for any other cause, that men are willing to kill and be killed."[22]

This point is borne out by the very names of the organizations of radical Islam. The term "Al Qaeda" means "the foundation" or "the base," which in this case refers to the foundation of a worldwide Islamic resistance. The largest group of radical Islam, with chapters throughout the Middle East, is called the Muslim Brotherhood; one of its famous slogans is "The Koran is our constitution." Hezbollah, the Iran-supported group that launched the 2006 rocket attacks against Israel from Lebanon, has a name that means "Party of God." Its motto is taken directly from the Koran. The Palestinian terror group Hamas gets its name from an Arabic acronym for "Islamic resistance movement"; the word itself means "enthusiasm" or "zeal." Muslim radicals in Algeria, who almost took over the government in the 1990s, called themselves the Islamic Salvation Front.

All these groups identify their struggle primarily in religious terms. Their activists speak of themselves as "holy warriors" for Islam. Their communiqués typically begin with the Muslim invocation "In the name of Allah, the Merciful, the Compassionate." The commentaries of radical Islam adopt the tradition of Islamic historical narrative in reporting the death of Muslims with phrases such as "Peace be upon him" or "God have mercy on him." These writings routinely refer to the adversary as the "enemies of God." Their references to America and the West are peppered with terms like "unbelievers" and "infidels." Curses like "vile unbeliever" and "accursed infidel" are not perfunctory slogans or stylistic exaggerations but are deeply meant. The deaths of Western infidels are reported with undisguised enthusiasm and typically accompanied by phrases like "God speed his soul to hell." Bin Laden's writings and video recordings are filled with this rhetoric, and the religious emphasis and terminology are not incidental to his message: they are his message.

Virtually every statement made by a Muslim attacker or suicide bomber testifies to an Islamic motivation. We know that the 9/11 terrorists left behind diaries professing their piety and hopes for heavenly reward, and giving detailed instructions of what prayers and ritual washings they should perform before boarding the planes and what religious chants they should make while killing those who stood in their way. Mohammad Sidique Khan explained his participation in the London bombings as an act of "obedience to the one true God." Muhammad Bouyeri told the Dutch court that his assassination of Theo van Gogh was in fulfillment of "the law that instructs me to chop off the head of anyone who insults Allah or the Prophet."[23]

As these statements make clear, in order to understand Islamic radicalism it is necessary to understand Islam. Even a basic knowledge can help unravel mysteries that would otherwise remain unsolved. For instance, while both Christianity and Islam share a concept of martyrdom, the martyr in Christianity is one who voluntarily endures suffering and death rather than relinquish the faith. In Islam, by contrast, a martyr is one who dies fighting for the faith. This helps to explain the statement I quoted earlier from the Gaza physician who is against suicide bombings but feels helpless in condemning those who carry them out. However terrible he finds their conduct, he cannot reasonably deny that these Muslims are making the ultimate sacrifice for their religious beliefs. From his point of view, there may be grounds for disagreeing with their strategy, or for deploring the consequences of their actions, but their status as martyrs remains secure because they have indeed given their lives fighting for Islam.

SOME CONSERVATIVES AND liberals, who recognize the importance of Islam in shaping Islamic radicalism and terrorism, nevertheless fall into various types of errors. These too are typically the product of an ethnocentric mind-set. On the conservative side, partisans of Samuel Huntington's "clash of civilizations" thesis tend to posit a war between Western civilization on the one hand and Islamic civilization on the other. As Huntington argues, culture is rooted in the cult and therefore the tension between Islam and the West is fundamentally religious. Huntington goes so far as to suggest that the West's seventy-year conflict with Soviet communism was a brief historical detour and now the centuries-old struggle between Islam and Christianity has resumed.[24] As we will see in the next chapter, this is very close to the way that bin Laden and the Islamic radicals view the conflict. This agreement does not, of course, discredit Huntington's analysis, but neither does it enhance its credibility. Overall, I think Huntington is wrong.

One problem with Huntington's thesis is that, as we saw in the previous chapter, the West today is not the religious civilization it once was, and today it is more divided than ever before. Not only are there bitter divisions between America and its major European allies, notably Germany and France, but in addition America itself is deeply split between liberals and conservatives, between blue America and red America. A second shortcoming of the "clash of civilizations" viewpoint is that it treats Islamic society as monolithic whereas, as we will see, there is an important chasm in the Muslim world that parallels the profound cleavage in America. It is time to move past Huntington to recognize the internal clashes within the West and within Islam. Neither "our" behavior nor "their" behavior can be understood without specifying which "us" and which "them."

Huntington's fallacy is part of a broader misperception on the right. This view holds that since pious Muslims are the ones launching attacks against Europe and America, Islam is to blame and Islam is the problem. Ibn Warraq and Oriana Fallaci both blame Islam for fostering the fanatical mind-set that leads to terrorism, and some Christian conservatives have gone so far as to allege that Islam is a "wicked religion" and that "Muhammad was a terrorist."[25] Even Pope Benedict in a September 2006 speech cited a medieval emperor to the effect that Islam was an evil faith founded and sustained by violence. If these views seem churlish and exaggerated—and they are—the misperception of Islam among many American liberals is no less egregious.

Several liberals who recognize the importance of Islam as a galvanizing force tend to draw from this the conclusion that "religion is the problem." Sam Harris writes in *The End of Faith* that on 9/11 "the evil that finally reached our shores . . . is the evil of religious faith." Nobel laureate Steven Weinberg argues that since religious people believe in an afterlife, they are more likely to participate in suicide attacks because they don't really expect to die as a consequence. The same point was made by Richard Dawkins: "To fill a world with religion is like littering the streets with loaded guns. . . . Religion teaches the dangerous nonsense that death is not the end."[26] According to this view, religion when taken too seriously leads to fanaticism and fundamentalism, and this has become a serious problem in the Muslim world, as it has become a serious problem in America.

The problem with this argument is that no other religion has displayed the characteristics that we see in today's Islam. Christianity in all its history has never had suicide bombers, and neither has Judaism, Hinduism, or Buddhism. Nor can anyone reasonably assert that Islam is intrinsically the problem. Despite the religious enthusiasm of many suicide bombers, Islam has been around for more than a thousand years, and for most of its history it produced neither suicide attackers nor terrorists. It is only contemporary Islam that provides an inspiration for suicide missions and attacks on civilians. Consequently we need to ask: what is the situation in Islam today that has given rise to a new kind of radicalism and terrorism?

To understand Islamic radicalism, we need to understand the culture from which it grows. Many Americans—liberal as well as conservative—seek to identify Islamic fundamentalism as a distinctive feature of either the Sunni or the Shia groups. Which of these groups—I am often asked—is theologically susceptible to the doctrines of Islamic radicalism? The problem with the question is that it presumes there are doctrinal or creedal differences between Sunni and Shia Muslims. This assumption reflects the Western tendency to understand Islam through the lens of the Catholic-Protestant divide. But unlike the Catholics and the Protestants, who fought hard over fine points of doctrine, there are no meaningful theological distinctions between the Sunni and the Shia.

Their real disagreement is over the issue of legitimate succession. It is a debate over the authentic Islamic family tree. Shia Muslims believe that the true line of descent passes through the Prophet Muhammad's son-in-law, Ali. Sunni Muslims recognize the legitimacy of the various caliphs and sultans who have ruled Islamic empires through the centuries. Admittedly the Sunni and the Shia have different styles of worship. The notion of martyrdom is much more deeply rooted in Shia history, whereas it is a recent development in Sunni Islam. Certainly the two groups sometimes fight each other for political and economic power—as they are doing in Iraq. But these are not religious disputes and the two groups remain united on the main tenets of Islamic belief and practice. The crucial point is that Islamic radicalism, with its insurgents, holy warriors, and suicide attackers, has arisen out of both groups. The Khomeini revolution arose in Shia-dominated Iran, and radical groups like Hezbollah are made up of Shia. Al Qaeda and the Iraqi insurgents are mainly Sunni.

Another common illusion, held across the American political spectrum, is that the Muslim world is divided into "liberals" and "fundamentalists." This distinction suffers from two limitations. First, there are virtually no liberals in the Muslim world. I am not referring here to classical liberalism—a belief in free markets, voting, or religious toleration—but rather to modern liberalism, which is characterized by doctrines such as "Men and women should have the same roles in society," "Freedom of expression includes the right to publish material that is sexually explicit or blasphemous," or "Government should not seek to promote religion or legislate morality." Liberalism of this sort is confined to a small number of Muslim intellectuals whose voice is amplified in the West but who have no influence in Islamic countries.[27] Throughout the Arab world and in most of the Muslim world, liberalism as a political force simply does not exist.

A secular liberal like Salman Rushdie has no constituency in the Muslim world. Author Thomas Friedman says the West desperately needs Muslim leaders who will reject the concepts of jihad and martyrdom and instead "embrace religious diversity" and "affirm that God speaks multiple languages."[28] My reaction to this is: Good luck, Tom. Contact me, or my descendants, when you find such Muslims. I do not deny that there are feminists and secularists and perhaps even advocates of unrestricted free speech and homosexual marriage in Muslim countries, but I deny that they have any political significance. I admit that there are a sizable number of feminist and secular Iranians, but they live in Los Angeles.

But what about those liberals who voted for the reformist president Muhammad Khatami, and who continue to press for change in Iran? We can get a better sense of this group by following the debate over the past several years between "hard-liners" and "moderates" over the issue of public flogging for adulterous women. The hard-liners hold that public flogging is essential because this is what the holy law mandates, and moreover, an example has to be made of blatant offenders. The moderates counter that public flogging has given Iran a bad international image and therefore it would be better to have the floggings administered in private. Some moderates argue that Islamic law is a bit vague on the precise nature of the punishments that should be administered, and therefore the regime could consider other alternatives, such as fines or imprisonment.[29] One may say that the spectrum of debate in Iran is between the right and the far right.

The term "fundamentalist" is not a useful term of distinction in the Muslim world. The concept is derived from Protestant Christianity. In America, a fundamentalist is one who believes the Bible is the literal, unadulterated word of God. By this definition, however, all Muslims are "fundamentalists" because all Muslims believe that the Koran is the literal, unadulterated word of God given in the Arabic language by the angel Gabriel to the Prophet Muhammad.[30] The term Koran means "recitation" and Muslims hold the suras of this holy book to be divinely composed and strictly speaking untranslatable. If you don't believe these things, you're not a Muslim. Unlike in the West, the term "fundamentalist" has no negative connotation in Islamic society. The Saudi ruling family, for instance, never refers to its religious and political enemies as fundamentalist because it saves the description for itself. I realize that the term "fundamentalist" has become so widely used in the contemporary political discussion about Islam that it is unavoidable. When it is used, however, let us seek to define it clearly or at least be aware of its limitations.

The real divide in the Muslim world is between Islamic radicals and traditional Muslims. Traditional Muslims are not well known in

America, so let me offer a brief anecdote to illustrate who these people are and what they believe. While I was growing up in Mumbai,
we had a Muslim family that rented the ground floor of our house.
We lived on the next floor and my grandparents on the top floor.
One year, my grandfather decided not to renew the Noorani family's
lease. Since the Nooranis were reluctant to leave and were protected
by rent control laws, my grandfather offered them a sum of money
to leave in a year. But a year later, property values had surged, and
the Nooranis felt they could extract some more compensation from
my grandfather, so they showed no signs of leaving. My grandfather
approached a local Muslim minister, who confronted the patriarch
of the Noorani family. "Mubarak, did you give your word that you
would leave?" the minister asked. "Yes," Noorani replied, "but that
was before the prices—" He could not finish his sentence because
the minister interrupted him. "You gave your word and you are still
here? You call yourself a Muslim? You are a disgrace to Islam! I ad-
vise you to start packing." Within a month, the Noorani family was
gone. I narrate this episode not to demonstrate the moral character
of traditional Muslims—who are in this respect no better or worse
than anyone else—but to show the respect that even ordinary Muslims show for Islam's moral code.

Traditional Muslims are not "moderates." Many of them are just as
zealous in their religious faith and practice as radical Muslims. Traditional Muslims are best understood as those who practice Islam in the
way that it has evolved in the centuries since Muhammad. By contrast, radical Muslims are those who believe that Islam has reached a
point of crisis and that violent conflict is both the inevitable and desirable outcome of this crisis. (When I use the term "fundamentalist"
in this book, I am always referring to the radical Muslims.) What are
the theological differences between traditional Islam and radical Islam? On the fundamental religious questions, there are none. What
are the political differences? In general, there are few. Remarkable
though it seems, traditional Muslims and radical Muslims agree on
the threats faced by Islam, on where those threats come from, and
even on the general solution. The main area of disagreement is that
Islamic radicals are willing to pursue insurgency and terrorism to

achieve the shared goals. This program includes a new form of jihad against the infidels, a category that includes not only Westerners but many Muslims as well.

So far traditional Islam remains, as Seyyed Hossein Nasr writes, "the norm in the Islamic world."[31] It is the majority group, estimated at between 60 and 75 percent of the Muslim population. But traditional Islam has been losing members to radical Islam, which is advancing not just in the Middle East but in all the countries of the Muslim world. Once we understand what the Islamic radicals are saying, we can discover what it is they hate about America, what they intend to do about it, and why they continue to win recruits and converts to their cause.

FOUR

"The Head of the Snake"

The Islamic Critique
of Western Moral Depravity

THE ATMOSPHERE IN the Islamic world today is a strange mixture of Muslim piety and Western influence. The piety is unmistakable, not only in the mosques and public buildings, which reflect the distinctive imprint of Muslim civilization through the centuries, but also in the everyday clamor of streets, the schools, and the market square. It is visible in the attire of the women, audible in the muezzin's call to prayer. Crowds fill up stadiums throughout the Muslim world to hear recitations of the Koran. It's an art form, but what impresses the outsider is less the virtuosity of the speakers than the realization that they have committed the entire Koran to memory. (Koran memorization is a common educational requirement in Muslim schools.) At Shia gatherings, mullahs tell stories about ancient battles in which Shia saints were martyred by infidels, and the crowd breaks into sobs, calling on Allah to give them similar opportunities to make sacrifices for Islam.

Yet outsiders and Muslims are equally struck by the degree to which Western culture has penetrated the Islamic world. This is obviously true in Indonesia, Malaysia, and Turkey. Istanbul was recently named by *Newsweek* as one of Europe's coolest cities, with international shopping and throbbing nightclubs. But the West has also made its way into the heart of the Middle East. In Egypt and the Palestinian territories, young people listen to hard rock and rap music. A group called Palestinian Rappers describes itself as "the first rappers from Gaza." In Iraq, a new radio station called Radio Al Mahaba plays Mariah Carey and Jennifer Lopez songs, and features candid and previously taboo public discussions of subjects like divorce and women pursuing careers. Founded by an American feminist from New York, Radio Mahaba seeks, in the words of one of its producers, Ruwaida Kamal, to "affirm women's rights." Even in Iran, two and a half decades into the Khomeini revolution, Internet cafés are buzzing late into the night and almost everyone seems to own a satellite dish providing access to foreign television channels and movies. *Baywatch* and *Dallas* are off the air in America, but these shows, and others like them, continue to captivate audiences from Tunis to Tehran. At Tehran airport, journalist Elaine Sciolino found copies of Danielle Steele romance novels.[1] Even in the holy city of Qom, just down the street from the mosque, you can buy Wrangler jeans, American CDs, computer programs, and videos.

Talk to the young Muslims wearing jeans and New York Yankees T-shirts and you will discover that many of them admire Osama bin Laden. They regard bin Laden in much the same way that an American teenager might regard a Hollywood celebrity or rock star. Nor is this enthusiasm restricted to the younger generation. Across the Muslim world—among young and old, men and women, Sunni and Shia—bin Laden is celebrated and in some cases even revered. A poll taken by the Pew Global Attitudes Project in 2004 found that bin Laden is viewed positively by 45 percent of the people in Morocco, 55 percent in Jordan, and 65 percent in Pakistan. Bin Laden has his critics, notably among traditional Muslims who disagree with his tactics, or think that he is harming the cause of Islam. But even bin Laden's enemies seem to give him a grudging respect, and qualify their objections with qualities that they admire in him. Muslim writer Jamal Ismail conveys a common sentiment: "Although we may disagree with Osama about his ideological and political views, no one can place him among the enemies of the Islamic community and its aspirations."[2]

Why is bin Laden so popular? Senator Patty Murray, Democrat of Washington State, thinks she has it figured out. "He's been out in these countries for decades, building schools, building roads, building infrastructure, building day-care facilities, building health-care facilities, and the people are extremely grateful."[3] Here is liberal ethnocentrism in full gear. In Murray's view, bin Laden is revered for promoting across the Muslim world the liberal, welfare-state causes that Patty Murray happens to advocate in the United States. In reality, bin Laden hasn't built any schools, hospitals, or day-care facilities. His popularity stems from two sources. First, just about everyone who has met bin Laden describes him as a quiet, well-mannered, thoughtful, eloquent, and deeply religious person. Even those who oppose bin Laden characterize him in these terms.[4] For many Muslims, it is remarkable that a man born into a multimillion-dollar empire, a man who could be on a yacht in San Tropez with a blonde on one arm and a brunette on the other, has chosen to live in a cave in Afghanistan and risk his life for his beliefs. Second, bin Laden is popular because of what he is fighting for: he is standing up for Islam and striking out against the United States.

At first, I was reluctant to credit effusive descriptions of bin Laden's personality and courage. My impression of bin Laden, formed largely in the aftermath of 9/11, was one of a dark-eyed fanatic, a gun-toting extremist, a monster who laughs at the deaths of three thousand innocent civilians. I thought of bin Laden in much the same way that I envisioned the ayatollah Khomeini, his unforgiving, fanatical visage imprinted on my mind since the days of the hostage crisis in 1979 and 1980. Somewhat to my surprise, I discovered that this is not at all how Khomeini is perceived, even today, in his home country.

In Iran, for the past quarter century, Khomeini has been widely regarded as a great and noble man, a veritable modern prophet or imam. The Muslim scholar Hamid Algar conveys a common Muslim view that "this man is a kind of embodiment of the human ideal."[5] Khomeini's face, which looks down at you on Iranian streets and in public buildings, is not in the least frightening but rather is gentle, avuncular, even giving the hint of a smile. Many people who live in Iran revile the mullahs who are now ruling the country, but Khomeini remains popular even with critics of the revolution. Khomeini's gravesite near Tehran draws tens of thousands of devoted visitors each year. Unknown to most Americans, before Khomeini became the ruler of Iran, he was famous both as a scholar and a mystical poet. Like bin Laden, Khomeini is highly regarded for his modest demeanor, frugal lifestyle, and soft-spoken manner. He, too, is hailed for his willingness to undertake great personal risks for Islam, and for his bravery in challenging the country he called the "Great Satan," the United States.

Khomeini and bin Laden are the two most important figures in the history of modern Islam. To understand them—their ideas, goals, and popularity—we must begin with their statements and writings. But we must also go beyond them to understand the full force of the argument for radical Islam, an argument that is winning converts throughout the Muslim world and gaining political ground for radicals against traditional Muslims in every Islamic country, including "moderate" countries like Malaysia and "secular" countries like Turkey. One way to understand radical Islam is to travel through the Muslim world and converse with Muslims. Another is to peruse news and commentary on popular Islamic Internet sites, or in the various outlets of the Muslim press: the Qatar-based TV channel Al Jazeera, the independent news satellite station Al Arabiya, the Iranian channel Al Alam, the Egyptian newspaper *Al Ahram*, and so on. But perhaps the best way to learn about Islamic fundamentalism is by studying the influential thinkers who are shaping radical minds in the Muslim world. This has been my focus for the past few years.

Who are these thinkers? Khomeini is an original and influential thinker in his own right, but bin Laden is not, and neither is his chief deputy and strategist, al-Zawahiri. Most of the Islamic radicals are planners and executors who are trying to implement the vision and the political program of the leading thinkers of Islamic radicalism: Khomeini and Ali Shariati in Iran, Maulana Mawdudi in Pakistan, Sheikh Muhammad Husayn Fadlallah in Lebanon, Hassan Turabi in the Sudan, and the man who has done the most to inspire Islamic radicalism around the world, Sayyid Qutb of Egypt. These thinkers, anchored in the Islamic tradition and yet well versed in the ways of the West, have developed a critique of America and the West that is far more sophisticated and comprehensive than anything produced by the Marxists and the communists. They are the brains behind bin Laden and the intellectual juggernaut behind the global resurgence of radical Islam. Some of them may seem obscure in the West, but we can be sure that they are carefully read by people who plot to kill Westerners. If we want to understand "why they hate us," it is time that we pay attention to these intellectual architects of 9/11.

IF YOU CAREFULLY read bin Laden's statements, not to scoff at the ravings of a maniac but to genuinely understand what the man is trying to communicate, two major themes emerge. One is that the Islamic world and Islam itself are gravely threatened, and the other is that America is the chief threat to the survival of both. In 1998 bin Laden claimed that "since God put down the Arabian peninsula, created its desert, and surrounded it with its seas, no calamity has ever befallen it" like the one it faces now. That same year bin Laden warned that the danger was not just one of political control but that "our religion is under attack." In a videotape released shortly after 9/11, bin Laden revealed how serious he considers the attack: for the first time since Muhammad, he warned, Islam faces a threat to its very survival. The war on terror, bin Laden has repeatedly said, is an intrinsic part of the "Zionist-Crusader war on Islam."[6]

This threat to Islam cannot be due to American troops in Mecca, since there are no American troops in Mecca. The American base in Saudi Arabia is more than five hundred miles from Islam's holy sites, and the troops there rarely venture off their bases and have nothing to do with Saudi society. Nor can Islam be threatened because of the presence of Israel, a small irritant within the vast expanse of Islamic territory. Consequently, bin Laden's occasional condemnations of Israel, as well as his demand that American troops be withdrawn from Saudi Arabia, must be understood in a metaphorical sense. Bin Laden views Israel's presence, and its ability to pistol-whip the entire Arab world, as symptomatic of a deeper malaise confronting Islam. It is for the purpose of saving and restoring Islam that bin Laden seeks the removal of American and Western influence not only from Saudi Arabia but also from the rest of the Middle East. The reason for bin Laden's emphasis on America emerges from his second main theme, which is that America is, in his words, "the worst civilization in the history of mankind." Moreover, as he sees it, America aims "to get rid of Islam itself." America is, in bin Laden's memorable phrase, the "head of the snake."[7] Therefore, he concludes, Islam can survive only if America is driven out of the Muslim world or completely destroyed.

Contrary to the assertions of many on the left and even some on the right, bin Laden's primary objection is not to American foreign policy. The suicide bombers of radical Islam are not blowing themselves up because they are distressed over the Gulf War of 1991 or because they are in solidarity with the Palestinians. These are some of the reasons why liberals have held protest marches in the West, but they have little to do with the grievance of the Islamic radicals. From bin Laden's point of view, the Gulf War was a response to one infidel regime (Saddam Hussein's Iraq) invading another infidel regime (Kuwait). Consequently for America to intervene in favor of the latter to get rid of a former was, for bin Laden, a matter of indifference. What bin Laden objected to was America staying in the Middle East, importing with it the immoral ingredients of American values and culture. In order to keep the United States out, bin Laden volunteered to assemble an army of Muslim true believers to eject Saddam Hussein from Kuwait. When the Saudi government refused his request, bin Laden became an outlaw. In a December 2004 audiotape, addressed to the people of Saudi Arabia, bin Laden condemned Saddam Hussein as "a thief and apostate." At the same time, he attacked the Saudi regime for adopting Western laws that amount to "changing our religion" and producing "educated slaves who will be loyal to America."[8]

So what about the Palestinians? Surely—many will insist—bin Laden is enraged by Israeli occupation and supports the idea of

Palestinian self-determination and a Palestinian state. Yet as of this writing Al Qaeda has not launched a single attack against Israel. Abdel Bari Atwan, a Muslim journalist who has interviewed bin Laden, remarks that bin Laden hated Arafat and condemned the Palestine Liberation Organization (PLO) as an atheist group inimical to Islam. Yes, bin Laden opposes Israeli occupation because in his view it constitutes foreign rule over Muslims. But as bin Laden sees it, the deeper problem is a conspiracy on the part of Israel and America to take over the Muslim world. This is what bin Laden means by the "alliance of Zionists and Crusaders" that he warns is swarming across the Muslim world "like locusts, eating our fruits and wiping out our plantations." If bin Laden opposes Israeli occupation, however, he does not do so in the name of Palestinian sovereignty or Palestinian self-determination. In fact bin Laden opposes Palestinian self-determination and a Palestinian state. Bin Laden is not a nationalist: he has repeatedly called for the integration of Muslims into a global Islamic community. When bin Laden uses the term "nation" he means "the Muslim nation."[9]

For bin Laden and other Islamic fundamentalists, the issue has always been the fate of Islam and the perceived existential threat to Islam. Here, however, we are confronted with a critical fact. American foreign policy may oppose Muslim interests on this or that point, but it has no way to threaten the existence of Islam. Yet bin Laden speaks of the United States as a nation worse than the Nazis, worse than the communists, the worst civilization in history. How is this possible? Bin Laden himself supplies the answer. America, he asserts, is "the modern world's symbol of paganism." In his writings bin Laden periodically refers to "the American devils" and to America's allies as "the helpers of Satan."[10] Of course the Nazis and the communists were also pagans, but bin Laden's point is that these are vanquished forms of paganism, while America's paganism is of the powerful, successful kind that threatens to overrun Islam and take over the world.

In his "Letter to America," released in November 2002, bin Laden enumerates his grievances against the United States. Contrary to "the deceptive lie that you are a great nation," bin Laden informs the

American people that theirs is a country based on "oppression, lies, immorality, and debauchery." He calls on Americans to "reject the immoral acts of fornication, homosexuality, intoxicants, gambling, and trading with interest" and instead to embrace "manners, principles, honor, and purity." American culture, he says, had become a kind of "abyss." Specifically, "You are a nation that permits acts of immorality and you consider them to be pillars of personal freedom." Bin Laden cites, as an example of this, "President Clinton's immoral acts committed in the Oval Office." Moreover, "You are a nation that permits gambling in all its forms . . . the sex trade in all its forms." According to bin Laden, the United States is the world's largest consumer of alcohol and drugs. He accuses America of generating, through its sexual immorality and drug use, "diseases such as AIDS that were unknown to man in the past" but now are being spread throughout the world. In addition, "You are a nation that exploits women like consumer products" after which "you then rant that you support the liberation of women." Finally, bin Laden calls America a civilization in rebellion against God because "you separate religion from your policies" and thus "contradict the absolute authority of the Lord and Creator."[11]

Does the radical Islamic case against America, then, not have a foreign policy component? Of course it does. But as bin Laden and his associates see it, U.S. foreign policy is the vehicle for the coercive transmission of corrupt American values to the Muslim world. Abu Musab al-Zarqawi, Al Qaeda's former head of operations in Iraq, charged that "America came to spread obscenity and vice and establish its decadence and obscene culture in the name of freedom."[12]

Other stated objections to U.S. foreign policy by bin Laden and his lieutenants have a similar moral thrust. Thus in his "Letter to America" bin Laden faults the United States with being "a nation without principles" because it tries to prohibit other countries from possessing weapons of mass destruction while America and Israel possess untold numbers of such weapons. Moreover, America calls those who oppose its policies "terrorist," while its own war crimes and those of Israel against Muslim populations are ignored and excused. America's casualties, as at 9/11, provoke worldwide grief and mourning—

"The entire world," bin Laden writes, "rose and has not yet sat down"—while the deaths of Muslims, although far greater in number, do not inspire any American sympathy. Through force, bin Laden alleges, the United States supports corrupt infidel governments in Muslim countries, and they introduce the immoral ways of the West, "preventing our people from establishing the Islamic *sharia*." America—a nation without faith, honor, decency, and respect—has declared war on Islam, which bin Laden describes as "the nation of monotheism . . . the nation of honor and respect . . . the nation of martyrdom."[13]

From the point of view of the Islamic radicals, the issue of "terrorism" is a smokescreen. Bin Laden calls this "accusing others with your own affliction in order to fool the masses."[14] It is illuminating for us to try and see why. For us in the West, a terrorist is a member of an outlaw group or community that is willing to kill civilians, even women and children, in pursuit of its political goals. This is regarded, across the political spectrum in the West, as utterly reprehensible. The Islamic radicals complain that the West has cleverly defined terrorism so that the resistance of Muslims to occupation and oppression is automatically considered evil while the state-sponsored massacres of a far greater number of Muslims by the American and Israeli war machines is never understood as "terrorism"—only a justified reaction to Muslim atrocities.

No matter how many women and children Israel kills, bin Laden says, "the United States stops any efforts to condemn Israel." He reminds Muslims that America firebombed numerous German and Japanese cities during World War II, killing hundreds of thousands of civilians. In his 1997 interview with Peter Arnett, bin Laden spoke of the civilian horror produced when America dropped atomic bombs on Hiroshima and Nagasaki: "The United States does not consider it a terrorist act to drop atomic bombs . . . which killed so many women and children that up to this day the traces of those bombs remain in Japan."[15]

Bin Laden's point is not that America is failing to live up to its moral standards, or that terrorism is bad no matter who engages in it. Rather, his point is that terrorism can be good or bad depending on *who is being terrorized*. As bin Laden said in one of his interviews, "Terrifying and terrorizing innocent people is clearly not right" whereas "terrorizing oppressors, criminals and thieves is necessary . . . to abolish tyranny and corruption." It is in light of this distinction that we can better understand bin Laden's otherwise cryptic assertion that "the terrorism we practice is of the commendable kind."[16]

To those in the West, and in the Muslim world, who ask how supposedly religious Muslims can justify killing innocent civilians, bin Laden answers that the civilians who are targeted are not innocent. In bin Laden's view, attacks on Iraqi civilians or foreign workers in Iraq are warranted because these are the people who support the governing infrastructure established by the infidel occupying power. Even attacks on civilians in America are justified, bin Laden argues, because in a democracy the citizens are not detached from the actions of their government. The basic idea of democracy is that the people *are* the government. As bin Laden puts it, "It is a fundamental principle of democracy that the people choose their leaders, and as such approve and are party to the action of their leaders." The American people are ultimately accountable, he contends, because "they chose their government, and voted for it despite their knowledge of its crimes."[17]

To Americans who feel outraged that they have become the target of terrorist attacks, bin Laden asks: Who is funding the Israeli government's war machine against Muslims? Who is backing and paying for the marauding actions of the U.S. military? Whose debauched values of promiscuity, pornography, family breakdown, and separation of church and state are being thrust—via military rule and corrupt local dictators—on the Muslim people? In each case bin Laden's answer is: You, the American people, are responsible. These are your morals, your government, your policies, that are threatening the future of Islam.

The indignation that bin Laden frequently expresses toward the United States surprises the Western observer. "Even ravenous animals," bin Laden writes, "do not do the deeds" routinely performed by Americans.[18] Such rhetoric is incomprehensible without recognizing that bin Laden is using a different compass to assess America than Americans use to assess him. American outrage toward bin Laden's actions usually focuses on the issue of killing noncombatants. Drawing on a long tradition of Western warfare, most Americans consider this inexcusably barbaric. Few Americans are likely to be persuaded by bin Laden's rationalizations for the murder of civilians. Bin Laden's outrage, however, is focused on the issue of proportionality. An old concept, respected in many cultures, proportionality simply means "measure for measure." As a well-known verse in the Koran has it, "Whoever transgresses against you, respond in kind." The moral doctrine here is that aggression should be punished according to the scale of the original crime: if I raid your tribe and kill ten people, you have the right to raid my tribe and kill ten people. But you do not, in this view, have the right to raid my tribe and kill ten thousand people. This would be utterly disproportionate to the original offense.

Proportionality is not an unfamiliar notion in the West, but it is often set aside because of another common belief in America, pointed out by military historian Victor Davis Hanson.[19] This principle says, in effect, "If you start it, we have the right to wipe you out completely." So if the Japanese attack Pearl Harbor and kill a few thousand Americans, America will not retaliate and kill an equivalent number of Japanese; rather, America will engage in a "fight to the finish," even to the point of killing hundreds of thousands of Japanese, both combat soldiers and civilians, until Japan unconditionally surrenders or is completely obliterated. As Hanson points out, Americans see this sort of unmitigated carnage as a fair and reasonable way to fight. According to bin Laden, however, it is an abomination.

Here is his way of reasoning. How many Americans did Muslims kill on 9/11? Around three thousand, every victim counted, every death mourned, every victim's family generously compensated. How many Muslims has the United States killed in response? Many thousands in Afghanistan, and tens of thousands in Iraq so far. It's possible that the death toll in those two countries has already topped fifty thousand. No one knows for sure, and few Americans seem distressed over these numbers. From bin Laden's point of view, these levels of carnage show that the United States is barbaric in its rules of war, a nation "without principles or manners." As he sees it, the immorality of America expresses itself in the way that America fights. Consistent with a country that has no God and no ethics, America refuses even to respect the norms of savage tribes: it kills without any measure of justice or restraint. The U.S. and Israel, bin Laden says, are like crocodiles ferociously devouring the children of Islam. In bin Laden's view, no amount of persuasion or pleas can be expected to dissuade the crocodile. "For does a crocodile understand any language other than arms?"[20]

Bin Laden concludes, "Just as you lay waste our nation, so shall we lay waste yours." The goal, he says, is a "balance of terror." And in this campaign the 9/11 attacks are just the beginning. Without revealing the basis for his calculations, an Al Qaeda spokesman asserts that Muslims would have to kill 4 million Americans, about half of them children, in order to achieve proportionality for all the Muslims who have died at the hands of America and its sidekick Israel.[21] Presumably the only way to do this would be for radical Muslims to detonate a nuclear bomb.

IN ORDER TO more fully understand bin Laden, it is necessary to examine the general outlook of radical Islam, which has formulated a comprehensive philosophy and strategy that is now the blueprint for Muslim activism, insurgency, and suicide bombings throughout the world. In discussing radical Islam, I will cite several thinkers but I intend to focus on the work of the Egyptian thinker Sayyid Qutb. Originally a traveler in literary and pro-Western circles, Qutb became fiercely anti-American after living in the United States. He returned to Egypt, joined the Muslim Brotherhood, and advocated Islamic radicalism as an antidote to what he perceived as American decadence. Although he died in 1966, martyred for his opposition to Nasser's secular socialist regime, Qutb's work has continued to grow in influence; indeed, no single person has done more to shape the minds of Islamic radicals.

The Muslim fundamentalists who planned and carried out the assassination of Anwar Sadat were inspired by Qutb. The blind sheikh Omar Abd al-Rahman, now incarcerated for terrorism in the United States, routinely cited Qutb in his sermons. Bin Laden's mentor Abdullah Azzam was a fiery advocate of Qutb's ideas, and one of bin Laden's professors at King Abdul Aziz University in Jedda was Qutb's brother, Muhammad Qutb. Bin Laden's deputy, Ayman al-Zawahiri, is an acknowledged disciple of Qutb. In his essay "Knights Under the Prophet's Banner" Zawahiri writes, "Sayyid Qutb was the spark that ignited the Islamic revolution against the enemies of Islam at home and abroad."[22] Here, then, with an emphasis on Qutb, are the two key elements of radical Muslim thought.

"Islam is the solution." This is now the most popular slogan in the Muslim world, and has become a sort of rallying cry for radicals. At first glance the notion that Islam is the solution may seem absurd to Western observers—especially Western liberals—for whom Islam and Islamic "fundamentalism" are viewed as part of the problem. But let's try and see things from the point of view of the Islamic radicals. The Islamic world, they concede, is in miserable shape. It is weak. Israel has shown that it can defeat the combined force of all the Arab countries. It is disunited. Despite a common religion the Muslim world has been rent by internecine conflict, such as the Iran-Iraq war, and by opportunistic alliances that set one Islamic country against another. It is poor. According to the Unified Arab Economic Report, published by a consortium of Muslim organizations, per capita income in the Arab world is around $2,000 a year. Unemployment is high and there are no jobs for young people coming out of the schools and colleges. Moreover, the Arab world has seen a declining standard of living at a time when everyone else— not only the West but also India and China—has gotten richer.[23] If you don't consider oil income, which after all is the product of luck and which will not last forever, the Arab world would join sub-Saharan Africa as the least developed, most insignificant part of the globe.

The Islamic radicals know all this. Their question is, how have we reached this low point? To answer this question, they look at history.

Unlike sub-Saharan Africa, the Muslim world once had a rich, sophisticated, and powerful civilization. By the time of the Prophet Muhammad's death all of Arabia was united under the Islamic banner. The early converts to Islam conquered the rest of the Middle East, defeating the Sassanid dynasty in Persia and pushing back the Byzantine Empire. The Islamic armies then drove into Asia, Europe, and Africa. Within a few centuries after Muhammad's death the Muslims had established an empire from the Himalayas to the Pyrenees that rivaled in size the Roman Empire.

Muslim fundamentalists ask, how did the Muslims do this? What accounts for the "miracle in the desert" that gave rise to a new faith and a new form of monotheism that surpassed the reach of Judaism and Christianity and established a new kind of human community throughout the known world? Their answer: Islam. It was their religious conviction that inspired the armies of Muhammad to create the great Islamic empire. It was religious conviction and not just force that won over tens of millions of converts to Islam. It was religious conviction that built the resplendent civilization stretching across three continents. Western historians in general agree with this.

How, then, did Western civilization grow so strong and Islamic civilization so weak? Western historians emphasize the internal changes in the West—the Renaissance, the Reformation, the Enlightenment, the Scientific Revolution, and so on. Islamic fundamentalists concede that the West discovered a new form of power: technology, created out of the dynamic interaction between science and capitalism. But they stress that if the West has solved the economic problem, it has not solved the moral problem. Although Islam may not be relevant in creating prosperity or military success, it is relevant in showing human nature the way to justice, goodness, and happiness. In the words of Qutb, Islam represents "an unparalleled revolution in human thinking" and far from being superseded or outdated it provides the only solution to "this unhappy, perplexed, and weary world."[24]

The Islamic fundamentalists argue that the distinctive contribution of Islam to the world was religious and moral. Coming after, and in a sense transcending, Judaism and Christianity, Islam in this view finalized the triumph of monotheism over polytheism and paganism, and it introduced to the world a new concept of a universal moral law, or sharia, that reflects divine rules for human behavior and human happiness. Consider how Islam transformed the Arabian desert. Before Islam, there was the age of what the Koran calls *jahilliya.* The term, which means "ignorance," refers to the state of pagan barbarism in the bedouin tribes before the arrival of the Prophet Muhammad.

According to the fundamentalists, the main characteristics of the bedouins of sixth-century Arabia were brutality, immorality, and polytheism. Looting and pillaging were their primary way of acquiring property. The bedouins were famous for never-ending feuds. The bedouins worshiped the sun, the moon, trees, and stones; they had no concept of an afterlife. Reputed for their heavy drinking, the bedouins were also known for their sexual adventurousness, not only with women but also with men and on some occasions with their animals. This carousing promiscuity is celebrated in the *Mu'allaqat, a* collection of sixth-century Arab poetry. One of the courtship styles of the bedouins was to capture a woman from another tribe, stupefy her with blows, and then drag her screaming into a tent. Where the bedouins live, the great Muslim historian Ibn Khaldun writes, "civilization decays and is wiped out."[25]

Islam, the fundamentalists point out, civilized these barbarians. It brought them together into a single community unified not by race or tribe but by allegiance to a monotheistic faith and its universal moral law. In addition, Islam outlawed bedouin practices such as rape, adultery, and homosexuality, as well as the bedouin custom of killing infant girls. Charity and almsgiving, unheard of among the tribes, became a legal requirement for Muslims. While the desert Arabs kept no track of time, the Muslims introduced the Islamic calendar. The Prophet Muhammad did not prohibit slavery, but he advocated the emancipation of slaves who converted to Islam, and he insisted on humane treatment for all slaves. Polygamy was not outlawed either, but men were limited to a maximum of four wives, and Muhammad issued strict guidelines for equitable treatment, including a just distribution of inheritance and conjugal favors.

Fundamentalists stress that, for all its rules, Islam is best understood not in terms of obedience but rather in terms of voluntary submission to a divinely established moral order. In his book *Social Justice in Islam* Qutb tells the story of a man and woman who came to the Prophet Muhammad and said, "Messenger of Allah, purify us." Muhammad asked, "From what am I to purify you?" They replied, "From adultery." Muhammad asked whether the couple was mad or drunk. Assured that they were not, Muhammad asked them again, "What have you done?" And they said they had committed adultery. Then Muhammad gave the order, and they were stoned to death. While the couple was being buried, onlookers scorned them, but Muhammad silenced the scoffers. The couple had repented, he said, and now they were in heaven.

"This is Islam," Qutb wrote. Analyzing the incident, he pointed out that no one had witnessed the adultery, and the prophet initially sought to attribute the couple's confession to the influence of alcohol or mental disturbance. Still, they had persisted. Finally Muhammad had no choice but to have them stoned in accordance with God's law. Qutb posed an interesting question: why did the couple demand to be stoned? His answer: "It was the desire to be purified of a crime of which none save Allah was cognizant. It was the shame of meeting Allah unpurified from a sin which they had committed."[26]

The moral outlook of Islam, the fundamentalists say, is codified in a way of life based on the divine government of society. This worldview requires that religious, economic, political, and civil society be based on the Koran, the teachings of Muhammad, and the holy law. In this analysis, Islam cannot be confined to the private or spiritual domain; rather, it governs the whole framework of life. The ayatollah Khomeini noted that "the ratio of Koranic verses concerned with the affairs of society to those concerned with ritual worship is greater than a hundred to one." In addition to regulating religious belief and practice, Islam also regulates the administration of the state, the conduct of war, the making of treaties, divorce and inheritance, property rights, and contracts. Khomeini writes that Allah has "laid down injunctions for man extending from before the embryo is formed until after man is placed in the tomb. . . . There is not a single topic in human life for which Islam has not provided instruction and established a norm."[27]

Qutb argues that an Islamic society is not merely one that contains a majority of Muslims, or even one in which Muslims govern themselves. Rather, he says, "There is only one place on earth which can be called the home of Islam and it is that place where the Islamic state is established and the *sharia* is the authority and God's rules are observed and where the Muslims administer the affairs of state with mutual consultation."[28] This is what the fundamentalists mean by an Islamic society.

None of this means that Islam cannot embrace science, commerce, or modern technology. Qutb himself praises science and writes that even when it poses dangers, those dangers must be faced because there is no real alternative to scientific and technological development. The real difficulty, the fundamentalists say, is not with "catching up" to Western modernity. Anyone can do this, as the Chinese, the Indians, and many others are demonstrating. Many of the Muslim radicals are themselves scientifically literate and technically trained. The real challenge, in their view, is to embrace modernity without moral degradation. For all his enthusiasm about science, Qutb concedes that modern institutions like capitalism and science, invented in the West, must be integrated into an Islamic ethical framework that puts them at the service of full human development and the common good of society. Material development must not be at the expense of religious truth or social morality.

In fact, the Muslim radicals believe that the Islamic restoration will bring not only unity and happiness but also economic and political success. According to Maulana Mawdudi, founder of the Jamaat-i-Islami (Islamic Society) in Pakistan, the Koran promises that if Muslims follow the teachings of Allah they will have prosperity in this world and paradise in the next world. And for a thousand years, Mawdudi wrote, this was true. Islam was winning. But now, he sighed, Islam is losing, and why is that? Mawdudi's simple answer has become very famous throughout the Muslim world: it is because we have stopped following the teachings of Allah. Muslims have fallen away from the true faith, a faith understood not merely as a creed but as a system of government and a way of life. Mawdudi's conclusion is that only by recovering true Islam and restoring Islamic societies under the rule of sharia can Muslims recover their wealth, strength, and former glory.[29]

"AMERICA IS THE GREAT SATAN." This is the second great theme of Islamic radicalism. In the view of the radicals, Muslims are prevented from reestablishing Islamic society by two factors. The first is what Iranian sociologist Ali Shariati calls *gharbzadegi*. The word means "intoxication with the West" or, since the West is the place where the sun sets, "intoxication with darkness." Shariati, who was one of the intellectual architects of the Khomeini revolution, was himself Western-trained, having earned his doctorate at the Sorbonne. Shariati's argument is that ordinary Muslims become so mesmerized with the wealth and power of the West that they become blinded to its severe defects. Moreover, they become ashamed of their own religion and culture. Consequently they become vulnerable to Western occupation, control, and influence. They are seduced by Western propaganda that identifies Westernization with "progress" and "freedom."[30]

This freedom, the ayatollah Khomeini contended, is nothing better than the "freedom of debauchery." Addressing the West in 1979, Khomeini said, "You, who want freedom, freedom for everything, the freedom that will corrupt our youth, freedom that will pave the way for the oppressor, freedom that will drag our nation to the bottom. You do not believe in any limits to freedom. This is a freedom that would lead our country to destruction."[31]

The second obstacle to the revival of Islam, fundamentalists say, is the well-orchestrated campaign by the United States to impose its values on the Muslim world. Thus even Muslims who wish to reject Western values and American culture are prevented from doing so. Fundamentalists argue that America does this partly through force, by occupying countries like Afghanistan and Iraq and then pressing them to adopt American institutions and values. "The West wants to distract you with shiny slogans like freedom and democracy," Kadhem al-Ebadi, a Muslim clergyman, told his congregation after the fall of Baghdad. "Infidel corruption has entered our society through these concepts."[32]

Another way that America thrusts its values on Muslims, fundamentalists say, is through the United Nations and various nongovernmental organizations (NGOs). In a 1997 interview, the radical sheikh Omar Abd al-Rahman accused America and other Western nations of "allocating huge amounts of money to the United Nations conference on population that came out with resolutions allowing adultery, abortion and homosexuality, resolutions encouraging girls to give up their honor and chastity, resolutions to weaken the authority of parents over children." Americans, Rahman suggested, promote their immoral practices without regard to the desire of other societies to protect the morality of their institutions. Consequently, Rahman concluded, Americans "have freedom for themselves, but they do not allow any freedom to others."[33]

A further mechanism for the imposition of American values is the rule of U.S.-supported dictators like Musharraf in Pakistan, Mubarak in Egypt, and Abdullah in Jordan. These dictators typically restrict or even eliminate Islamic laws and rules, replacing them with Western laws and institutions. In this way, the ayatollah Khomeini said, "they strive to annihilate Islam." Khomeini gave the example of the shah's decision in 1976 to abolish the Islamic calendar and replace it with a secular calendar. The Islamic calendar dates time from the Prophet Muhammad's migration from Mecca to Medina in the year 622 of the Christian era. The shah instituted a new calendar based on the supposed date on which Emperor Cyrus established his monarchical rule over ancient Persia. Khomeini also condemned the shah for getting rid of sharia rules regarding marriage and divorce, and extending voting rights in local elections not only to women but also to non-Muslims. Khomeini was most vehement in castigating the shah for decriminalizing alcohol, gambling, and adultery, noting that "Islam makes no provision for the orderly pursuit of these illicit activities."[34]

The general charge that fundamentalists make against despots past and present is that in exchange for U.S. military and political support for their regime, they open up their countries to the polluting influences of American social institutions and popular culture. Fundamentalists charge that in every case, the United States seeks to strengthen those forces that are operating in the Muslim world to secularize the society, destroy the family, corrupt the children, and degrade the culture.

Here, then, is the heart of the radical Muslims' case against America and the West. Fundamentalists portray America as a nominally Christian but de facto atheist society. Although people in America call themselves Christian, Qutb writes, their actions prove that they are indifferent to God and that their real religion is materialism. In this respect, "The materialistic outlook on life is the same in Communism and in the civilization of the West." Moreover, Qutb says, even when Americans do go to church it is usually for social display or to meet members of the opposite sex. Protestant preachers, he writes, are mainly entertainers who put on all kinds of circus antics to attract listeners and then measure success by how many people come marching down the aisle.[35] Qutb is especially revolted by the fact that in America religion has been driven out of public life and has nothing to do with the institutions of government. So the de facto atheism of the people is reinforced by the de jure atheism of the laws. As a consequence of the American doctrine of separation of church and state, Qutb writes, "God's existence is not denied, but His domain is restricted to the heavens and his rule on earth is suspended."[36]

The best indication of American depravity that Muslim fundamentalists point to is the collapse of the traditional American family. Qutb writes, "If free sexual relationships and illegitimate children become the basis of a society; and if the relationship between man and woman is based on lust, passion, and impulse, and the division of work is not based on family responsibility and natural gifts; and if

the woman is freed from her basic responsibility of bringing up children; and if, on her own or under social demand, she prefers to . . .
spend her ability working for material productivity rather than in
the training of human beings, because material production is considered more important, more valuable and more honorable than the
development of human character, then such a civilization . . . cannot be considered civilized, no matter how much progress it makes
in industry or science."[37]

Recently Sheikh Fahd Rahman al-Abyan, a prominent radical
preacher, took up the theme of family deterioration in a sermon at
a mosque in Riyadh. In America and the West, he said, "it has
reached the point where the woman gives the orders, and there is
no wonder that the women have become masculine. But what is
amazing is that some men have become feminine. These ideas . . .
have caused the downfall of entire societies." Sheikh Yusuf Qaradawi, an influential figure who is regularly featured on Al Jazeera,
recently focused on the prospect of homosexual marriage and its effect on the traditional family. "There are strong tendencies in the
West to destroy the family," Qaradawi said on his Al Jazeera program. "An example of this is the marriage of men with men, and
women with women. Unfortunately some clergymen welcome this
and perform these marriage ceremonies. In addition, several Western parliaments have permitted this practice that all religions oppose. They want to make homosexuality seem natural. They want to
make this perversion widespread. This is what they want."[38]

Finally, Islamic fundamentalists point out that these trends are
openly fostered by America's popular culture. As a result of American influence, Qutb writes, "Humanity today is living in a large
brothel. One has only to glance at its press, films, fashion shows,
beauty contests, ballrooms, wine bars, and broadcasting stations. Or
observe its mad lust for naked flesh, provocative postures, and the
sick, suggestive statements in literature, the arts, and the mass media." Qutb's followers point to the increasingly blatant materialism,
vulgarity, and decadence of American popular culture. The distinctive feature of this culture, they say, is its shamelessness. It is ob-

sessed with sex and bodily functions. It promotes promiscuity and adultery. This is the culture that, according to the ayatollah Khomeini, "penetrates to the depths of towns and villages throughout the Muslim world, displacing the culture of the Koran."[39]

Masoumeh Ebtekar, the highest-ranking woman to serve in the Iranian government, condemns the "degradation" of what she terms the "Hollywood lifestyle" and asks, "Must we all conform to Hollywood's view of human nature, which mostly stresses what is base rather than noble in humanity?" In a harsher vein, one Islamic radical who lived in California, Majid Anaraki, describes the United States as "a collection of casinos, supermarkets, and whorehouses linked together by endless highways passing through nowhere." Far from feeling inferior to modern America, Qutb argues, true Muslims should feel revulsion and contempt. "The believer from his height looks down at the people drowning in dirt and mud." Speaking of Western civilization in general, Shariati writes, "Let us leave behind this Europe that always speaks of humanity but destroys human beings wherever it finds them."[40]

In a formulation that has become extremely influential among Islamic radicals, Qutb argues that America represents a new form of *jahilliya*—the same kind of barbarism and immorality that the Prophet Muhammad encountered in Arabia in the seventh century. In Qutb's view the new barbarism is worse because at least the bedouins were ignorant. The bedouins didn't know about monotheism, they hadn't yet encountered Islam. By contrast, Qutb argues, the new *jahilliya* is far worse because it is based on knowledge; it represents "aggression against God's governance on earth."[41] In this view, the United States has willfully rejected Christianity and chosen to celebrate a pagan culture and a depraved system of morality. Qutb concludes that it is one thing for America to degrade itself, and quite another for America to use its wealth and power to impose ruin on the rest of the world.

Islam, the fundamentalists say, is the real target of America's immoral fury. In the words of Muhammad Husayn Fadlallah, the spiritual leader of Hezbollah, "The enemies are after Islam, not the official Islam that moves freely in the royal palaces, but the Koranic Islam. These are the committed Muslims that the enemy seeks to destroy, calling them extremists, radicals, and terrorists."[42] In the view of Muslim fundamentalists, the reason for America's hostility is quite simple: the Muslims are the last of the true believers. Of all the monotheistic religions, only Islam continues to maintain its hold on its members. Most Jews and Christians are only nominally religious, and at best, their religion takes up one part of their existence. But for Muslims all over the world, even today, Islam remains central to their lives. As the fundamentalists see it, Islam represents the last bastion of monotheism in a pagan world. No wonder, they say, that the U.S. has gathered up all its forces to destroy Islam. If Islam falls, the rule of Satan on earth will be achieved, and its name will be Planet America.

FIVE

Innocence Lost

Liberalism and the Corruption of Popular Culture

THE ISLAMIC HOSTILITY to American culture, shared alike by radical and traditional Muslims, raises a simple but disturbing question: are they right? Does Western culture promote immoral values that corrupt people, especially the young? Is American culture now so decadent and depraved that it is a danger to the world, especially to the traditional cultures of Asia, Africa, and the Middle East? If we wish to understand the vehemence of anti-Western feeling among traditional cultures, these questions cannot be ignored. They are critical to formulating an approach to the problem of anti-Americanism around the world. The charge of cultural depravity is one that we should take seriously, not because America needs to persuade radical Muslims to like us, but because America needs to persuade traditional Muslims not to become radical Muslims.

The accusation of decadence against the West is obviously valid in one sense: Western societies (including America) are not reproducing themselves. Western civilization is decadent in the quite literal sense that its people are slowly dying out. Europeans are having so few children that their populations are shrinking. The only way that

Europeans are moderating this population loss is through immigration—mainly Muslim immigration. We in the West are accustomed to thinking of our society as strong due to its affluence and technology. But another measure of a civilization's strength and self-confidence is its desire to perpetuate itself. As Patrick Buchanan writes, "The Islamic world retains something the West has lost: a desire to have children and the will to carry on their civilization, cultures, families and faith. Today it is as difficult to find a Western nation where the native population is not dying as it is to find an Islamic nation where the native population is not exploding."[1]

In this chapter, I examine the charge of decadence, not in the sense of population decline, but in the sense of moral decline. Imagine how American culture looks and feels to someone who has been raised in a traditional society where unmarried men and women do not shake hands, where modesty and decorum are highly prized, where girls who are not virgins cannot find men to marry them, where homosexuality is taboo and against the law. Economist Deepak Lal relates an episode from a few years ago, when he was staying in Beijing with the Indian ambassador to China: "Beijing was hosting a UN Conference on Women, and the female delegates were housed in a large tent city. One night the ambassador was woken by an agitated Chinese official asking him to rush to the tent city as the Indian delegates were rioting. On getting there he found that the trouble began when some American delegates went into the tents of their Third World sisters and tried to initiate them into the joys of gay sex. With the Indians in the lead, the Third World women chased the American women out of their tents, beating them with their slippers."[2]

My mother, who is in her early seventies, lives in Mumbai and watches a good deal of television. Many of the shows regularly broadcast on Indian TV are American. My mom finds them fascinating and repulsive at the same time. "It's quite extraordinary how people who have just met each other start taking their clothes off and having sex," she tells me. "I also find the language to be coarse. Some of it is very disgusting, the things that they talk about." Confronted by talk-show episodes of the Jerry Springer variety, my mother cannot help concluding that "these Americans seem very weird and abnormal." I remind my mother, of course, that this is entertainment. Most Americans don't live this way. My mother's point is, "Yes, but I'm surprised to see all of this indecency on television. Imagine if someone came into our living room and started talking like that. What would we think of such a person? I would ask him to leave the house! Don't Americans have any sort of standards?" Her reaction is not unique. One American academic who teaches in Southeast Asia writes about how appalled young Cambodians, who are struggling to survive, must be to confront American TV dilemmas: "My God, did you see the way that Buck looked at Latrice? And isn't it just sad the way that Skippy is so controlling toward his boyfriend Allan?"[3]

We have heard a great deal from critics of globalism about how America is corrupting the world with its multinational corporations and its trade practices. But surveys such as the Pew Research Center studies of world opinion show that non-Western peoples are generally pleased with American products. In fact, the people of Asia, Africa, and the Middle East want more American companies, more American technology, and more free trade. Their objection is not to McDonald's or Microsoft but to America's cultural values as transmitted through movies, television, and music. Huge majorities of more than 80 percent of people in Indonesia, Uganda, Kenya, Senegal, Egypt, and Turkey say they want to protect their values from foreign assault. The Pew study concludes that there is a "widespread sense" that American values, often presented as the values of modernity itself, "represent a major threat to people's traditional way of life." These sentiments are felt very keenly in the Muslim world. As an Iranian from Neishapour told journalist Afshin Molavi, "People say we want freedom. You know what these foreign-inspired people want? They want the freedom to gamble and drink and bring vice to our Muslim land. This is the kind of freedom they want."[4]

We sometimes assume that the Muslim critique applies to American mass culture and are sometimes startled to see that it also applies to American "high culture." In her best-selling book *Reading*

Lolita in Tehran, Azar Nafisi describes a group of Iranians who gather regularly to discuss "great books." They are discussing *The Great Gatsby* when a man named Nyazi explodes with the following rant. "This book preaches illicit relations between a man and woman. First we have Tom and his mistress, the scene in his apartment—even the narrator, Nick, is implicated. He doesn't like their lies, but he has no objection to their fornicating and sitting on each other's laps, and those parties at Gatsby's . . . remember, this Gatsby is the hero of the book—and who is he? He is a charlatan, he is an adulterer, he is a liar. . . . He earns his money by illegal means and tries to buy the love of a married woman. . . . This is the man Nick celebrates and feels sorry for, this destroyer of homes. This book is supposed to be about the American dream, but what sort of a dream is this? What kind of model are we setting for our innocent and modest sisters, by giving them such a book to read? The only sympathetic person here is the cuckolded husband, Mr. Wilson. When he kills Gatsby, it is the hand of God. He is the genuine symbol of the oppressed, in the land of the great Satan."

Interestingly, Nafisi describes the uncomfortable reaction to Nyazi's barrage on the part of several of the others who enjoyed reading the book. "Perhaps our honorable prosecutor should not be so harsh," a woman named Vida says. "Gatsby dies, after all, so one could say that he gets his just deserts." Rejecting the attempt at conciliation, Nyazi replies, "Is it just Gatsby who deserves to die? No! The whole of American society deserves the same fate." At this point the author herself weighs in, seeking to expose Nyazi's tirade as unsophisticated. "You don't read *Gatsby* to learn whether adultery is good or bad but to learn about how complicated issues such as adultery and fidelity and marriage are. A great novel heightens your senses and sensitivity to the complexities of life and of individuals and prevents you from the self-righteousness that sees morality in fixed formulas about good and evil." To this pompous bromide, Nyazi delivers this crushing response: "There is nothing complicated about having an affair with another man's wife. Why doesn't Mr. Gatsby get his own wife?"[5]

The radical Muslim critique embodied by Nyazi is disturbing. It does not attack American culture at its outer limits for "excesses" that can be found in any culture. Rather, it attacks American culture at its best, accusing Fitzgerald of trying to distinguish "good adultery" from "bad adultery" and employing his acknowledged talents to rationalize "good adultery." Nyazi's distress is not over the portrayal of the subject of adultery; rather, it is over the fact that there seems to be no moral standard condemning it. This, more than anything else, confirms in his mind the degeneracy of American culture.

Confronted by the accusation that American culture is decadent and immoral, many Americans respond defensively, even angrily. Liberals become especially indignant because they recognize that American popular culture is, for the most part, liberal culture. The values it celebrates—such as openness, diversity, and the uninhibited cultivation of individuality—are liberal values. Libertarians, who are champions of the free market, also become defensive because they are committed on ideological grounds to the view that if the market produced a particular result, it must be wonderful. Even conservatives tend to rush to the defense of American culture because it is, well, American. Some conservatives feel a patriotic duty to uphold American culture, especially against accusatory Muslims.

Consequently the response of many Americans to charges of cultural depravity is to dismiss those concerns as reflecting Muslim hypocrisy or a Taliban-like devotion to censorship and social control. Indeed, the Taliban banned music, television, the Internet, photography, card playing, and even kite flying. Public executions were one of the few permitted forms of mass entertainment. Women were forced to wear the burqa, and there were even regulations prescribing the lengths of men's beards. The Taliban, however, is hardly representative of the Islamic world or even of radical Islam. While the Taliban's rules met bin Laden's approval, they were considered ridiculous and extreme throughout the Muslim world, even by the mullahs in Iran. Of course, the ruling regime in Tehran has produced its own idiocies. At one point Iran had a blind censor who was in charge of reviewing plays and films. The man would sit in the theater or movie house while an assistant described to him the action on the stage or screen, and then he would decide which parts needed to be eliminated. Traditional Muslims ridiculed the censor, but not on grounds of "free speech" or opposition to censorship per se. Rather, the point of traditional Muslims was that the man was in no position to discriminate between what should be allowed and what should be forbidden.

Moreover, hypocrisy is a charge to which most traditional Muslims, and even some radical Muslims, would plead guilty. Post-Khomeini Iran offers some revealing examples. Journalist Elaine Sciolino was surprised to discover that the ruling mullahs of Iran often exchange dirty jokes in private. One ayatollah is especially famous for his sexual innuendos. Asked why his conversations with his colleagues reflected such an extreme obsession with sex, the ayatollah replied, "Because I do not have any of it." Sciolino gives other examples where rules and standards are abridged in practice. She notes that dancing, which is forbidden in Iran, is routinely taught under the guise of "exercise lessons." Sciolino attended a wedding reception at a large villa, where the drinking and revelry were broken up by Iranian police who accused everyone of violating the law. Members of the rock band jumped over the wall into the next garden. The guests took refuge in the house. The bride's father accompanied the police to jail and agreed to pay a fine. No sooner did the police leave than the bride's relatives recalled the band, which resumed playing, and the party continued.[6]

It is a commonplace in traditional cultures that people who espouse high moral standards sometimes indulge in the same wrongs they have publicly condemned. Many Americans took special glee in noting that the 9/11 hijackers went to strip clubs in Las Vegas, where they consumed alcohol and paid for lap dances.[7] One of the chief architects of 9/11, Khalid Sheikh Mohammed, reportedly visited the Philippines during the 1990s, where, posing as a businessman and using another name, he socialized in bars with Manila women. Traditional Muslims will acknowledge these lapses while insisting on a public norm that condemns them as lapses. Hypocrisy is not viewed as a major vice in traditional cultures. The reason is that it is considered better to uphold moral standards, while falling short, than to relinquish all standards on the grounds that human beings do not always live up to them.

Muslims may be hypocritical and support censorship, but these facts provide no basis for a defense of Western or American cultural depravity. An accusation cannot be refuted by pointing out that the accuser is guilty of the same offense. Moreover, the Muslims are not guilty of the charge that they launch against the West. Muslim societies can be faulted—I would fault them myself—for being excessively harsh or repressive in the enforcement of their standards. I cannot approve of the kind of censorship that is routinely tolerated throughout the Muslim world. Traditional societies can also be exposed for failing to conform to their own standards. But they cannot be accused of not having standards. Muslim leaders charge that Western culture—and specifically American culture—has no moral norms that it is willing to defend or uphold. In this view, the offenses of Western culture are especially frightening because they have no built-in remedy. Many people in traditional societies regard Western culture as a kind of malady for which there is no antidote or cure.

Some in the West appear to confirm the fears of the Muslims. A few years ago the Dutch politician Pim Fortuyn was assassinated. Newspapers in America portrayed Fortuyn as "right wing extremist" on account of his opposition to Muslim immigration. Fortuyn famously said that immigration should be halted because "Holland is full." But as Europeans recognized, Fortuyn was no right-winger. Instead, he was a flamboyant homosexual whose argument was that Muslim immigrants were, on account of their religious beliefs, threatening the core values of Holland. In Fortuyn's view, these core values were legal drugs, legal pornography, legal prostitution, and widespread social acceptance of homosexuality. If Fortuyn was a "conservative," these were the values that he sought to conserve. Theo van Gogh, who was murdered by the Moroccan Muslim Muhammad Bouyeri, was a friend and admirer of Fortuyn. A foul-mouthed man who publicly called Muslims "goat fuckers," van Gogh was also famous for his sexual promiscuity and cocaine use. Following Fortuyn, van Gogh blasted Muslims for their "primitive" beliefs in contrast with Holland's "progressive" ideals. Like Fortuyn, van Gogh cherished Holland for embodying precisely those values that traditional societies consider degenerate and immoral.[8]

Here in America, a longtime man of the left, Christopher Hitchens, argues that modern America represents the values of secularism, feminism, and homosexuality. An outspoken atheist, Hitchens is the author of a book vilifying Mother Teresa titled *The Missionary Position*. It is "godless hedonistic America" and the state of Massachusetts's recent sanction of practices such as homosexual marriage, Hitchens gleefully points out, that provoke "the writhing faces and hoarse yells of the mullahs and the fanatics." It is in defense of this godless, hedonistic America that Hitchens supports the Bush administration's war on radical Islam.[9]

Is this, then, what the war on terrorism is all about—to impose the values of secularism, feminism, homosexuality, prostitution, and pornography on the world?

REMARKABLY, THERE HAS been no serious debate in America over the moral content of American popular culture. America has witnessed huge changes in its culture over the past few decades, changes that put contemporary American values sharply at odds not only with non-Western cultures but also with the values of America's own past. Some of these changes are, of course, for the better. American culture is more varied, spirited, and individualistic than in previous generations. There is an infectious spirit of freedom that Americans and non-Americans find irresistible. At the same time, there has been a coarsening, a debasement, a collapse of standards in American culture that makes much of it intolerable to older Americans, repulsive to most immigrants from traditional cultures, and alarming to many parents.

One small indication of this is in the use of language. Terms that would never previously have appeared on television, such as "ass," "bitch," and "bastard," now routinely appear even during the early evening, when children are watching. Only in rare cases can the use of obscenities be justified as necessary to character or plot development. In many cases the mere use of obscenity is intended to be humorous. Indeed the f-word is now so gratuitously common in films that some movie characters would be rendered virtually mute if they didn't use the term.

Talk shows on television have sunk so low that I am virtually nostalgic for *The Phil Donahue Show*. Not that I was a fan of earnest, gaseous Phil, but at least he tried to discuss legitimate social questions. Donahue was rudely pushed off the air by the likes of Sally Jessy Raphael, Geraldo Rivera, Rikki Lake, Oprah Winfrey, Montel Williams, Maury Povich, and Jerry Springer. Each tried to outdo the other. "My Mom Had an Affair with My Man." "Women Who Fall in Love with Gay Men." "Women Who Marry Their Rapists." Finally Oprah moved to more uplifting programming. Even Geraldo concluded that "I went too far . . . I used up my quota on deviant behavior"[10] and joined Fox News Channel as a foreign reporter. But the others continue their daily routine of exploiting mostly poor, highly screwed-up guests—all under the guise of helping them. "So tell us, Jolene. When did you find out that the man you had been having sex with was your real dad? And how did that make you feel?" Seeking distinctiveness in the talk-show lineup, Jerry Springer developed his trademark shows in which guests—typically men who are having sex with the same woman, or women who are having sex with the same man—come to blows while the audience appreciatively chants, "Jerry! Jerry!" For sheer shock value, however, it is hard to outdo Howard Stern, who has developed a huge and virtually cult following. Stern's show regularly features an endless parade of women who are asked to take off their clothes, let Howard touch their breasts, let Howard evaluate their ass, let Howard shave their private parts, and so on. Occasionally, to vary the pace, Stern will conduct a "Spot the Jew by His Nose" contest or "Man with the Smallest Dick" contest.

Television sitcoms have reached a new level of polymorphous promiscuity, as some recent examples show. On the CBS show *Two and a Half Men*, Charlie gets together with an old girlfriend, only to discover that she is now a he. This is intended to be very funny. The humor deepens when Charlie discovers that the former girlfriend, now a man, is having sex with Charlie's middle-aged mom. Charlie faces a moral dilemma: whether to tell his mother that "Bill" used to be "Jill." On NBC's prime-time hit show *Will & Grace*, a young woman named Tina confesses to Will that his father, with whom she is having an affair, is cheating on her with another woman. When Will offers to help Tina, she is extremely grateful, because, as she explains, "I have no one else to go to. I'd go to my girlfriends but I've slept with all their husbands." Hilarious. Eventually we discover that Will's father is cheating on Tina with his ex-wife, Will's mother. Time for a showdown between the two women? Not at all. We find out that Will's mother is so openminded that she doesn't mind sharing. She tells Tina, "I'll take George Mondays, Wednesdays, and Fridays." Tina adds, "And I'll keep him on the weekends. We'll give him Tuesdays and Thursdays to rest." The laughter at this point has reached its crescendo.

Shocking the morals of the American public—"pushing the envelope"—is a central theme of contemporary entertainment, although the public has become so desensitized that this is becoming increasingly difficult to do. Madonna perfected the genre in the 1980s, not just because of her salacious lyrics and dance routines, but also because she juxtaposed those with the symbols of traditional morality and religiosity. Her name is "Madonna"—a reference to the Virgin Mary. She often wore highly revealing outfits with a large cross necklace bouncing on her breasts. Even her videos, with titles such as *Like a Prayer,* and her songs, with titles such as "Like a Virgin," evoke traditional religion and morality if only to mock them. Madonna's appeal rests on a kind of blasphemy: she is a pagan goddess who is posing as the Virgin Mary. Madonna made headlines recently for her openmouthed kiss with Britney Spears on the MTV Video Music Awards show. As was no doubt intended, the kiss made headlines around the world, including the front page of *USA Today*. Entertainment sages informed the public that Madonna was symbolically anointing Britney Spears as her successor.

Britney Spears's participation in "the Kiss" was significant because of Spears's status as a pop icon for very young girls. Her audience reaches down to girls as young as eight. Yet parents who bother to listen to the words in her songs are often startled by their content. Spears has gone from moderately titillating lyrics like "I'm not that innocent" and "Hit me baby one more time" to more explicit recent fare like "The Hook Up" and a song about masturbation. These topics, from her famous kiss with Madonna to her masturbation melody, are now openly discussed by "serious" journalists like Diane Sawyer. Here, for instance, is Sawyer interviewing Spears about "the Kiss" on *Primetime Thursday:*

Sawyer: You said there's no tongue action there.
Spears: Oh, of course there was no tongue. Gosh, no.
Sawyer: Well, it looked like it. It looked like there was.[11]

Much has been said about the filthy language, sexual exploitation, and violence that are central themes in today's rap music. Here is a relatively mild example from the white rapper Eminem:

Slut, you think I won't choke no whore
Till the vocal cords don't work in her throat no more?
Bitch I'm a kill you! Like a murder weapon, I'm a conceal you
In a closet with mildew, sheets, pillows and film you.

Recently the *New York Times* pointed out that for rappers, serving time for violent crime is a "resume booster" that often leads to higher sales. The *Times* noted: "On Tuesday C-Murder released his newest album. The sticker boasts: Behind Bars! Still Thugging! C-Murder has been locked up since 2003, when he was convicted of second-degree murder. Next week the Philadelphia rapper Beanie Sigel is to release *The B. Coming,* recorded last year before he began his one-year sentence for weapons possession. And one of the season's most eagerly anticipated albums is by Jah Cure, who has been in prison since 1999, convicted of robbery, gun possession, and two counts of rape."[12]

I want to emphasize that the examples I am giving are neither rare nor extreme. It would be easy to provide hundreds of examples, and to find many far more explicit than the ones I have given.

American culture offers a pattern so reliable that I can often make sound predictions about it, even when I have very limited information. For example, if I walk into my daughter's room with the TV on and hear the word "God" mentioned, there is a 99 percent chance that the character is swearing ("My God!" "Good God!") rather than praying. If I turn on an episode of a daytime soap or evening drama in which two characters are having sex, I can safely bet that they are not married—at least not to each other.

Behind the innumerable examples of excess, immodesty, and immorality there is an ideology. Here are some of the ingredients of that ideology, which constitutes Hollywood's understanding of how the world is, or should be. Children are usually wiser than their parents and teachers, who are often portrayed as fools and bunglers. Homosexuals are typically presented as good-looking and charming, and unappealing features of the gay lifestyle are either ignored or presented in an amusing light. As countless movie plots confirm, the white businessman in the suit is usually the villain. Prostitutes are always portrayed more favorably and decently than anyone who criticizes them. Small towns are the preferred venue for evil and scary occurrences, and country pastors are usually portrayed as vicious, hypocritical, sexually repressed, and corrupt. Notwithstanding the occasional appearance of the stereotypical Elmer Gantry, nobody goes to church. Religion is simply not a feature of the lives of movie and television characters. Lots of film and TV characters have premarital sex, but very rarely does anyone contract a sexually transmitted disease. "Prudes" are always the subject of jokes and ridicule. One of the central themes of American movies and television is the glamorization of adultery. Adultery is almost always portrayed sympathetically, so that if a woman cheats on her husband, the husband is generally shown to be vicious, unscrupulous, abusive, impotent, or in some way deserving of the fate that befalls him.[13]

Where, then, are the moral standards in American popular culture? It seems that there are none, just as the Muslims allege.

* * *

SO FAR I have greatly understated the Muslim case against American popular culture. The triviality, coarseness, and vulgarity in movies, in music, and on television are bad enough. But it is far worse for a culture when those trends, far from being denounced and deplored, are actually praised and celebrated by influential figures in the society. This is precisely the case with American popular culture, which is actively championed by leading voices on the cultural left. Moreover, as Tipper Gore found out, anyone who attempts to criticize cultural depravity is vehemently denounced by the cultural left. In short, the cultural left is the political guardian of the depraved values of American popular culture.

To understand this, it is important to notice what the cultural left says and does, but also what it doesn't say and doesn't do. Critics on the left will deplore violence when it appears in a movie that promotes traditional religious faith, such as Mel Gibson's *The Passion of the Christ*. The liberal critic for the *New York Daily News* found the violence in this movie "grotesque . . . savage . . . sickening." But the left will praise violence when it appears in movies that promote liberal or avant-garde values, such as *Pulp Fiction, Natural Born Killers,* or *Kill Bill*. The same critic who found Mel Gibson's movie hard to endure has written a glowing biography of the moviemaker who virtually specializes in gruesome violence, Quentin Tarantino.[14] Politicians on the cultural left, like Hillary Clinton, understand the tactical value of siding with parents who are concerned about the harms of popular culture. But while she frequently speaks of a V-chip to enable parents to control the violent programming to which their children are exposed, Clinton has never called for an S-chip to enable parents to monitor sexually explicit programming. Thus Clinton tacitly conveys her indifference to the goal of protecting childhood sexual innocence.

Some on the left have sought to deflect blame for the moral depravity of American popular culture to American business. "It is because of the market," Thomas Frank writes, "that TV is such a sharp-tongued insulter of family values and such a zealous promoter of every species of social deviance."[15] But if this is so, then the silence of the cultural left in criticizing the entertainment business is especially revealing. The left, after all, constantly denounces American business for various types of financial corruption. It is unfailingly vigilant in exposing business for polluting the natural environment. But when is the last time a liberal denounced Hollywood or the music industry for polluting the moral environment? When is the last time someone on the left scorned the music industry in the same way that liberals scorn Tyco and Enron? Why don't liberals treat the movie companies with the same belligerence that they treat the cigarette companies? The movie business and the music industry appear to be the two forms of capitalism that are generally exempt from liberal criticism. It seems that the cultural left opposes capitalism except when it produces moral degeneracy.

Moreover, the most passionate advocates of cultural and moral decadence are on the left. "Indecency is part of an American birthright," writes Frank Rich, the culture columnist of the New York Times and one of the most influential liberal critics in the country. Rich is reviewing a play that he describes as "featuring incest, bestiality and almost every conceivable bodily function." Predictably, he loves it. One should not assume from his praise of obscenity that Rich is incapable of moral indignation. He is indignant about what he terms "the indecency crusade," about those who oppose obscenity. And what do these nefarious people seek? According to Rich, they seek a "repressive cultural environment" in which movie, theater, and music producers may actually restrain themselves. "Our new Puritans," Rich darkly warns, seek to "stamp out . . . everything that is joyously vulgar in American culture."[16]

Several years ago the social critic Henry Louis Gates, who is the chairman of the Black Studies Department at Harvard University, offered a highbrow apologia for the rap lyrics of the group 2 Live Crew. At first glance, the group's music might seem difficult to defend. The songs hail the pleasures of forced intercourse: "I'll break you down and dick you long," "So we try real hard just to break the walls," "I'll bust your pussy, then break your backbone," and so on. Much of the content is simply grotesque.

Suck my dick, bitch, and make it puke
Lick my ass up and down
Lick it till your tongue turn doo-doo brown.

Gates argued that 2 Live Crew's music was "brilliant . . . astonishing and refreshing . . . exuberant hyperbole." For Gates, the group's "so-called obscenity" was comparable to Shakespeare's lyrics. "Many of the greatest classics of Western literature contain quote-unquote lewd words," Gates declared, adding that 2 Live Crew's lyrics were "part of a venerable Western tradition."[17]

Admittedly most American liberals and leftists are not partial to such vulgar fare as the songs of 2 Live Crew. Many liberals speak condescendingly about Jerry Springer, Howard Stern, and even *Will & Grace*. Their objection is not that these shows feature moral depravity, but that the moral depravity is not highbrow enough for their taste. Sophisticated liberals prefer plays like *The Mistress Cycle*, described by *New York Times* reviewer Miriam Horn as featuring "four women from remote places and times, all of whom have slept with men not their husbands." Here one finds just the right mix of obscurity and depravity that liberals love. Horn has nothing but praise for these women. "These are mysterious, original, daring women." In one of her essays, philosopher Martha Nussbaum gives the example of the Athenian thinker Crates and his lover, Hipparchia, who "copulated in public and went off together to dinner parties." For Nussbaum this couple demonstrates "the life of the cosmopolitan" at its best.[18]

When photographer Robert Mapplethorpe was criticized for some of his offensive subjects, such as his portrait of himself with a bullwhip protruding from his anus, liberals rushed to celebrate Mapplethorpe's genius and to bullwhip his critics. Social critic Susan Sontag wrote a fawning introduction to a book of Mapplethorpe's photographs. Another liberal hero of recent years was Andres Serrano, who came to public attention for his work *Piss Christ*, featuring a crucifix suspended in a jar of the artist's own urine. Liberals did not merely defend these artists' right to produce their work; they defended their right to receive grants from the federal government through the National Endowment for the Arts. Many liberals denounced Mapplethorpe and Serrano's critics as advocates of "censorship." Here censorship was defined not as government suppression of a work of art but rather as government refusal to subsidize the kinds of art that liberals like.

I am not suggesting that, in their personal behavior, liberals act any worse than conservatives or anyone else. Some years ago, liberal congressman Barney Frank answered a personal ad in the *Washington Blade* in which a male prostitute, Stephen Gobie, drew public attention to his "hot bottom" and "large endowment." Frank began to pay Gobie for sex and even invited Gobie to move in with him. When the arrangement soured, Gobie revealed to the press that he had been running a full-service prostitution ring out of Frank's Capitol Hill apartment.[19] Conservatives savored the Frank story, but as they know—and as left-wing writer Joe Conason gleefully details in his book *Big Lies*—there have been numerous cases of misbehavior involving outstanding conservative members. During the period when Clinton was sharing his cigar with Monica Lewinsky, former House Speaker Newt Gingrich was cheating on his second wife with a congressional committee staffer. Congressman Robert Livingstone was forced to withdraw his name for Speaker shortly after his extramarital dalliances with female lobbyists became public. When the press reported conservative congressman Henry Hyde's adulterous affair with Congresswoman Helen Chenoweth, Hyde dismissed it as a "youthful indiscretion" even though he was forty years old at the time.

Divorce rates are high in red America as well as blue America, and some liberal states, like Massachusetts, have lower divorce rates than conservative states like Wyoming.[20] Moreover, in its habits of cultural consumption, red America is quite similar to blue America. Shortly after the 2004 election the *New York Times* ran a front-page article, "Many Who Voted for Values Still Like Their Television Sin." The article revealed that shows like *Sex and the City* and *Desperate Housewives* are equally popular on the liberal coasts and in the conservative heartland.[21] So the contrast that some on the right draw between a decadent liberal coastline and a virtuous conservative heartland seems to be invalid. Liberal values have penetrated the heartland. In this sense liberals are the dominant side in the "culture war."

The real difference between liberals and conservatives is not over the practice of vice or even its cultural consumption. The real difference is over the advocacy of vice. Conservatives, even while they divorce or engage in homosexual conduct, will not generally praise divorce or homosexuality. Many on the right will concede that vulgarity and excess are popular, but they do not share liberal enthusiasm over this. Conservatives are hardly immune to the vicarious thrills provided by sexual infidelity on television, but they are not likely to champion infidelity as an esthetic or social value, or to attack traditional morality.

Recently the executive producer of *Desperate Housewives* revealed that "at its core, our show is about what it means to be a wife and mother. It's about the millions of women leading lives of quiet desperation." This notion that marriage is an iron cage and infidelity is the escape from the cage is the voice of social liberalism. Caryn James of the *New York Times* praises shows like *Desperate Housewives* for recognizing that "monogamy has come to seem an impossible goal," so that "the new ideal is honesty about infidelity."[22] Not all liberals feel this way, of course. But only in the liberal community does monogamy seem an impossible goal; only among liberals does a confession of infidelity become a hallmark of virtue.

ANOTHER AREA WHERE liberals are active promoters and apologists for cultural depravity is pornography. The topic is relevant to a discussion of American culture because the culture has become increasingly pornographic. Pornographic themes have entered advertising and movies in a way that would have seemed unthinkable even a decade ago. Smut virtually thrusts itself upon us, most notably through e-mails and Web pop-ups that are more persistent than any other form of online advertising. Liberals, of course, have not caused the porn revolution. But they are, along with pornographers, its biggest promoters and defenders.

Pornography is, of course, an ancient vice. There is very little that our contemporary pornographers depict that was unknown to the ancient Greeks and Romans. Even child pornography—showing, say, men having sex with young boys—would not have surprised the Greeks, who did after all practice pederasty. What is new, and what would have amazed our Greek forebears, is the mainstreaming of pornography and the kinds of arguments that some liberals make in defense of it.

Pornography is now big business in America. You no longer have to go places to find it; it now finds you. Once confined to "dirty old men" and seedy areas of town, pornography has now penetrated the hotel room and home. The Internet and cell phone have made pornography accessible everywhere, all the time. The spread of porn is not surprising, and neither is its popularity. It is not the appeal of sex, but the appeal of voyeurism. After all, the actors in porn films seek to gratify not themselves but the viewer. The spectator finds himself in an unnatural position of being witness to a sexual act that is conducted fully for his benefit. While it is customary to refer to pornography as "adult material," there is in fact nothing "adult" about pornography. Rather, pornography provides the juvenile fantasy of the ever-willing and ever-horny female who wants to have sex with every man she sees. Traditionally porn has been considered debasing and immoral because it reduces sexual love to bodily functions. Pornography promotes a trivialization and dishonesty about sex that is unhealthy for human development.

In a manner that the older generation of Americans finds scandalous, porn has become socially acceptable and lost its moral stigma. A good example of this cultural cachet is that today a porn star like Jenna Jameson appears on billboards and on the cover of magazines like *Vanity Fair*. In some liberal intellectual circles, the advocacy of porn is now viewed as a mark of sophistication. Recently *The New Yorker* reported on an event held at the Mary Boone Gallery in Manhattan where "artists, collectors, literati, and other art world regulars mingled seamlessly with adult-movie producers and directors and quite a few of the performers themselves." The purpose of the event was to celebrate the publication of the book *XXX: Porn Star Portraits*. The pictures in the book are accompanied by appreciative essays by leading figures on the left like Gore Vidal, John Waters, and Salman Rushdie.[23]

The liberal defense of obscenity and pornography began many decades ago as a defense of great works of literature and of free speech. It began, in other words, as a noble cause. Pressured by philistines, ignorant prosecutors brought obscenity charges against works like James Joyce's *Ulysses*, Flaubert's *Madame Bovary*, and D. H. Lawrence's *Lady Chatterley's Lover*. These are not works of equivalent value: Lawrence, for instance, is markedly inferior to Joyce and Flaubert, and literary culture would not suffer greatly if any of his books had been suppressed. The liberal claim that artistic flourishing requires the widest possible freedom of expression seems dubious: historically art has fared better under conditions of moderate repression (Renaissance Italy, Elizabethan England) than it has under complete freedom. Even so, I'm glad that liberals fought to defend Joyce, Nabokov, and Picasso from efforts at unreasonable censorship. Some traditional Muslims may want to censor all books and artworks that portray immorality or explicit sexuality, but such works may have genuine merit, and so this is too suffocating a standard for a healthy and vibrant culture.

The fanaticism of contemporary liberalism can be seen in the insistence that all forms of obscenity are equally deserving of legal protection and that no restriction of pornography should be allowed. This is the position urged in former ACLU president Nadine Strossen's book *Defending Pornography*. As liberal pundit Wendy Kaminer puts it, in her foreword to the book, "You don't need to know anything about art—you don't even need to know what you like—in order to defend speech deemed hateful, sick or pornographic." Kaminer even takes the view that child pornography should be permitted because "fantasies about children having sex are repellent to most of us, but the First Amendment is designed to protect repellent imaginings."[24] This should not be taken to reflect what the First Amendment actually says—the framers were concerned to protect political speech and not depictions of pedophilia—but it is a good reflection of how some liberals would like to interpret it.

Groups like the ACLU have taken the approach that pornography rights, like the rights of accused criminals, are best protected at their outermost extreme. This means that the more foul the obscenity, the harder liberals must fight to allow it. By protecting expression at its furthest reach, these activists believe they are fully securing the free speech rights of the rest of us. It is a long way, for instance, from James Joyce to a loathsome character like Larry Flynt, the publisher of *Hustler* magazine. There would seem to be an obvious distinction between fighting to include Joyce in a high school library and insisting that the same library maintain its subscription to *Hustler*. For the ACLU, however, the two causes are part of the same free speech crusade. In a sense, the ACLU considers the campaign for *Hustler* a more worthy cause because if *Hustler* is permitted, anything is permitted, and therefore free speech has been more vigorously defended.

In recent years, leading liberals have gone from defending Flynt as a despicable man who nevertheless has First Amendment rights to defending Flynt as a delightful man who is valiantly fighting against the forces of darkness and repression. "What I find refreshing about Larry Flynt is that he doesn't pretend to be anything other than a scumbag," Frank Rich says. "At least Flynt's honest about what he's doing."[25] These liberal virtues—honesty and openness about being a scumbag—are on full display in Milos Forman's film *The People vs. Larry Flynt*. The movie sanitizes Flynt in order to make him a likable, even heroic figure. In reality Flynt is short and ugly; in the movie he is tall and handsome, played by Woody Harrelson. In life Flynt was married five times. One of his daughters has publicly accused him of sexually abusing her, a charge Flynt denies. All of this is suppressed in the movie, where Flynt has one wife and is portrayed as an adoring and supportive husband. *Hustler* features a good deal of gross and repellent material, such as its parody of Jerry Falwell having sex with his grandmother, or its picture of a woman being processed through a meat grinder. The movie, by contrast, features mostly tasteful erotica; if Flynt goes over the line, it is always presented as mischievous fun. If there is anyone who is despicable in the movie, it is Flynt's critics, who are unfailingly shown as smug, hypocritical, vicious, and stupid.

Some on the left may object to being characterized as defenders and promoters of pornography. They might point out that a sizable minority of feminists have been vocal in their denunciation of pornography. If, however, you carefully read the work of antiporn feminists like Andrea Dworkin and Catharine MacKinnon, you will see that their only objection is on the grounds of equality. Pornography, MacKinnon writes, represents "an institution of gender inequality." She condemns pornography because it objectifies women and not men. One of MacKinnon's essays is titled "Not a Moral Issue."[26] She disassociates herself from the traditional view that pornography is morally corrupting. Presumably if men and women were degraded in the same manner and to the same degree, MacKinnon's objection to pornography would vanish.

Nor should liberal enthusiasm for pornography be confused with an absolute commitment to free speech. Liberals know that there are many cases—defamation, criminal solicitation, false advertising, copyright infringement, and so on—where speech is restricted. Liberals generally support these restrictions as compatible with the First Amendment. Moreover, many liberals frequently demand new restrictions on free speech when liberal values are threatened. Several left-leaning organizations support campus restrictions on "hate speech" that demeans minorities. Groups like the ACLU support restrictions on political donations—a form of political speech—in the name of campaign finance reform. Therefore when liberals tirelessly champion the cause of pornographers, it is difficult to resist the conclusion that these liberals do not consider obscene and pornographic expression to be especially harmful and in some cases even approve of it.

LIBERAL ARGUMENTS IN favor of contemporary cultural trends have led some conservatives to conclude that liberals are proponents of relativism or "anything goes," or that liberals are simply "against morality." But there are no liberals who believe that "anything goes," nor is the liberal position a repudiation of morality as such. Rather, liberals who champion pornography and cultural depravity are expressing a new morality. We should not miss the moral thrust of contemporary liberalism just because liberal morality differs so markedly from traditional morality. How, then, do we recognize this new morality? We can discover it by seeing the difference between the conduct of pornographers and the conduct of those who uphold the pornographers' "rights."

The pornographer generally knows that he is a sleazy operator. I have read interviews with men like Larry Flynt and Al Goldstein, the publisher of *Screw* magazine. Typically such men do not even try to defend the social value of what they do, other than to point out that there is a demand for it. It is only the ACLU and its supporters who celebrate the pornographer as a paragon of the First Amendment and a contemporary social hero. Social liberals like Frank Rich seem to have a much higher view of Flynt than Flynt himself. In this sense, the liberal defense of pornography is more perverted than the pornography itself.

Similarly the sexual deviant usually recognizes that he is doing something wrong. Bill Clinton admits in his autobiography that he understood that, as president, he should not be seducing the interns. Clinton also acknowledges that he lied about his actions, and he knew the lies were wrong. It is only in the liberal universe that Clinton's conduct—which all traditional cultures revile, and which the Muslims would punish by stoning or flogging—becomes a minor peccadillo that is of no public concern and that is permissible to lie about even in a judicial proceeding. Again, the liberal adopts a more forgiving view of presidential sex abuse than the abuser himself.

None of this is to suggest, either in the domain of pornography or in the Clinton scandals, the absence of liberal moral outrage. During the Clinton scandals, the behavior that really infuriated liberals was the "inquisition" conducted by independent counsel Ken Starr. Similarly, many liberals are genuinely indignant when they confront people who condemn cultural depravity, or who seek to restrict pornography. In such cases, liberal condemnation goes into high throttle: these people are not merely mistaken or overzealous but unscrupulous, dangerous, and, yes, evil. The temperature of ideological indignation, and the language of good and evil, shows the presence of a rival morality. Call it liberal morality. It is highly instructive to contrast liberal morality with traditional morality. By doing this, we can better understand why liberals defend and promote values that are controversial in America and deeply revolting to people in traditional societies, especially in the Muslim world.

Liberal morality emerged in resistance to the traditional morality that holds sway in all traditional cultures and that constituted a virtual moral consensus in America prior to the 1960s. In America today, traditional morality is espoused mainly by religious and political conservatives. Traditional morality is based on the notion that there is a moral order in the universe, which establishes an enduring standard of right and wrong. All the major religions of the world agree on the existence of this moral order. There is also a surprising degree of unanimity about the content of the moral order. If we make a list of the virtues that are prized in various cultures, we discover that we are looking at pretty much the same list. Of course, some cultures give priority to promoting this or that virtue, or to eradicating this or that vice, but very rarely do we encounter virtues in one culture that are considered vices in another, or vices in one culture that are championed as virtues in another.

There is also widespread acceptance in traditional societies, as there was in America, that human behavior falls short of the universal moral code. The existence, even the pervasiveness, of violation was never considered an argument against the code. On the contrary, it is precisely because of the imperfection of human nature and the depravity of human conduct that an unwavering moral standard was considered indispensable to provide a guiding light for human aspiration and to bring forth "the better angels of our nature." Moreover, the traditional moral code was reflected in law. This is not to say that morality and law were ever identical. There are things that are immoral—like greed and selfishness—that are not, by themselves, illegal. There are actions that are against the law, like building without a permit or leaving your car in a No Parking zone, that are not necessarily immoral. Even so, the traditional understanding is that the law is a moral teacher and should generally reflect the precepts of the shared moral code.

Many liberals reacted against the traditional moral code because they viewed it as a burden, and an obstacle to freedom. Since the traditional code was so deeply entrenched in Western society, the first moral rebels were also social rebels. These were the bohemians, most of whom were artists of one sort or another: poets, writers, sculptors, painters, and so on. You could find them on the Left Bank of Paris in the nineteenth century, or in Greenwich Village in New York in the early twentieth century. Fitzgerald's Gatsby—a self-created individual who thinks nothing about pursuing a married woman because he obeys no rule other than the imperative of his inner imagination—is the classic expression of the high-flying bohemianism of the roaring twenties. The term "bohemian" was originally used to describe Gypsies, who were thought to have come from Bohemia in Central Europe. Like the Gypsies, the bohemians lived on the margins of respectable society and openly flouted its moral rules, which they spurned as "bourgeois morality." The bohemians lived in obedience to a new code, which has now become liberal morality.

This liberal morality did not become a mainstream phenomenon in the West until the 1960s, when bohemian values became the values of the counterculture. In a recent study, Elizabeth Wilson observes that "bohemian values have penetrated mainstream society to a degree unthinkable a hundred years ago," so that today we commonly encounter attitudes and behavior "once considered completely beyond the pale."[27] Some in America regard the counterculture as largely the product of the Vietnam War, although it also developed in Europe, where the Vietnam War had no direct relevance. It is also inaccurate to think of liberal morality as the product of movements of social liberation, such as the feminist movement and the homosexual rights movement. In many ways those movements were themselves the product of the new morality. Their success is inconceivable apart from liberal morality, because this morality supplied the ethical vocabulary in which the champions of sexual freedom and sexual equality articulated their deepest concerns.

What, then, is liberal morality? Its premise is that right and wrong reside not in some invisible external order but within the inner reaches of our own heart. Its operating maxim is the one that Polonius gives to Laertes in Shakespeare's *Hamlet*, "To thine own self be true." The crucial difference between the traditional view and the liberal view is not in the content of morality but in the source of morality. Liberal morality holds that in a given situation—as when faced with a moral choice—we should not consult some external set of rules but look within ourselves to our moral rudder. Plumbing our inner depths, we have access through our feelings to a kind of "second self" or "inner self." This is nothing other than our best self: it is the self uncorrupted by the evils of society. Indeed it can be viewed as the voice of nature within us. In the liberal view, human nature is in its original sense good but has been distorted by society. That is why liberals so often excuse irresponsible and even criminal behavior by saying, in effect, "Society made him do it."

As philosopher Charles Taylor puts it, the morality of the "inner self" is an attempt to achieve wholeness and self-fulfillment by "recovering authentic moral contact with ourselves."[28] This morality is very appealing, because it celebrates individuality and moral freedom and places very few burdens on behavior. It celebrates individuality because it presumes that each person has his or her own way of being, which is revealed through an inward sensibility. It offers moral freedom because although one is obliged to follow what his heart says, ultimately he is accountable to no one other than himself.

Moreover, liberal morality casts aside many of the old and restrictive rules that insist, in one way or another, "Thou shalt not." There is no longer an external moral authority to constrain people from watching pornography or coveting their neighbor's wife. What used to be considered sexually deviant or perverted under the old order becomes permitted as an expression of autonomy and individuality. Traditional forms of excess become excusable, even commendable, as modes of self-realization and self-discovery. This is not to say that morality becomes arbitrary. Consider some typical dilemmas. Do I, Jane, love Bill? Should I become a poet, or go to business school? The liberal view is not that any answer will do, or that all answers are equally right, but that there is a correct answer and your heart will tell you what it is. So morality is authoritative and at the same time subjective, because each person must decide for himself or herself what is right in a particular situation.

If there is a villain in the liberal story, it is traditional morality itself. The new code of individuality is fiercely intolerant of the old moral code—or indeed any code—that subjects individual choices to external judgment. Traditional morality and its defenders become objects of liberal antagonism, because they are viewed as "judgmental" and "repressive" and therefore as enemies of freedom. Consequently liberals become indignant whenever they encounter traditional morality, and many do whatever they can to subvert it. In this framework, transgressing the conventions and morals of traditional society becomes a virtue. This is why, when the comedian Ellen DeGeneres in 1997 publicly declared her lesbianism on national television, Vice President Al Gore praised her for her "courage" and her "contribution to society." Absent liberal morality, Ellen's behavior would be viewed as strange, and Gore's as even stranger. It would be as though a leading public figure had announced a press conference to declare his preference for oral sex. Such a revelation of his nocturnal habits would be regarded as a disgraceful breach of decency. Moreover, it would be unthinkable for one of the nation's top-ranking leaders to praise such a declaration for its boldness or value to society. He would be more likely to ignore it as beneath the dignity of comment. In Gore's view, however, Ellen's revelation was commendable because here was a glamorous figure and a role model asserting sexual autonomy and repudiating traditional morals.

The liberals' strongest charge against traditionalists is that they are hypocrites. This charge is easy to sustain because traditionalists inevitably fall short of the high moral bar that they set for themselves. By contrast, liberals are immune to the accusation of hypocrisy because in the sexual domain they do not espouse external moral standards at all. To sustain a charge of hypocrisy you cannot accuse a liberal of operating a prostitution ring; you have to accuse him of failing to pay the minimum wage! The contempt and even hatred that many liberals exhibit toward traditionalists gives liberalism its crusading zeal. Some conservatives mistakenly regard liberalism as "non-judgmental," but liberal morality is extremely judgmental in condemning traditional morality.

This explains, for instance, the scorn with which organizations like Planned Parenthood regard efforts to teach sexual modesty and abstinence to young people. Such programs, according to Carol Rose, executive director of the Massachusetts ACLU, are "dangerous to the health and well-being of teens." Abstinence advocacy is considered ineffective and even harmful because, in the liberal view, it has no chance of restricting teen sexual behavior. The liberal premise is that sex is natural and that young people are going to have it. Of course, modesty is also natural. Moreover, the liberal assumption is on its face implausible: young people were much less active sexually when abstinence was the moral norm, and they are much less active sexually in other cultures where abstinence remains the norm. Wendy Shalit argues that in traditional cultures unmarried young women are instructed to be ashamed of sexual experience, whereas in liberal culture they are induced to be ashamed of their sexual innocence.[29] It is liberal morality that teaches young people to suppress modesty and act upon their sexual impulses with the sole caveat that they use contraceptives or other forms of "protection." Liberal morality dispenses with traditional moral restraints and reduces the scope of sex education to matters of safety and hygiene.

Clearly this approach of resignation in the face of human tendencies is not the one that liberals take in other areas. Liberals do not say, "Prejudice is natural," and therefore racism and gay bashing on the part of young people should be accepted as inevitable. Rather, liberals typically condemn these tendencies and do what they can to suppress them, restrict them, and educate young people to resist them. When parents protest the exposure of their children to sexually explicit materials in school or in movies, liberals typically accuse them of "censorship." But when civil rights and gay rights groups protest the portrayal of blacks and homosexuals, liberals hasten to get the material withdrawn or rewritten, or to extract public expressions of repentance. The reasonable conclusion, therefore, is that many on the cultural left regard racism and gay bashing as evils that should be discouraged, whereas they regard premarital sex as a good that should be promoted.[30]

I will have more to say about the consequences of liberal morality in subsequent chapters. My conclusion at this point is that the depravity of American culture is defended and protected by the new liberal morality. This ethic has contributed to making American culture more trivial, debased, and degenerate. Now this gross underside of American culture is being exported to the world. Therefore it is no longer "our problem" but a global problem. Many liberals seem blind to the moral concerns of traditional people, such as their concern for childhood innocence and modesty, because they do not share the traditional view of right and wrong. What traditional cultures and specifically Muslim cultures consider deviant and disgusting, many liberals consider progressive and liberating. Thus, from the point of view of those cultures, liberals promote an "upside down" morality in which traditional forms of depravity become signposts of freedom. Traditional Muslims fear that freedom in the West means moral corruption, and liberals are the ones who are proving them right.

A World Without Patriarchy

Divorce, Homosexuality, and
Other Liberal Family Values

If you want to understand liberal family values, a good place to start is the Abu Ghraib scandal. For many Americans this statement may seem surprising. After all, Abu Ghraib is widely associated with prisoner abuse, lack of accountability, and torture. Once the scandal erupted in April 2004, with lurid photographs showing U.S. soldiers degrading and humiliating Iraqi prisoners, the American media portrayed the incident as a textbook case of the abuses of empire.

As many liberals saw it, the images of Abu Ghraib—Private Lynndie England leading an Iraqi man on a leash, naked Iraqi prisoners stacked into a human pyramid, captives being forced to masturbate in a public corridor, and so on—demonstrate the Bush administration's arrogant indifference to the misuse of power. As Mark Danner, author of *Torture and Truth*, puts it, "We've been offered a window into the realm of government decision-making having to do with interrogation and torture." Anthony Lewis saw Abu Ghraib as symptomatic of "the abandonment of America's commitment to human rights at home and abroad." Seymour Hersh traced "the roots of Abu

Ghraib" to torture memos drafted in the White House and torture policies approved by Defense Secretary Donald Rumsfeld.[1]

Conservatives did their best to minimize the significance of Abu Ghraib. President Bush said it "does not represent America." James Schlesinger characterized it as "Animal House on the night shift." Many conservatives pointed out that there was no moral equivalence between an admitted excess like Abu Ghraib and the terrorists' practice of chopping off captives' heads. Bernard Goldberg noted that liberals who whine about "so-called American atrocities . . . never seem to cry over the genuine atrocities that are commonplace throughout the Arab world." Some on the right defended Abu Ghraib as a way to get valuable tips about potential terrorist attacks. Rush Limbaugh claimed that "maybe the people who ordered this are pretty smart" because, as an interrogation technique, "it sounds pretty effective to me." Columnist Tammy Bruce wrote, "I'm all for whatever it takes to get information."[2]

Throughout the Muslim world, Abu Ghraib was viewed very differently. To see why, we need to take a closer look at the scandal. Fortunately we have a detailed picture of what happened, both from the military's five-hundred-page report and from the trials of Private England and Private Charles Graner, the two main figures involved. After marrying at age nineteen "on a whim," as she put it, England left her husband and enlisted in the military. There she met Graner, who was fresh from a divorce in which his wife had taken out three protective orders against him. Shortly before they went to Iraq, England and Graner partied together with another soldier friend in Virginia Beach. "They drank heavily," the *New York Times* reports, and when the other soldier passed out, "Private Graner and Private England took turns taking photographs of each other exposing themselves over his head." In Iraq, the two began an affair that they continued even though both were warned that their sexual trysts on the night shift violated military rules.

Soon Graner and England began to make videos of their sex acts. They circulated the videos among their friends, and even mailed some to friends back in America. In October 2004, Graner persuaded several other soldiers to join him in staging and photographing prisoners. They made Muslim men strip naked and simulate various sex acts for the camera. They ordered male captives to put on female underwear, sometimes on their heads. They compelled prisoners to masturbate while they watched. At one point England said of a detainee, "Look, he's getting hard." Graner said he was the one who took the infamous photograph of England holding a leash around the neck of a crawling prisoner. "Look what I made Lynndie do," Graner boasted in an e-mail with the photo attachment that he sent to someone he knew. Graner said the pictures he took of inmates masturbating were a "birthday gift" to England. Graner made another unexpected present to England: he made her pregnant.

England discovered the pregnancy two days after she broke up with Graner. The reason for the breakup was that Graner was having an affair with another woman, Specialist Megan Ambuhl. During their courtship Ambuhl e-mailed Graner an article headlined, "Study Finds Frequent Sex Raises Cancer Risk." She commented, "We could have died last night." The army sent England home on account of her pregnancy, and by the time the baby was born she was no longer speaking to Graner. Graner proposed marriage to Ambuhl during his court-martial, and England found this out from her lawyers. Graner got ten years in prison, England three years. The other soldiers received lesser sentences. Paul Arthur, the military investigator who was the first to question England, quoted her giving a simple motive for her actions. "It was just for fun." Arthur added, "They didn't think it was that serious. They didn't think it was a big deal. They were joking around."[3]

Now we are in a better position to understand the Muslim reaction to Abu Ghraib. Most Muslims did not view it as a torture story at all. Muslims were not outraged at the interrogation techniques used by the American military, which are quite mild by Arab standards. Remember that Abu Ghraib was one of Saddam Hussein's most notorious prisons. Tens of thousands of people were held there and many were subject to indescribable beatings and abuse. Twice a week, there were hangings outside the prison. This is what Muslims mean by torture, not the lights-on, lights-off version that American liberals are so indignant about. Moreover, Muslims realized that most of the torture scenes in the photographs—the hooded man with his arms outstretched, the prisoner with wires attached to his limbs—were staged. This was simulated torture, not real torture.

The main focus of Islamic disgust was what Muslims perceived as extreme sexual perversion. For many Muslims, Abu Ghraib demonstrated the casualness with which married Americans have affairs, walk out on their spouses, and produce children without bothering to take responsibility for the care of their offspring. In the Muslim view, this perversion is characteristic of American society, and is the root of family breakdown in America. Moreover, many Muslims viewed the sexual degradation as a metaphor for how little Americans care for other people's sacred values, and for the kind of humiliation that America seeks to impose on the Muslim world. Some Muslims argued that such degradation was worse than execution because death only strips a man of his life, not of his honor. As these Muslims saw it, there was in fact no moral equivalence between the sexual humiliation of Abu Ghraib and the decapitation of hostages by terrorists: the former was worse!

A writer on one Muslim Web site termed Abu Ghraib "a mirror of the pornographic lifestyle of America that has fun while it tramples on Muslim hearts." Anouar Abdel Malek, a columnist for the Egyptian newspaper *Al-Ahram*, wrote that Abu Ghraib reflects the kind of sexual depravity that is normal in America but that revolts the conscience of traditional Muslims. As Muslims, he wrote, "We feel as though we are knocking on the gates of hell, and all hope is about to abandon us."[4] A Muslim businessman told me in Istanbul, "Abu Ghraib showed a side of America that many of us have suspected but tried not to believe. Now we see that it is true. There is a sickness in American society that goes beyond a few soldiers who got carried away. What that female American soldier in uniform did to the Arab man, strip him of his manhood and pull him on a leash, this is what America wants to do to the Muslim world."

Although I do not believe that Abu Ghraib reflects America's predatory intentions toward the Muslim world, I can see why Muslims would see it this way. In one crucial respect, however, the Muslim critics of Abu Ghraib were wrong. Contrary to their assertions,

Abu Ghraib did not reflect the shared values of America, it reflected
the sexual immodesty of liberal America. Lynndie England and
Charles Graner were two wretched individuals from red America
who were trying to act out the fantasies of blue America. Casting
aside all traditional notions of decency, propriety, and morality, they
simply lived by the code of self-fulfillment. If it feels good, it must be
right. This was bohemianism, West Virginia–style.

At some level, the cultural left recognized this, which is why most
of its comments about Abu Ghraib assiduously avoided the issue of
sexual deviancy. The left's embarrassment on this matter seems to
have drawn on class prejudice. For some liberals, soldiers like Graner
and England were poor white trash getting into trouble again. Of
course if Graner and England were professors at an elite liberal arts
college, their videotaped orgies might easily have become the envy
of academia. If they were artists staging these pictures in a loft in
Soho they could have been hailed as pioneers and encouraged by
leftist admirers to apply for a grant from the National Endowment
for the Arts. But being low-life Appalachians, Graner and England
inspired none of these elevated thoughts. Instead, liberals moved op-
portunistically to attack the military and discredit its prisoner interrogation policies—even though these policies had nothing to do
with what actually happened. Conservatives completely missed the
significance of Abu Ghraib. Chagrined because they knew how bad
the incident made America look, conservatives sought desperately to
minimize Abu Ghraib, to call it a prank, to explain it as an interrogation technique, to say it wasn't typical. In trying to defend the
indefensible, conservatives became cheap apologists for liberal debauchery.

IN A DEEPER sense, the Muslim anguish over Abu Ghraib reflects
a broader Muslim concern about American sexual depravity. Many
Muslims believe that Americans are sexual perverts, that sexual perversion destroys the family, and that the United States is trying to
impose its deviant ways on the Islamic world. Islamic radicals continually exploit these issues. Referring to the Americans, bin Laden

said in a 1998 interview, "They want to skin us from our manhood." By encouraging women's liberation and the free mixing of the sexes, Iran's supreme leader, Ali Khamenei, charges, America is trying "to spread cultural values that lead to moral corruption." In this way, he said, the United States is trying to emasculate Muslim men and weaken Islamic society. Speaking at a mosque in Riyadh, the radical sheikh Fahd Rahman al-Abyan said, "The West is a society in which under-age girls know what married women do and more, a society where the woman does as she pleases even if she is married, a society in which the number of illegitimate children approaches and sometimes surpasses the number of children from permitted unions. These putrid ideas . . . are being pushed on us in the name of women's rights."[5]

Years ago Sayyid Qutb wrote that no society that undermines the family can be considered to be civilized. Sexual depravity is the essence of *jahilliya,* Qutb argued, because it destroys the elemental unit of civilization. Among the bedouins in pre-Islamic Arabia, he wrote, "Fornication was rampant in various forms and was considered something to be proud of." Qutb noted that a typical bedouin woman had relations with so many men that when she became pregnant, the tribe would wait for the child to be delivered and then determine the father with the assistance of "an expert in recognizing resemblances." Qutb suggested that precisely this kind of sexual and social chaos is increasingly characteristic of America. The new *jahilliya* is the consequence of "this animalistic behavior which you call the free mixing of the sexes, this vulgarity which you call the emancipation of women."[6]

Critiques of this sort strike a deep chord among traditional Muslims today. Tariq Ramadan points out that, even in the West, many young Muslim women "wear headscarves and give visible signs of the modesty in which they wish to be approached." In Ramadan's view these Muslims represent "a liberation movement within Islam," a movement that seeks liberation from Western feminism. If freedom is defined in the West as sexual liberation, then Muslims have decided to adopt "another way of freedom."[7] In Muslim countries this resistance is nearly universal. The Turkish sociologist Nilufer Gole says that most Muslims have concluded that freedom in the West basically means freedom from the marriage contract, "the freedom of seduction."

The distinguished Muslim scholar Seyyed Hossein Nasr writes, "The most basic right of a child is to have two parents, and this right is taken away from nearly half of the children in Western society." America's social system, he remarks, "places the desires of the individual above responsibility in marriage to one's spouse and children." Nasr argues that the idea that people own their bodies and can do as they please with them "is totally alien to Islam." Even so, Nasr charges that this is precisely the doctrine that America is trying to impose on the Muslim world.[8]

Imagine the outcry if Muslim countries routinely convened international conferences that featured testimony and resolutions on social life in America. One can envision the testimony of American children wounded by divorce, or graphic details of the various sexual diseases that homosexuals routinely contract, or vivid images of American women aborting their offspring. Imagine if Islamic countries funded massive programs to increase or decrease the American population, change the status of American women, pass laws to alter the structure of authority in the American family! No doubt Americans would be outraged and would act swiftly to stop such arrogant meddling. Muslims charge that the United States is interfering in precisely this way to destroy the patriarchal family in the Islamic world. As one Western-educated Muslim told me in India, "I wish you Americans would take your family values and shove them up your ass."

It is not hard to understand why many Muslims might feel this way. There is widespread agreement in America that the family is in crisis. The divorce rate in America is 50 percent. One in three American children is born out of wedlock. One-third of American children are living apart from their biological father. Even in two-parent families, two-thirds of women with young children have full-time jobs, so most children under school age are cared for in day-care centers. There have been more than 30 million abortions in America in the past three decades. The very concept of family no longer seems to refer to a married couple with children—it is now an umbrella term covering cohabiting couples, "blended families" resulting from divorce and remarriage, single-parent households, lesbian couples with adopted children, and so on. Americans are fairly accustomed to all this, but from the Muslim point of view, might not America's social reality reflect precisely the *jahilliya* that Qutb warned about?

It may seem odd, given the state of the American family, that a group of Americans would seek to attack and transform the domestic institutions of other cultures where the family remains intact, most children grow up with two parents and a host of relatives, and where divorce rates remain extremely low. Yet for the past three decades, the cultural left has been conducting a global campaign to impose liberal family values on non-Western cultures. Nicholas Kristof expresses the rationale for this enterprise: "The central moral challenge we will face in this century is to address gender equality in the developing world." The problem, Ronald Inglehart and Pippa Norris confess, is that most of the world subscribes to traditional values. Therefore, "Cultural change is a necessary condition for gender equality." Feminist Ellen Willis calls for a "serious long-range strategy" to combat what she calls "authoritarian patriarchal religion, culture, and morality . . . all over the world, including the Islamic world."[9] Consequently the family has become ground zero in the global culture war.

The campaign to undermine traditional values worldwide is spearheaded by feminist groups like the Association for Women's Rights in Development, population control groups like Planned Parenthood International, homosexual rights groups like InterPride, philanthropic organizations like the Ford Foundation, and human rights groups like Amnesty International. Most Americans, who are well aware of the spread of American popular culture abroad, know very little about this campaign. Planned Parenthood, an organization that receives one third of its funds from the U.S. government, has clinics all over the world that distribute condoms to young people and provide abortions to teenage girls without their parents' permission or knowledge. When homosexuals are arrested in Muslim countries for conduct that violates the law of those countries, groups like Amnesty International and Human Rights Watch demand their immediate release and sometimes pay for their legal defense. Feminist groups provide funding and legal support to indigenous activists seeking to pressure non-Western courts and governments to make divorce as easy to obtain as it is in the West.

With the help of ideologues like Mary Robinson, the former president of Ireland who served as U.N. high commissioner for human rights, the left works through international agencies to pass resolutions undermining the traditional family. This campaign has been going on since 1979, when the Convention on the Elimination of All Forms of Discrimination Against Women (CEDAW) first defined women's rights in opposition to the family and proposed abortion as a "reproductive right" protected by international law. These rights were affirmed and extended at the 1994 Cairo conference on population, the 1995 Beijing conference on women, and the 2002 U.N. Convention on the Rights of the Child. Armed with the proceedings of these international meetings, the left proclaims a whole set of newly enacted rights and then browbeats non-Western governments to change their laws or be declared in violation of international norms and treaties. For the cultural left, "international law" provides a mechanism to penetrate the otherwise-opaque barrier of national sovereignty.

What are the values the left seeks to impose on the rest of the world? One is population control. The left wants to achieve this by providing easy access to contraception to all women, including teenage girls and unmarried women. A second is the legalization of prostitution, a cause that Hillary Clinton has championed on the international stage.[10] A third is no-fault divorce, so that one partner can dissolve the marriage without the other partner's consent. A fourth is abortion, which feminist groups regard as central to female autonomy. A fifth is the elimination of the concept of the husband as the head of the household—this is seen as a violation of gender equality. The left also seeks to prohibit parents from using corporal punishment in the home. Finally the left seeks to give cohabiting couples and homosexual couples the same rights as married couples.

Seeking to avoid the stigma of foreign intervention, the left prosecutes its agenda through local "front groups." One such group is Women Living Under Muslim Laws, an international network that promotes feminism and abortion rights in Islamic countries. While the group poses as an indigenous effort, and is typically described that way in the press, its base is in London. Its funding comes largely from the West. The affiliates listed on its Web site constitute a menagerie of Western leftist organizations: the Netherlands-based Women's Global Network for Reproductive Rights, the San Francisco–based Global Fund for Women, the London-based Women Against Fundamentalisms, the New York–based Equality Now, the Belgium-based International Gay and Lesbian Human Rights Commission, and the New York–based Al-Fatiha Foundation for gay, bisexual, and transgender Muslims.

Recognizing the controversial nature of its project, the left promotes its agenda through neutral-sounding rhetoric. Once the language is adopted, leftist organizations then spell out the implications and claim the rights implicit in the benign-sounding generalities. Rather than call for non-Western women to have fewer children, the left speaks of a woman's right to determine the number and spacing of her pregnancies. While handing out contraceptives to unmarried young girls in traditional cultures, Planned Parenthood claims it is merely providing "equal access" to "family planning services." Even as they file lawsuits to promote no-fault divorce, feminist groups justify their actions as part of an international campaign against domestic violence. (Human Rights Watch claims that domestic violence occurs in 90 percent of Muslim homes in Pakistan, a charge that virtually declares the Muslim family pathological.)[11] When Planned Parenthood advocates abortion rights and performs abortions abroad, the term "abortion" is rarely mentioned; instead, the group speaks of "reproductive rights." Patriarchy is undermined through resolutions asserting a woman's right to "equal respect" and "equal status" in the home. Rather than insist that parents stop using corporal punishment, the left promotes "children's rights" that include a right against cruel and unusual punishment—defined to include all forms of corporal punishment. The left seeks to legalize prostitution by speaking of "workers' rights" and then defining the term to include "sex workers." Feminist and gay rights groups seek to legitimize cohabitation and homosexual marriage by calling for the elimination of "discrimination" in family status, and then re-defining the concept of family to include unmarried and homosexual couples.

Despite the left's camouflage, many non-Western people are now aware of the agenda that is being thrust upon their cultures against their will. The left's campaign against the traditional family has pro-duced widespread social disruption and political protest in many tra-ditional cultures. When an international coalition of liberal groups recently convinced the South African high court to legalize homo-sexual marriage, South Africa became the only country with a majority nonwhite population to permit gay marriage. The decision has been vociferously protested in this socially conservative coun-try. Along the same lines, protests have erupted in Latin America over lawsuits filed by the U.S.-based feminist group Women's Link Worldwide. Funded by the Ford Foundation and George Soros's Open Society Institute, this group seeks to overturn relatively stringent divorce and abortion laws on the grounds that these laws violate international human rights provisions. Recently the group suc-ceeded in convincing Colombia's high court to strike down the country's comprehensive antiabortion law. Asian countries trying to reduce sexual trafficking have heatedly complained about resolu-tions at international conferences establishing prostitution as a basic right.

Let us remember that in most of the non-Western world the fam-ily is not a venue for self-expression; it is the basic unit of survival. Marriage is venerated as a social institution because children depend on their parents to raise them, and parents depend on their children to support them in old age. There is little or nothing available in the way of social security and none of these societies provides welfare to single mothers. Children are generally viewed as a blessing in non-Western cultures. In poorer societies children—especially male children—can work to supplement the family income. A large fam-ily provides better social insurance for parents as they become dependent. Very few people in traditional societies share the Western liberal view that they should have fewer children because they cannot afford more, or because children will get in the way of their life's plans, or because birth control is a moral duty owed to the planet.

Drawing on the World Values Survey, a comprehensive study of global opinion, Ronald Inglehart and Pippa Norris write that in non-Western cultures "both men and women willingly adhere to the traditional division of sex roles in the home. Men in these societies are not actively restricting and silencing women's demands. Instead, both sexes believe that women and men should have distinct roles." As a consequence, "There is a growing gap between the egalitarian beliefs and feminist values of Western societies and the traditional beliefs in poorer societies." Rejection of homosexuality is "deeply entrenched" in the non-Western world. According to the survey, the practice is opposed by 71 percent in India, 92 percent in China, 94 percent in Iran, and 99 percent in Bangladesh and Egypt. Nor is the gap on social issues between the West and the non-West shrinking. While younger people in the West tend to be more liberal than their elders on questions like premarital sex, divorce, and homosexuality, Inglehart and Norris find that in non-Western cultures "there is usually little difference between younger and older cohorts, with the exception of abortion, where there is evidence of a shift toward greater disapproval among younger generations."[12]

Nowhere is the resistance to the cultural left's agenda more vehement than in the Muslim world. Commenting on the global feminist agenda on an Islamic Web site, Khalid Baig writes, "It is hard to imagine a more diabolical and wicked program to destroy Muslim societies from within, and create the same mess there as is visible in the Western world."[13] While Muslims have no objection to family planning, they are deeply insulted by the efforts of Western groups to pressure Muslim families to have fewer children. Abortion is another issue in which there is virtual unanimity among Muslims. One of the Prophet Muhammad's most celebrated reforms was to stop the bedouin practice of killing newborn girls. Muslims view their opposition to abortion as deriving from a principle of life's sacredness that was established at the very beginning of Islam. Consequently many

Muslims are enraged when leftist groups like Planned Parenthood use American money and influence to promote abortion rights and abortion services in Muslim countries.

Muslim revulsion reaches its apex on the issue of homosexuality. The Koran describes homosexuals as "people of the wrath of Allah," and most Muslims find the notion of legitimizing what they perceive as sinful conduct to be disgusting and unspeakable. One can only imagine the Muslim reaction to televised scenes of homosexual men exchanging marriage vows in San Francisco and Boston. A columnist for the Egyptian newspaper *Al Akhbar* describes homosexuality as "one of the most loathsome acts of which anyone can be accused." Another writer for the same publication remarks, "What moral debasement has been reached? And yet there are people in the West who defend them, claiming human rights! What human? What rights?" A writer for another Egyptian weekly says of homosexuals, "All the Eastern cultures despise them, just as we do in Egypt. They arouse our loathing and nausea." A lecturer at Cairo's Al Azhar University comments, "We must caution our children against this accursed disease. If these perverts proliferate, the honor of the entire society will be violated."[14] However uncharitable these sentiments—and I find them appallingly so—they do not indicate Arab unfamiliarity with homosexuality. Some Arabs are quite familiar with it, and more. "You have no idea what goes on in the desert," one Saudi businessman told me. "But this does not mean we endorse it as a society. If we accept homosexual marriage, what comes next? Are we then going to have to legalize marriage between a man and his camel?"

MUSLIM PROTESTS AGAINST interference in their social institutions have not gained much sympathy in the West because the Muslim family has such a bad reputation. So negative is the image of the Muslim family that even conservatives take pride in championing women's rights and sometimes even homosexual rights in the Muslim world. Laura Bush pointed to the liberation of the Afghan women as one of the great benefits of the overthrow of the Taliban

in the aftermath of 9/11. While we can all rejoice in the sight of
Afghan women who are now free to uncover their faces, travel outside the home, vote, and work, we should remember that women
enjoy these rights in most Muslim countries, including fundamentalist Iran. So the strong prejudice of many Americans against the
Muslim family still requires explanation.

I think one reason for it is the Muslim practice of polygamy. For
Americans across the spectrum, even homosexual marriage is a less
freakish prospect than polygamy. The typical American woman cannot even imagine living in a household where she shares her husband's affection with other wives. Americans are also offended by
other forms of gender discrimination that seem religiously mandated
in Muslim countries. Sharia law decrees that Muslim women inherit
half of what men inherit, and the testimony of a Muslim woman in
court carries half the weight of the testimony of a man. Muslim men
can easily divorce women, but Muslim women cannot easily divorce
men. Women are concealed in veils and burqas while men do not
hesitate to wear Western-style clothing. Male infidelity is ignored
while women who are suspected of premarital sex or adultery bring
shame and dishonor on their families. Sometimes such dishonor is
avenged by "honor killings," in which the disgraced family wreaks
their vengeance either on the girl or her mate. These honor killings
provoke unmitigated revulsion in the West.

In order to assess Islamic society, we should be on guard against
the blinders of ethnocentrism. This problem is illustrated by Under-
secretary of State Karen Hughes's visit to Saudi Arabia in September
2005. Speaking before a carefully screened group of upper-middle-
class Saudi women, the kind of women who would normally be
sympathetic to America, Hughes introduced herself as a "working
mom" and proceeded to enlighten the Saudis about ways in which
they were being oppressed by Islam. "I believe women should be
free and equal participants in society," Hughes said. "I feel that as an
American woman, my ability to drive is an important part of my
freedom." Many American women, Hughes added, "can't imagine
not being able to drive ourselves to work."[15]

To her amazement, Hughes felt a wave of derision and hostility from the audience. She subsequently discovered that the women didn't feel oppressed by Saudi driving laws because, like other well-to-do women in non-Western societies, most of them had drivers. Thus they were no more outraged than affluent American women would be if they were informed that they were denied the privilege of taking out the garbage or mowing their own lawns. Moreover, these Saudi women were not attracted by Hughes's "working mom" model because they did not perceive work outside the home to be a form of liberation. What is the joy of going to work and being ordered around by a boss when you can stay home and order around the domestic servants? The attitude of the Saudi women was much like that of the Russian women who, after the fall of communism, declared their freedom as one of *not* having to work.

When we take off the ethnocentric sunglasses, we see that in its structure of authority, the Muslim family is patriarchal, as the Western family once was. Many of the practices that are perceived in the West as "discrimination" are simply the consequence of a system that assigns different social roles to men and women. Seyyed Hossein Nasr writes, "Islam sees the role of the two sexes as complementary. . . . The role of women is seen primarily but not necessarily exclusively as preserving the family and bringing up the children, and that of men as protecting the family and providing economically for it. . . . Although usually the Muslim male dominates in economic and social activity outside the home, it is the wife who reigns completely in the home, where the husband is like a guest."[16] There is nothing "Islamic" about this. It is not even "religious." It is the way that all traditional cultures conceive family relationships. I am not a Muslim, and I grew up in India in a society like this. I can testify from personal experience that traditional systems of this sort do not breed passive, submissive women. My two grandmothers were both tyrants who ruled over their husbands. Patriarchy doesn't make women less powerful—it merely diverts their power to the domain of the household.

Practices like arranged marriage and even polygamy are also not distinctively Islamic. They too are characteristic of patriarchal cultures.[17] Even today marriages are frequently arranged throughout the non-Western world, as they used to be in Europe as well. We know from the Bible that in ancient Israel men had multiple wives as well as concubines. More recently in America, polygamy was permitted and practiced by the Mormons. Islam allows polygamy but limits the number of wives to four. Some Americans may be surprised to learn that the practice of polygamy is quite rare in the Muslim world. The reason is that Islam places strict conditions on it. The Prophet Muhammad insisted that a Muslim man must treat his wives equally in inheritance, in attention, and even in conjugal favors. The vast majority of Muslim men have decided it is easier and less expensive to have only one wife.

The veil, too, is not a custom native to Islam. The practice of veiling was common in ancient Judaism and early Christianity. The Muslims adopted the custom from the Persian and Byzantine societies. The term *hijab* means "hide" or "conceal," and the Koran instructs women to "lower their gaze and guard their modesty" so as to "display their beauty only to their husbands." But the Koran does not demand the veil nor does it provide specific guidelines. The Taliban required the full-body covering, or burqa, but most Muslim countries are content with the headscarf. Defenders of the Muslim dress code, like Masoumeh Ebtekar, the first woman to serve as a vice president of Iran, argue that "modest dress is to the benefit of women, not something imposed by men. The point is to avoid one sex being exploited by the other." Oddly, some Islamic radicals argue that the veil makes it possible for Muslim women to pursue careers and enter public life while escaping the unwanted attention of men. Western visitors are often startled to discover that even in Islamic regimes like today's Iran, many women run their own businesses and hold prominent positions in law, universities, and government. When the Muslim woman is veiled, Hassan Turabi contends, "she is considered a human being, not an object of pleasure or an erotic image."[18]

There is, of course, no excuse for the abuses of patriarchy and traditional Islamic teaching that occur far too commonly in the Muslim world. The most abominable are the "honor killings." These are not unique to the Muslim world, but that is where they are most common today. Female circumcision too is not an Islamic practice; it is an African custom, and not surprisingly we find it in Muslim North Africa. Another practice that cannot be condoned is that of child marriage. Since the Khomeini revolution, the marriage age for girls in Iran was lowered from eighteen to nine, and then raised to thirteen. The notion of forty-year-old men marrying fourteen-year-old girls is deplorable, even taking cultural differences into account.

Although polygamy allows men multiple avenues to meet their sexual needs, some Muslim men have found an alternative means to find gratification when they travel away from home or go on pilgrimages. The practice is called *sigheh* (in Farsi) or *mut'a* (in Arabic), and it refers to "temporary marriage," which is permitted in Shia Islam but forbidden in Sunni Islam. Under the rules of *sigheh*, men can pay a bride price and contract marriage for a specified time. The original justification for temporary marriage was that Muslim men needed marital companionship when they went off to war and were away from their families for years at a time. Whatever the original rationale, temporary marriage has been subject to widespread abuse in contemporary Iran. Some of the worst abusers are the mullahs. The traveling clergymen pick up women, pay them a small sum, and then contract to marry them for a few days or even a few hours. Here marriage becomes a disguise for prostitution. One Western journalist spoke to a woman in the holy city of Qom who takes an average of three temporary husbands a day.[19]

While some radical Muslims defend honor killings, child marriage, and temporary marriage, most traditional Muslims will condemn these practices as violations of their moral code. Responding to a question about honor killing, the Muslim site islamonline.net cites numerous Islamic authorities unequivocally condemning the practice.[20] It is important, however, to recognize what traditional Muslims are condemning. Traditional Muslims are outraged by honor killings, but they do not adopt the viewpoint of some American liberals who ridicule the concept of chastity and consider family honor to be a dubious notion not worth defending. Many traditional Muslims look with revulsion at the sight in their countries of young girls attached to men old enough to be their fathers—just as they would find such a sight revolting in the West. Most Shia Muslims disdain temporary marriage as a form of prostitution no different from that found in Las Vegas or Amsterdam's red light district. In short, Muslims condemn abuses of marriage not to demonstrate the deficiencies of traditional marriage, but in the name of traditional marriage.

Given their strong belief in the traditional family, many Muslims are convinced that women's liberation and sexual liberation, of the kind promoted by the cultural left, would be a disaster for their society. They contend that these foreign forms of "liberation" would undermine their religion, overturn their moral beliefs, and destroy their traditional families. In believing these things, of course, the Muslims are absolutely correct.

THE LIBERAL ASSAULT against family values in traditional cultures is typically conducted in the name of universal rights. Groups like Amnesty International and Planned Parenthood International invoke the universal right to sexual autonomy, the right to practice birth control, the right to abortion, the right to bear children out of wedlock, the right to no-fault divorce, the right of mothers to have careers, the right of children against corporal punishment, the right to social recognition for homosexuals, and the right to gay marriage. But these are not universal rights, and in some respect they are not rights at all. You can look in vain for them in the universal rights doctrines of the founding philosophers of liberalism, such as Locke and Montesquieu. You will not find them enumerated in the Declaration of Independence or the Bill of Rights. They are entirely absent from the Universal Declaration of Human Rights ratified by the United Nations, which instead affirms that "the family is the natural and fundamental unit of society and is entitled to protection by society and the state."[21] True, some of these rights are claimed—or at least artfully implied—in the documents of recent international conferences, such as the Cairo population conference or the Beijing women's conference. But it is the cultural left that put them there. To say that they are not universally accepted would be an understatement. It would be more accurate to say that, outside the West, these rights are almost universally rejected. For the cultural left, rights are a tactical weapon that is used in the moral crusade against the patriarchal family.

It is important to recognize that the cultural left does not view itself as "antifamily." It views itself as profamily. That is why many liberals are so deaf to heartfelt protests from the Muslim world. "We accept the basic framework of democracy and you keep pushing us," complains Salah Abd al-Karim, an opposition leader in Egypt. "Americans are promoting free sex, homosexuality, things which go to the very roots of human society and are not even accepted by everyone in America. For God's sake, what are you trying to do to us?"[22] The liberal answer is, in effect, "We are trying to produce in your society the wonderful progress we have achieved with the family in the West."

To understand what liberals have accomplished, we need to reconsider the great revolution in family life that has occurred in United States. According to feminist historian Stephanie Coontz, marriage has changed more in America in the past few decades than it has during the previous three thousand years.[23] As late as 1960, the traditional family was the unquestioned norm and the predominant reality in America. The divorce rate was 5 percent. Illegitimacy was rare. Virtually all children lived in two-parent households. The vast majority of mothers stayed home to look after their children. How did this change, and why does the cultural left think of the change as "progress"?

What's new in America is not single parenthood, divorce, working mothers, homosexuality, or abortion. What's new is how widespread these things have become. Even more novel is the concept that these are good things that should be defended and in some cases even encouraged. These changes reflect the triumph of liberal morality, the morality of the "inner self."

There was plenty of single parenthood in colonial America. But it was seen as a tragedy, resulting mainly from the death of a parent due to disease or the travails of childbearing. There was a fair amount of divorce in America from the founding through the 1950s. But divorce was widely regarded as a violation of a solemn oath and a sign of personal failure. Many couples having marital problems tried to keep the family together, at least until the children were grown and independent. Women have worked since the days of the first settlers, but for most of American history mothers worked mainly out of necessity. Millions of American women took full-time jobs during World War II to help with the war effort, but most of them went back to full-time homemaking when the war ended. Homosexuality has existed longer than the republic, but it has generally been considered deviant, a form of behavior that may be permitted but should not be publicly sanctioned or encouraged. Abortion, even when available, has traditionally been regarded as a wrong that should be socially discouraged and prudentially regulated by law.

But according to liberal morality, these traditional wrongs become expressions of autonomy and self-fulfillment. Now you hear people say things like, "I feel called to leave my marriage. My life would be wasted if I stayed." Today many couples refuse to preserve their marriages for the children's sake. They defiantly say, "How can my children be happy if I am not happy?" Author Barbara Dafoe Whitehead calls this "expressive divorce," divorce as a form of spiritual and personal growth.[24] Today many American mothers work, not because they have to, but because they want to. Many mothers choose to have a career because it is more self-fulfilling than the life of a full-time mom. The same is true of people who bear children out of wedlock. "I want to have children, and why should I let the fact that I'm not married stop me?" Homosexuality is no longer a mere sexual proclivity but something like an ideology. The homosexual declares his identity through his sexual preference, proclaiming, in the words of Yale law professor Kenji Yoshino, "the freedom to be who I am."[25] And when the fetus gets in the way of a pregnant woman's plans for her life, even abortion becomes a mode of self-fulfillment. "I simply don't feel ready to have a child. This pregnancy is really going to mess up my life."

* * *

HOW DID THE new liberal morality succeed in undermining the traditional family? Why did the traditional family prove so vulnerable? For all its benefits, the nuclear family did not satisfy everyone. Polygamous males were constrained under the monogamous code of the "nuclear" family. Singles who did not want to marry at all felt marginalized, as did homosexuals. These groups became nonconformists, and they assembled into communities that went by the name of bohemia. Excluded by traditional society, the bohemians fought back by sneering at the mores and morals of traditional society. Theirs was the morality of the "inner self," the morality of authenticity. Even the most untalented bohemians proclaimed themselves to be "artists" whose paintings, journals, and doggerel reflected the unique expressions of their inner voice. When bohemians did things that have traditionally made people ashamed, such as abandoning those who loved and relied on them, they justified their actions as manifesting an elevated and lofty freedom above petty notions of propriety and responsibility.

According to historian Gertrude Himmelfarb, the sex lives of these social rebels were so bizarre and convoluted that diagrams are needed to trace their heterosexual and homosexual associations. Many of the bohemian women, passed from one self-styled "artist" to another, felt used and degraded by their men. These women had little ground for complaint, however, because they accepted the liberal moral code. In their liaisons as in their work, the men claimed to be following the call of their inner selves.[26] The only liberation conceivable within this framework was for women to demand the same right to self-fulfillment as the bohemian men. Feminism in this sense meant "the right to do things that men have always done." Sexual freedom, and the freedom to work, became the defining hallmarks of the women's movement.

The bohemians were the founders of the cultural liberalism of today's left. Starting in the early twentieth century, these bohemians began a campaign against the nuclear family. Three champions of the bohemian lifestyle were social activist Margaret Sanger, anthropologist Margaret Mead, and sex researcher Alfred Kinsey. Sanger, the founder of Planned Parenthood, left her husband and children to devote herself to the cause of birth control. She promoted contraception and abortion as part of her campaign to liberate the sexuality of women from the consequences of childbearing. She was the one who invented the idea that a woman is not free if she does not "control her own body." Mead went to Samoa and claimed that the South Sea cultures had a culture of free love that did not suffer from the repression and hangups of American society. "They laugh at stories of romantic love, scoff at fidelity . . . adultery does not necessarily mean a broken marriage . . . divorce is a simple, informal matter. . . . Samoans welcome casual homosexual practices. . . . In such a setting, there is no room for guilt."[27] Kinsey authored famous studies—a strange mixture of lewdness and pedantry—showing that various forms of "deviant" sex, such as adultery, homosexuality, incest, pedophilia, and bestiality, were much more common than anyone suspected. Quite the sexual pervert himself, Kinsey's objective was to use the prevalence of sexual deviancy to establish its legitimacy.

Sanger, Mead, and Kinsey were sexual revolutionaries with a clear agenda. Sanger was a social Darwinist who was determined to reduce the breeding rate of blacks and other minorities. Mead and Kinsey were scientists, which gave their work public credibility. Subsequent research found that Mead was completely wrong about Samoan free love. Anthropologist Derek Freeman showed that virtually all her claims about Samoa were contradicted by the facts. In a classic lapse of ethnocentrism, Mead seems to have written more about what she wanted to believe than about what was really there. Kinsey was a sadomasochist who collected much of his evidence by interviewing prisoners, child molesters, prostitutes, and regulars in gay bars. Kinsey passed off their experiences as representative of the national population. Even so, Sanger, Mead, and Kinsey are celebrated on the cultural left as pioneers of sexual "openness." The latest paean is Bill Condon's film *Kinsey*, a canonization of Kinsey that sends movie critic A. O. Scott in the *New York Times* into raptures: "Where Many Were in Darkness, He Shone a Light."[28]

Starting in the early 1960s, a group of women calling themselves feminists intensified the attack on the traditional institution of marriage. In 1963 Betty Friedan published *The Feminist Mystique*, which portrayed the housewife as the inhabitant of a "comfortable concentration camp." The only way for women to escape, Friedan said, was to seek fulfillment through full-time careers. Germaine Greer wrote *The Female Eunuch*, which scorned the contented housewife as a sexless "eunuch." Greer called on women to realize their authentic nature by pursuing the same sexual freedom that men have always enjoyed. "The chief means of liberating women is . . . by the pleasure principle. The essence of pleasure is spontaneity. Spontaneity means rejecting the norm, the standard that one must live up to. Liberation will not happen unless individual women agree to be outcasts, eccentrics, perverts."[29] Scholars like Jessie Bernard and Carolyn Heilbrun, and columnists like Gloria Steinem and Helen Gurley Brown, echoed these sentiments. Through academic writings and popular journalism, feminists championed a revolution to overthrow the regnant patriarchy.

Reading these feminist "classics" today, one is struck by their crudeness, their intellectual weightlessness, their virtual unreadability. Even so, the social transformation they sought did occur. The first change involved the laws governing divorce. Pressed by feminist groups such as the National Association of Women Lawyers, most states passed no-fault divorce laws allowing spouses to divorce without showing cause or even without the other spouse's consent. Suddenly marriage became the only contract that one party could breach without suffering any penalty for doing so. Ironically, the partner initiating the divorce often received custody of the children. Equally strange, divorce allowed one parent to relinquish both parents' decision-making authority to the courts or the state. Important as these legal changes were, the bigger transformation was in social mores. Divorce became increasingly acceptable, and couples contemplating it were often urged by friends and family to go their separate ways. Most Americans came to believe that parents should leave unhappy marriages, not preserve the marriage simply for the welfare of the children. Mothers were expected to work and leave their children in day-care centers.

How did feminist groups and their allies on the cultural left achieve these changes so easily? The conventional answer is technology, but this is only a partial answer. Yes, the technology of time-saving appliances and the contraceptive pill made it possible for women to have careers, whereas in the past this was impractical for most women. Even so, technology is no more a full explanation of the success of the women's movement than the invention of printing is a full explanation of the Reformation. In both cases, technology made the revolution possible, but the root cause of these momentous events must be found in the ideas and activism of the people who championed them.

I believe the reason feminism prevailed so easily is that from the beginning, the feminists had the tacit support of many men. Contrary to the predictions of the feminists, the patriarchy offered no serious resistance to women's liberation. Many men realized that feminists were championing something men have always sought, something that the ethic of the nuclear family denied them. Men discovered in women's liberation a means to have sex with many women without having to marry or support any of them. This was even better than polygamy, which allowed men to have multiple wives but required the husband to look after all of them. Consequently many men—especially rich, powerful men looking to expand their options—enthusiastically backed the feminist goal of liberation.

As a few feminists like Germaine Greer have now recognized, this liberation has proved a mixed blessing for women.[30] Relationships between men and women have been unhooked from the old social restraints, and are now largely subject to market forces. What this means is that as the man grows older, more sophisticated, and earns more, he no longer feels obligated to stay with the spouse who has devoted her "best years" to him. Many men now feel free to leave their wives and find younger women who are attracted to their status and power. Call it "men's liberation." The women who are left behind rarely have the same options that the men have. The plight of the abandoned forty-five-year-old housewife with three children is easy to contemplate. But even older women, who are successful and sophisticated, find that their "market value" is much lower. The law of nature, which neither liberalism nor feminism can repeal, has decreed that men of all ages generally prefer a sexy woman in her twenties or early thirties to the charms of an aging career woman.

As people in traditional societies have always recognized, the real victims of women's liberation and men's liberation are the children. Every child considers its particular family irreplaceable. Children lose their childhood on the day that parents divorce. They become vulnerable to a host of social pathologies that are well known. Judith Wallerstein's landmark twenty-five-year study shows that the problems of divorce persist even into adulthood. Children of divorce are typically reluctant to form enduring relationships and are more likely themselves to divorce and to bear children outside of wedlock. Years and even decades later, they harbor feelings of self-doubt, loneliness, and hostility toward their parents, especially toward the one who initiated the divorce.[31] No child would choose divorce, and the sons and daughters of divorce never wish this for their children. If children had the vote, there would be no such thing as divorce. Children are to the right of even the Muslims on this issue.

AMERICA IS NOW witnessing a new wave of opposition to the traditional family, with effects that are being felt throughout the world. This is the campaign for homosexual marriage, presented by the left as the civil rights issue of our day. The first wave of gay activism focused on getting rid of statutes criminalizing homosexuality, and on winning the battle for social tolerance. These are causes that I support. But now, in a second wave of activism, the cultural left is pushing for complete social approval of homosexuality. This campaign goes beyond tolerance. It seeks to stigmatize all moral criticism of homosexuality as "discrimination" and "homophobia." Gay marriage is the centerpiece of this campaign, and its implications are well known to its advocates. Andrew Sullivan writes, "Granting homosexuals entrance into this institution is tantamount to complete acceptance of homosexuality by American society."[32]

Sullivan's point is dramatized by a recent controversy at Joseph

Estabrook elementary school in Massachusetts. The parents of several second-graders were outraged to discover that the teacher was reading to the children stories that promote homosexual marriage. One such book, titled *King and King,* featured a prince who rejected the proposals of several beautiful maidens in order to finally select, for his mate, another prince. This twenty-first-century fairy tale ends with the two men kissing. "My son is only 7 years old," complained parent Robin Wirthlin. "They're intentionally presenting this as a norm, and it's not a value that our family supports. By presenting this kind of issue at such a young age, they're trying to indoctrinate our children." School superintendent Paul Ash agreed, but argued that such indoctrination is a good thing. "Same sex marriage is legal," he said, and the school district is committed to promoting acceptance of diverse sexual lifestyles "by teaching children about the world they live in."[33]

With a straight face, liberal scholars like Michael Walzer present gay marriage as a profamily concept. "True defenders of family values," he writes, "are those who promote . . . gay marriage." Columnist Jonathan Rauch goes even further, writing in *The New Republic* that "gay marriage is good for kids." Senator Ted Kennedy accuses people who oppose gay marriage of "bigotry" for their willingness to "deny gays and lesbians the right to marry."[34] I wonder if these men have any idea how radical their schemes sound to people beyond their social circle. Certainly outside the West, their arguments would be considered to be bordering on madness.

While there have been a variety of family forms throughout history—the nuclear family, the polygamous family, the extended family, even the incestuous family—no society has ever permitted homosexual marriage. Only in recent years have a number of European countries—accompanied, of course, by our own state of Massachusetts—legalized the institution. The entire swath of cultures stretching from South America to Africa to the Middle East to South Asia to the Far East regards homosexuality as wrong or disordered. The general view is, we know that homosexuals exist and there may be good reasons to leave them alone. At the same time, this view holds, why would a sane people jeopardize an indispensable and already fragile institution such as marriage by redefining it away from its central purpose? Is the point of marriage to ensure that children have a father and mother, or is it to make Edgar and Austin feel more accepted by society?

In America, sad to say, we are inured to the debris of the broken family. We accept that the traditional family is no longer the norm, it is now something like an "alternative lifestyle." We invite Edgar and Austin to our dinner parties. But in the Middle East, Abdul and Ali do not go out on dates. The traditional family remains the norm, both in the statistical sense and in the moral sense, in the non-Western world. Many Muslims believe that we should stop parading our perversions as an example to the world, and we should stop all efforts to export our way of life to other cultures. As they see it, if we in America want to wreck our families and ruin the lives of our children, that is our choice. But we don't have the right to wreck their families and ruin the lives of their children.

When Osama bin Laden champions the veil and denounces America as morally corrupt, he is appealing not only to traditional Muslims but also to traditional people around the world who support the idea of the patriarchal family. When Americans attack the Muslim family for being hierarchical, backward, and oppressive, many traditional folk in Asia, Africa, and the Middle East view their cherished values and institutions as being attacked. A good deal of bin Laden's support comes from non-Western people who see him as defending a traditional social order. It is an article of faith on the cultural left that Bush's policies, such as his invasion of Iraq and the use of torture, are fueling Muslim hostility. The irony is that it is the cultural imperialism of human rights groups and the left that is the deeper source of Muslim rage. In attempting to "liberate" Muslim cultures from patriarchy, the cultural left has provoked a cultural blowback that has strengthened the hand of America's enemy.

SEVEN

A Secular Crusade

Yes, There Is a War Against Islam

WHEN THE DANISH newspaper *Jyllands-Posten* in September 2005 published a dozen cartoons lampooning the Prophet Muhammad and linking him to terrorism, the editors believed they were making a point about free speech. The cartoons were provocative—one showed Muhammad with a turban in the shape of a bomb, another showed him turning away suicide volunteers with the admonition "Stop, stop, we're running out of virgins." Even so, they were relatively mild by the standards of Western religious caricature. The Danish newspaper wanted to affirm that Islam, like Christianity, should not be above public criticism.

To the consternation of its editors, the newspaper provoked an avalanche of anger and protest throughout the Muslim world. Islamic clergy from Morocco to Malaysia condemned the cartoons. There were boycotts of Danish goods throughout the Middle East. Saudi Arabia recalled its ambassador to Denmark. The Jordanian parliament condemned the drawings. Demonstrators in Pakistan burned effigies of the Danish prime minister and cried, "Death to the West. Death to America." To counter the chilling effect such protests might have on freedom of the press, dozens of European and even a few American newspapers reprinted the cartoons. The editors wanted to show their solidarity with the embattled Danes and affirm their commitment to press freedom. These actions provoked an even more intense explosion of Muslim rage. Western embassies in Syria, Lebanon, Indonesia, and Iran were attacked. In Khartoum, fifty thousand enraged marchers chanted, "Strike again, bin Laden. Strike again."[1]

To many in the West, the cartoon riots were utterly incomprehensible, a seeming confirmation of the unbridgeable gulf between Western civilization and Islamic civilization. For most Western commentators, the issue was simple: freedom of expression. Many in the West pointed out that newspapers routinely lampoon religion, which is considered a legitimate target. As *France-Soir*, a newspaper that reprinted the cartoons, editorialized, "We have the right to caricature God." A German publication championed "the right to blaspheme." *Jyllands-Posten* announced that it would demonstrate its fairness by printing a series of caricatures of Christ. The Bush administration accused "extremists" of exploiting the controversy and fanning the fires of anti-Western prejudice.

This was a charge to which the Islamic radicals would happily plead guilty. As Sheikh Nayef Rajoub, a leader of Hamas, told *The New Yorker*, the caricatures were "a weapon of the Western Crusaders." Sheikh Hassan Nasrallah of Hezbollah pledged to demonstrators in Beirut, "We will defend our Prophet with our blood." The controversy was a godsend for radical Islam, because it corroborated a point that Islamic radicals have been making for two decades: there is a war against Islam. Pointing to the cartoons, radical mullahs were able to say, "Look, this is what they think of our Prophet in the West. This is what they mean by freedom of speech. This is the kind of society that the West wants to bring to the Muslim world—a society that permits and even approves of blasphemy against our religion." This argument found a receptive ear among traditional Muslims. Most traditional Muslims conducted peaceful protests. But except for the usual suspects—Irshad Manji, Salman Rushdie—no Muslims could be located by the Western media to defend the cartoons. For traditional Muslims, free speech was not the issue. The newspaper may have a right to publish the cartoons, but it should not have exercised that right. During the controversy, a prominent Muslim leader declared at an international conference on Islam, "The demonization of Islam and the vilification of Muslims, there is no denying, is widespread within mainstream Western society." The speaker was Malaysian prime minister Abdullah Badawi, a traditional Muslim who is widely considered a moderate.[2]

Radical Muslims win points with traditional Muslims by showing them incontrovertible evidence of Western hypocrisy. Iranian president Mahmoud Ahmadinejad took exquisite relish in pointing out that while the Muslim world has religious taboos, the West has secular taboos, such as racism and the Holocaust. While this claim was pooh-poohed by Western commentators, it is undoubtedly accurate. Imagine if a reputable American newspaper—say the *Boston Globe*— were to publish a series of cartoons showing, say, Martin Luther King as a pimp, a drug dealer, a drive-by shooter, and a street thug. (If it is within the parameters of acceptable satire to blame Muhammad for the pathologies of radical Islam, why is it not within those same bounds to blame King for the pathologies of inner-city black America?) Surely the publication of the King cartoons would provoke immediate howls of outrage from the African American community and throughout the country. Civil rights activists would fulminate that the cartoons demonstrate the bigotry that is endemic in American society. There would be irresistible pressure on the newspaper to apologize, to fire the responsible parties, and to announce measures to rectify its institutional racism. It is not inconceivable that there would be race riots, and then there would be commissions to study the root causes of the grievance and to propose jobs programs and sensitivity education to prevent such bigotry from rearing its ugly face again. What is the chance that dozens of other American newspapers would reprint the cartoons "in solidarity" with the *Boston Globe*? No way. The entire discussion would focus on racism, on hate speech, on the content of the message. I doubt the First Amendment would even come up.

The cartoon controversy should not be taken as evidence that we in the West believe in free speech and they in the Muslim world do not. What it showed was that Westerners have become inured to Christianity being mocked and therefore are surprised to see Muslims react so strongly when Islam is mocked. Yet Western civilization has its own sacred cows that enjoy protected status—only they are all secular. Traditional Muslims saw the whole episode as evidence of the atheism that is characteristic of the once-Christian West. Moreover, the cartoon controversy confirmed the suspicion of many Muslims that throughout the West there is a systematic hostility to Islam. From this premise, it is easy to conclude that the "war against terrorism" is a continuation of the "war against Islam." As one Muslim scholar put it, "Ultimately, it is not possible to eradicate Islam from the hearts of the Muslims. It is possible only to annihilate the Muslims themselves."[3]

RADICAL ISLAM'S MOST serious charge is that there is a war against Islam being waged by America, the fountainhead of atheism. It is this accusation—and this accusation alone—that explains why Muslims would fly planes into buildings or blow themselves up in suicide attacks against American targets. Only when people perceive their deepest beliefs to be under attack are they willing to take extreme measures of this sort. "It is our duty to preserve Islam," Khomeini wrote in his book *Islam and Revolution*. "This duty is more necessary than prayer and fasting. It is for the sake of fulfilling this duty that blood must sometimes be shed."[4]

In his first public statement after 9/11, bin Laden described America as "the modern world's symbol of paganism." Bin Laden regularly refers to Americans as "devils" or "helpers of Satan." The manifestos of radical Islam regularly describe America as the "house of unbelief" and the "enemy of God." It is because of this atheism, Muslim fundamentalists charge, that America will stop at nothing to destroy Islam. Islamic radicals justify terrorism as a legitimate response to this American enterprise. As Sheikh Omar Abd al-Rahman put it, "We must terrorize the enemies of God, who are our enemies too." The blind sheikh and others have pointed to the Twin Towers of the World Trade Center as representing the Tower of Babel, and they celebrate 9/11 as a kind of divine retribution that brought down this modern symbol of paganism.[5]

The charge that America is an atheist society waging war against Islam is a profound embarrassment to both liberals and conservatives. It is an embarrassment to liberals because it confounds the central premise of the liberal understanding of the war against terrorism. In the liberal view, the war is a clash of opposed fundamentalisms. Liberals typically define the conflict as one between Christian fundamentalism and Islamic fundamentalism. Many liberals consider these two groups as essentially equivalent, "kindred spirits," in the words of novelist William Styron. Al Gore finds in President Bush "the American version of the same fundamentalist impulse that we see in Saudi Arabia." According to Richard Dawkins, the dogmatic beliefs of each side lead to violent enmities that "fuel their tanks at the same holy gas station." In her book *The Mighty and the Almighty,* Madeleine Albright frets that "hardliners can find in the Koran and the Bible justifications for endless conflict." So, in the view of the left, Christian and Muslim religious fanatics are once again fighting each other, as they have done in the past. As Jim Wallis puts it in *God's Politics,* there is a close parallel between Islam's holy war against the West and Bush's holy war against Islamic terrorism.[6] From the perspective of the left, the best solution is for liberals to stand up for the principles of secularism and oppose both Muslim fundamentalism and Christian fundamentalism.

The liberal understanding is superficially supported by bin Laden's rhetoric declaring a religious war of civilizations. Bin Laden speaks of the world being divided into the "region of faith" and the "region of infidelity." At times bin Laden defines the clash as one between the Muslims and the Crusaders. But the context of bin Laden's arguments clearly shows that bin Laden is not speaking of a religious war between Islam and Christianity. In the same videotaped remarks where bin Laden posits these conflicts, he praises Christianity and observes that Islam respects the prophets of Judaism, Christianity, and Islam "without distinguishing among them."[7]

In the classical Muslim understanding, there is a fundamental distinction between Jews and Christians on the one hand and polytheists and atheists on the other. According to Islam, Judaism and Christianity are incomplete but genuine revelations. As monotheists, Jews and Christians have historically been entitled to Muslim respect and even protection. In every Islamic empire, Jews and Christians were permitted to practice their religion and in no Muslim regime has it ever been considered legitimate to kill them. By contrast, polytheists and atheists have always been anathema to Islam. The Koran says, "Fight the pagans all together as they fight you all together," and, "Slay the idolaters wherever you find them." These passages, which bin Laden frequently quotes, do not refer to Christians, because Christians are not considered pagans or idolaters. Rather, they refer to those, like the bedouins of ancient Arabia, who worship many gods or no god. Muslims are commanded to fight these unbelievers, especially when they threaten the House of Islam.

Muslim radicals could repudiate the entire Islamic tradition and argue that Christians and Jews are no different from atheists and deserve the same treatment. But this claim would undoubtedly alienate traditional Muslims. Sheikh Muhammad Tantawi, head of Al Azhar University, argues the traditional view that "Islam is not and will never be at war with Christianity." For bin Laden to declare war against Christianity would even divide the radical Muslim camp. The influential radical sheikh Yusuf Qaradawi has said that as Muslims, "We believe in the Jewish and Christian scriptures. Our Islamic faith is not complete without them." Over the past several years films like *The Last Temptation of Christ* have generated controversy in America because of their blasphemous portrayal of Jesus. Qaradawi's supporters have pointed out that only in the Muslim world were these films actually banned. (*The Da Vinci Code* is most likely headed for the same fate.) Even the hostility of Muslims to Israel, Qaradawi says, is "not about matters of faith" but entirely because "they seized our land." While Islam has theological differences with Christianity and Judaism, these are differences among people who worship the same God and are "not like atheism."[8]

Islamic radicals make their case against America and the West on the grounds that these cultures have abandoned Christianity. In his May 2006 letter to President Bush, Ahmadinejad faulted America not for being Christian, but for not being Christian enough. Many years earlier, Sayyid Qutb made the same point. The main reason for the West's moral decay, Qutb argued, is that in the modern era "religious convictions are no more than a matter of antiquarian interest." Other radicals today echo these arguments. The influential Pakistani scholar Khurshid Ahmad, leader of the Jamaat-i-Islami, argues, "Had Western culture been based on Christianity, on morality, on faith, the language and *modus operandi* of the contact and conflict would have been different. But that is not the case. The choice is between the divine principle and a secular materialistic culture."[9]

Even though Christianity has eroded, Muslim radicals contend that the ancient crusading spirit now infuses the pagan culture of the West. When bin Laden calls America a Crusader state, he means that America is on a vicious international campaign to impose its atheist system of government and its pagan values on Muslims. In this way, bin Laden argues, America is hell-bent on destroying Islam. It is the West's campaign against Islam that provides the religious and political basis for radical Islam's call to violent jihad. As Sheikh Muhammad al-Qaysi told his Baghdad congregation, urging them to fight the Americans in Iraq, "This war is no different than that of the polytheists against the Prophet."[10] Bin Laden holds the same view. In his 1998 declaration bin Laden called on Muslims to "launch attacks against the armies of the American devils" and to kill Americans, whom he identified as the "helpers of Satan." In a 2003 sermon, bin Laden praised the September 11 hijackers and compared the Twin Towers of the World Trade Center to the idols in the Kaaba that the Prophet Muhammad destroyed in the year 630 upon his victorious return to Mecca.

Thus the liberal doctrine that the war against terrorism is a battle of two opposed forms of religious fundamentalism is false. This is not why the Islamic radicals are fighting against America. From the perspective of bin Laden and his allies, the war is between the Muslim-led forces of monotheism and morality against the America-led forces of atheism and immorality.

* * *

CONSERVATIVES ARE JUST as embarrassed as liberals by the charge that America is an atheist society hostile to Islam. For more than a decade, leading figures on the right have insisted that America is one of the most religious countries in the world. In a recent book, Senator Rick Santorum cites polls showing that 90 percent of Americans profess a belief in God, and nearly 50 percent go to church every week. Santorum observes that, unlike in Europe, where the cathedrals are empty, "More people are in church in any given week in America than are in the stands at all professional sporting events in a year." Conservatives like to point out that the religious faith of Americans seems to translate into a politics of traditional values that is unknown in other Western countries. Certainly the overt religiosity of President Bush, who does not hesitate to quote the Bible or declare Jesus Christ the most important figure in his life, is virtually unthinkable for a European head of state. There are no groups in Europe that are remotely similar to the Christian Coalition or Focus on the Family. Abortion and homosexuality are accepted without controversy in Stockholm, Copenhagen, and London. There is no German version of Jerry Falwell, no French counterpart to Pat Robertson. In this sense, American "exceptionalism" appears to be largely a product of American Christianity.[11]

But the notion that America is the world's most religious nation is a fallacy. The World Values Survey, which measures the intensity of religious beliefs throughout the world, lists Nigeria as the most religious, followed by countries such as Uganda, the Philippines, El Salvador, Bangladesh, Egypt, Iran, Jordan, and Mexico. The United States ranks twentieth. Moreover, the conservative claim that America is more religious than Europe would hardly impress most Muslims, who know that Europe is not religious at all. No civilization seems to have generated within its boundaries as much unbelief. Only one in ten people in Britain, France, and Germany attend church on a regular basis, and surveys such as the Gallup Millennium study reveal that most Europeans regard God as irrelevant to their lives. It might even be accurate to say that Europeans are characterized by their animus toward religion. In drawing up the Constitution of the European Union, the drafters acknowledged the continent's extensive debt to Greece but refused to mention its equally significant debt to Christianity.[12] French hostility to religion, rooted in the anticlericalism of the French Revolution, seems especially notorious. Consequently when Muslim schoolgirls in France wanted to wear Islamic headscarves, the French said no, pointing out that, in the name of fairness, they would not permit Christians to wear crosses either. French justice, in this view, is defined by discriminating equally against all religions.

If Europe is resolutely secular, America seems to be, at best, half Christian. About 30 million Americans never attend church and have no formal ties to religion. This number has almost doubled in the past decade, suggesting that the ranks of the nonreligious are rapidly expanding.[13] Moreover, tens of millions of Americans—even some who are nominally religious—live their lives as if religion did not matter and God did not exist. In comparison with Muslim societies, America is not very religious and conservatives seem to have exaggerated the religiosity of the American people.

While American society has become more secular over time, Muslims throughout the world have become more devout. Seyyed Hossein Nasr writes, "There exists in the Islamic world today the widely-prevalent desire to preserve a religious and cultural identity, to reapply the divine law, to draw the various parts of the Islamic world together, and to reassert the intellectual, cultural and artistic traditions of Islam. These wishes must not be identified as fundamentalism. Most people who share these ideals are traditional Muslims." Even in the West, Tariq Ramadan writes, there is a "silent revolution" in the Muslim community so that "more young people and intellectuals are actively looking for a way to live in harmony with their faith."[14] That's why you see Muslim students wearing Islamic dress even on progressive American campuses.

Moreover, no amount of surveys about the religious convictions of the American people would convince Muslims, since this is not what Muslims mean when they charge that America is an atheist society. What they mean is that the public life of America—its government, laws, and policies—is intentionally divorced from religion. One influential Islamic writer argues that America has embraced "doctrines which banish religion from practical life and restrict it to a tiny corner of man's conscience so that it has no bearing whatsoever on society and its active life."[15] In the view of many Muslims, this is unacceptable, even unthinkable, because God is the ruler both of heaven and earth. Moreover, God is primarily a lawgiver, and it is the duty of a Muslim society to live by God's laws. For a society to forgo divine rules to the point of excluding any consideration of them from its institutions of government—this is the very definition of atheism.

Islamic radicals allege that their dictators, such as Musharraf in Pakistan, King Abdullah of Jordan, and Mubarak of Egypt, are responsible for importing secularism to the Muslim world. In a December 2004 statement bin Laden theatrically asks, "Is a Muslim supposed to rid himself of his religion to become a good citizen?"[16] Islamic radicals argue that Muslims should not abide despotism with their usual forbearance. The traditional Muslim approach to a despotic ruler has been "Yes, he is a scoundrel, but at least he is our scoundrel. He is a poor excuse for a Muslim, but at least he is a Muslim. Allah put him there. Let us put up with him and obey his rules, because even bad laws are better than anarchy." Sunni Islam, which is the most widely practiced form of Islam, is based on this combination of acquiescence and realism. The Islamic radicals, however, contend that this approach does not apply to dictators like Musharraf and Mubarak. As the radicals see it, these men are not just flawed Muslims, they are unbelievers! They are puppets who are being held in place by the greatest power of global atheism, which is America. They are pagans in disguise who are doing the Devil's work. In exchange for America's promise to keep them in power, these wolves in Muslim clothing are actually working to achieve America's objective of destroying Islam from within. Therefore jihad against these Little Satans and their foreign sponsor, the Great Satan, is not only permitted but mandated.

* * *

FOR MANY AMERICANS, the notions that there is a "war against Islam" and that secularism is a disguised form of atheism may seem both disturbing and implausible. Moreover, the Muslim solution, which is the rule of sharia, appears cruel and offensive. In the American mind, sharia conjures up fearsome images of Christians and Jews being persecuted, accused criminals having their limbs cut off, and homosexuals and "fallen women" being publicly whipped and stoned. It is hard for many Americans to see how a society based on sharia can be condoned, even if that is what the Muslims want for themselves. In order to see if this American belief is reasonable, we need to understand better the Islamic perspective on religion and government.

Islam is not simply a different religion from Christianity. Islam involves a different conception of the meaning of religion, and the place of religion in society. Sayyid Qutb writes that "the basis of the Islamic message is that one should accept *sharia* and reject all other laws. There is no other meaning of Islam."[17] This may seem like a radical view, but it is shared by many traditional Muslims. The sharia is not simply a canon law but also a constitutional, commercial, and civil law. It covers religious teachings as well as interest rates, business practices, inheritance, and divorce. Essentially sharia covers not only the domain of religion but also the domain of morality. All of life falls under God's laws and commandments.

To Americans, the notion of a comprehensive holy law enforced by the state seems frighteningly reminiscent of "theocracy." In a literal sense, this term means rule by divine authority of the priesthood or clergy. But until the Khomeini revolution, Islam has never had a governing priestly class. Rather, the caliph or sultan ruled as God's representative on earth. The closest regime to a theocracy is the Islamic Republic of Iran, where the mullahs do rule. Even candidates for parliament are screened by the clergy, and parliamentary laws can be vetoed by a religious council. In Iran, however, the power of the state and of the mullahs is limited by the specific rules set forth in the Koran and the Islamic tradition. The rulers themselves are bound by these laws. Khomeini once said that if the Koran establishes the penalty for prostitution as one hundred lashes, he did not have the power to reduce or increase the penalty by even one lash. If he did, he would be going against God's law, and Muslims would have not only the right but the duty to resist.[18]

Although traditional Muslims concede the stringency of their moral code, they emphasize that its rules are voluntarily embraced by those who practice Islam. While many in the West believe that Islam allows forced conversion, the Koran says "there is no compulsion in religion." Muslims have traditionally distinguished between conquering a country and bringing it under the rule of Islam—this is allowed—and forcing a person to accept Islam: this is not allowed. While Islam allows freedom for those who choose to convert in, however, Islam does not permit one who is a Muslim to convert out. That's why the government of Afghanistan was getting ready to try Abdul Rahman for converting to Christianity when American protest convinced the regime to drop the charges. Apostasy in Islam is less a matter of "wrong beliefs" or heresy and more a matter of treason, of betraying the Muslim community.[19]

In the Salman Rushdie case, for example, Muslims didn't care about his differences with traditional Islamic theology. They were outraged at the way a fellow Muslim mocked the Prophet Muhammad and his followers. Rushdie compared Muhammad to the Devil, envisioned him having sex with all the women of the world, gave his wives' names to prostitutes, and called Muhammad's companions "scum and bums." Rushdie denies any intention to offend. The insults he directed against the Prophet Muhammad, his wives, and his companions were, according to Rushdie, an ingenious literary device. In fact, Rushdie insisted, he was *defending* Islam. "Central to my purpose," he wrote, "is the process of reclaiming language from one's opponents."[20]

Most Muslims regarded this as a pathetic and cowardly defense, and they were right. In fact, it was amusing to see the liberal iconoclast Rushdie set about his usual business of slaughtering sacred cows only to end up whimpering, to save his hide, that he was really a subtle advocate for sacred cows. Rushdie could be considered brave if he had said, "Yes, I did blaspheme Islam, but I don't deserve to die for it." Since Muslim holy law establishes the penalty for apostasy as death, Khomeini's fatwa against Rushdie was entirely in line with Islamic teaching, and even traditional Muslims could not disagree with the ayatollah's verdict. Muslim disagreement with Khomeini was confined to issues of procedure. "Yes, but has Rushdie been given a judicial hearing in which the charges were established in a court of law? Yes, but shouldn't the execution be carried out by a legitimate authority rather than leaving it to any fortune seeker who is going after the financial bounty?" And so on.

The Rushdie case seemed to confirm the extreme religious intolerance of Islam. So did the infamous incident in which the Taliban dynamited the statues of the Bamiyan Buddhas, which had stood for two thousand years. Oddly enough, Islam was historically far more tolerant than Christianity. Medieval Christians had no place in their society for those who did not follow their faith. Jews in Catholic Spain had three choices: convert to Catholicism, leave the country, or be killed. By this standard, Muslim empires were beacons of tolerance. The Mughals in India ruled over a predominantly Hindu society, yet they allowed the Hindus to go to temple, celebrate their festivals, and follow their dietary rules. Under the Ottoman regime, Jews went to synagogue and Christians went to church. The Ottomans established a *millet* system in which each religious group lived in its own neighborhood, had its own leaders, operated its own schools, and administered its own laws. Only in the case of disputes involving Muslims, or intramural disputes between Jews and Christians, did the Islamic judge, or *qadi*, get involved.

Admittedly Islamic tolerance was always qualified. As historian Albert Hourani points out, no Muslim regime permitted equal rights to other religions. Judaism and Christianity, although regarded as genuine precursors to Islam, suffered moderate forms of discrimination. Jews and Christians were required to pay a special tax, although they were exempt from paying the religious tax levied on Muslims. No synagogue or church could be more prominent than the local mosque. No Christian or Jewish man could marry a Muslim woman. Other groups such as the Zoroastrians received less protection, and beliefs regarded as pagan or polytheistic received no protection at all.[21] Many Americans may regard this as a crude, bogus form of toleration, although as we shall see, it is precisely the form of toleration that today's brand of liberalism employs toward orthodox believers of all faiths.

Islam is notorious for the harshness of some of its punishments, such as cutting off the arms and legs of thieves, flogging adulterers, and executing drug dealers. In this respect one may say, with only a hint of irony, that Muslims are in the Old Testament tradition. Muslim courts require demanding standards of proof: when there is a charge of fornication or adultery, no circumstantial evidence is permitted and conviction can occur only on the basis of a confession or multiple witnesses. Even Muslim countries with a reputation for moderation, such as Malaysia and Indonesia, deal harshly with burglars and drug offenders. While admitting the severity of Islamic remedies, traditional Muslims point to their effectiveness as a deterrent. There are very few one-armed and one-legged people walking around the streets of Muslim countries, yet crime rates are very low by Western standards. Recently Maulvi Qalamuddin, former head of the Taliban's Department for the Prevention of Vice and Promotion of Virtue, defended the 1996 stoning of two adulterers in Kandahar. "Just two people, that's all, and we ended adultery in Kandahar."[22]

The regulations in Islamic countries covering sex and personal behavior are so detailed that they sometimes reach the level of the absurd. Even Orthodox Jews, with their elaborate codes of diet, dress, and conduct, cannot compete with Muslims in this matter. The Taliban—always out in front in these areas—declared that playing with birds such as pigeons was impious behavior, and ordered that all Afghans with non-Islamic names change them to Islamic ones. Even today, it is not uncommon to have clergymen on Iranian, Egyptian, or Saudi television solemnly discussing whether it is appropriate for a husband and wife to have anal sex, whether food may be consumed during intercourse, under what circumstances it is acceptable to laugh in public, or what the permissible ways are for a man to play with his beard. Muhammad Majlesi, an influential cleric of the Safavid dynasty, wrote on such matters as appropriate techniques for "plucking nasal hairs" and "proper ways of sneezing, belching and spitting."[23] I am not suggesting that most Muslims follow all, or any, of these procedures. They seem, however, to be the natural consequence of a worldview that places the entire orbit of life under religious scrutiny and possible state regulation.

The Islamic system of enforcing piety and virtue through the heavy hand of the law seems to me both unreasonable and imprudent. It does not concede the legitimacy of the secular life. It ignores the dangers of giving the state so much power over the lives of the citizens. It is open to grotesque abuses, which are apparently routine in countries like Saudi Arabia and Iran. In private conversation, many traditional Muslims agree with all of this. But Muslims like Tariq Ramadan point to a strange parallel. If it is wrong for fundamentalist Muslims to occupy the public square all by themselves, using law as their instrument, and pushing everyone else into the background, why isn't it equally wrong for devout secularists to occupy the public square all by themselves, using law as their instrument, and pushing everyone else into the background? If it is unfair to discriminate against the secular life, isn't it equally wrong to discriminate against the religious life? If Muslim regimes are too rigid about enforcing a fixed conception of morality, Ramadan argues, the Western system of separation of church and state enforces "a militant ideology opposed to any form of religious expression . . . in the public arena."[24] For many Muslims, whatever the flaws of the Islamic system, the American system is much worse.

American-style secularism, many Muslims believe, is being forced on the Muslim world. This belief is the basis for the allegation that Islam itself is under attack. In a survey of Muslim opinion, the Pew Research Center concluded, "The perception that Islam faces serious threats is widespread and growing among Muslims in many parts of the world. More than 9 in 10 Jordanian and Palestinian Muslims say their religion is threatened, and three quarters in Lebanon agree. While this view is somewhat less universal in Pakistan, Indonesia, Turkey and Nigeria, the proportion concerned about threats to their religion has risen significantly in all these nations."[25]

Many Muslims believe that America is imposing its atheism and paganism on the Muslim world. This missionary paganism works, they say, by proclaiming "rights" that are inconsistent with Islamic teaching, and then using those "rights" to attack and discredit the principles of Islam. Moreover, they charge that America and the West use the United Nations and other international agencies to pressure Muslim countries to get rid of Islamic laws and replace them with secular laws. Bin Laden alleges that "America's intention . . . is to change the beliefs, and morals of Muslims," which amounts to nothing less than "changing our religion."[26] Finally, Islamic radicals accuse America of propping up secular dictators who are undermining Islam within the Middle East. These dictators— from Atatürk and the shah of Iran to, now, Musharraf and Abdullah—open up their society to Western influences that are imported in the name of "freedom of speech" and "civil liberties." These same despots also regulate the mosques, appointing religious authorities who receive government salaries and, in exchange, provide religious blessing for the despot's anti-Islamic policies. In addition, the Islamic radicals say, the tyrants seek to suppress religious education in the madrassas, fearing those schools may teach young Muslims to rise up against their rulers and against America. The dictators are accused of seeking, with American blessing, nothing less than a systematic secularization of Muslim society.

Muslim fears of coerced secularization are based on concrete experience. In the past half century, there has been a thoroughgoing push to dilute or abolish Islamic law and replace it with secular law. Rulers such as Atatürk in Turkey and the shah of Iran tried to detach Muslim societies from their Muslim identity, and to give them new, secular, and Western-oriented identity. So determined was the shah of Iran to do this that he even changed the name of his country. For centuries, the country we now call "Iran" was known as "Persia." During the 1930s, a newly ascendant group in Germany, led by Adolf Hitler, sought to strengthen Germany's ties with Persia. The Germans informed the shah that "Iran," the ancient name for Persia, was derived from the same root as "Aryan." So by descent the Persians were actually European, and they even had a claim to be part of the master race! Delighted with this "discovery," and eager to affirm his country's identification with Germany, the shah got rid of his country's name, Persia, and gave it a new name, Iran.[27] One can hardly blame traditional Muslims for chafing under such extreme measures to transform their national and religious identity.

With the acquiescence if not support of ruling dictators, Western culture and Western liberal ideals have made deep inroads into contemporary Islamic society, weakening the influence of traditional Islamic mores. Some Americans blame "globalization" for all this, but that is an inadequate explanation. Globalization in this case has been driven by a powerful Hollywood effort to push American culture throughout the world. International agencies like the U.N. and its various spin-off groups have been active in asserting rights for women, children, homosexuals and others that directly contravene Islamic teaching. At U.N. conferences, liberal activists stress that religious objections cannot serve as legitimate grounds to restrict homosexual rights and reproductive rights. No doubt the most active agents of secularization are the dictators who are responsible for suppressing Islamic institutions and Islamic law. But even here the despots are routinely encouraged to liberalize by powerful forces inside and outside the American government.

It is important to realize that secular despots in the Middle East enjoy bipartisan support in America. On the right, the despots are supported largely for strategic reasons. Conservatives like the fact that they are pro-American, and don't ask many other questions about how they are ruling their countries. Liberals, on the other hand, tend to support the rulers' secular agenda. Indeed liberalism is behind the international campaign to introduce a secular way of life to Muslim societies around the world. Liberals tend to believe, as two leading scholars assert, that "an Islamic religious heritage is one of the most powerful barriers to the rising tide of gender equality."[28]

Many liberals agree with Rushdie's contention that "if terrorism is to be defeated, the world of Islam must take on board the secular humanist principles on which the modern is based." The influential philosopher Richard Rorty condemns Islam as a backward way of life and says that "the idea of a dialog with Islam is pointless" until there is an "Islamic Enlightenment" that produces a largely secular society in the Middle East. These attitudes even extend to democratically approved religious laws. Even though both men and women voted for Iraq's democratic government, the *New York Times* finds it "glaringly deficient in women's rights and minority rights" simply because it seeks to implement some forms of Islamic law. The *Times* demands that Iraq's constitution be rewritten so that women don't have to resolve family disputes in religious courts but can do so in secular courts.[29] In other words, even if Muslims want to live in an Islamic society under Islamic laws, the *Times* believes they should be denied that right. This is liberal cultural imperialism in its most naked form. What many liberals apparently seek is an Islamic world bereft of public expressions of Islam. Here, as many Muslims see it, is America's secular crusade against the Muslim religion.

HOW CAN PROMINENT liberals be so arrogant as to treat an entire civilization and one of the world's great religions in this contemptuous way? In general, they derive their confidence from the American idea of separation of church and state, which is regarded, by many liberals and even some conservatives, as a model for the rest of the world. America's contemporary church-state doctrine has been in effect for several decades now, and most Americans are so familiar with it that they do not see how weird it really is. A visitor from another place would be struck by the fact that a nation with a strong Christian heritage, where most of the population is at least nominally Christian, has expelled virtually all displays of Christianity from its public institutions.

Consider this: we live in a society where it is considered legitimate for homosexuals to press for state endorsement of their sexual orientation and beliefs, but not for Christians to seek the same for their religious orientation and beliefs. The government can fund any kind of project it wants, with the single exception of religious expression and activity. The public schools can teach and promote any ideas they choose; they can extol the blessings of masturbation and safe sex and even hand out the contraceptives. At the same time the public schools are absolutely forbidden to promote any ideas that are deemed religious. If a public-school teacher handed out copies of the Bible to each student, the practice would promptly be halted as a violation of the U.S. Constitution and a threat to the basic liberty of citizens.

Such policies would strike an outside observer as deeply strange, and it is hard to fault religious people for seeing in them an antireligious prejudice. Even so, there is a powerful movement in America to secure and defend them. This is the secular movement, led by activist groups like the ACLU, People for the American Way, and Americans United for Separation of Church and State. Unknown to many Americans, there is a "secular left" in this country today that is the political counterpart to the "Christian right." Who are these people? Democratic pollster Stanley Greenberg points out that more than 25 percent of voters go to church once a year or not at all. He notes that these secular voters constitute a bloc that is just as large as the voters who do attend church regularly. Greenberg calls this group the Secular Warriors. They are, he says, "the true loyalists" in the Democratic party.[30]

The distinguishing characteristic of the secularists is that they define their faith through the liberal code of personal autonomy. Years ago the sociologist Robert Bellah interviewed a woman named Sheila Larson, who described her faith as "Sheilaism." No church, no sacraments, no creed. "It's Sheilaism. Just my own little voice." This is not to say that there are no Christians in this group. But they tend to be tactical Christians who employ religious language in a secular way. As Hillary Clinton puts it, "The Good Samaritan parable is an example of compassion toward people who are of different backgrounds." In the same vein, Al Gore explained the significance of Christmas: "Two thousand years ago, a homeless woman gave birth to a homeless child." What unites the secular left is a denial of an external or transcendent moral order. This group affirms, with the Supreme Court in its *Casey* decision, an individual "right to define one's own concept of existence, of meaning, of the universe, and of the mystery of human life."[31] This doctrine may be termed "political atheism." Working through the courts, the secular left seeks to implement this political atheism in the public square.

So far it has been remarkably effective. American public schools may not have organized prayers, not even at graduation ceremonies or sporting events. Courts have ordered the removal of monuments with religious themes, such as the Ten Commandments, from public facilities. Some courts have even declared the Pledge of Allegiance, with its reference to "one nation under God," unconstitutional. The secular ethic favored by the left has permeated the culture: "Merry Christmas" is now "Happy Holidays," Christmas holidays are now winter break, and "friendship" trees have replaced Christmas trees. The left's religious exclusion campaign is not complete. Working through its allies in the judiciary, every year the ACLU and its allies seek to eradicate the remaining vestiges of religious influence from America's public institutions. Each Christmas we witness the surreal spectacle of liberal organizations filing lawsuits to dismantle Nativity displays, compel department stores to remove statues of Jesus from their stores, and stop public-school children from singing Christmas carols like "Silent Night." Groups like People for the American Way are also seeking to deny religious organizations access to government funding on the grounds that their faith inspires them to discriminate against certain groups, such as homosexuals, or to refrain from providing certain services, such as contraception and abortion.

Despite an occasional setback, the left's strategy of religious exclusion continues to win court victories. The reason it is so hard for public expressions of religion to survive judicial scrutiny can be seen from the recent Supreme Court case on two state monuments featuring the Ten Commandments. In order for religious displays to meet the court's constitutional standard, they must have a secular purpose. Attorneys for the states of Texas and Kentucky sought to convince the Supreme Court that the Ten Commandments were basically secular. This argument is, on the face of it, absurd. The Ten Commandments are a product of the Jewish and Christian faith. Moses is said to have received them directly from God. The first three commandments concern duties owed directly to God. Moreover, Justice Scalia told the Texas attorney general, "I would consider it a Pyrrhic victory for you to win on the grounds you are arguing."[32] Even if the states prevailed—as it turned out, Texas did and Kentucky did not—they could only do so based on a proposition that all religious people would find disheartening: religious displays

are permitted in the public square only if they can be proven to be
not religious at all. This is the secularism that liberal groups and their
judicial allies have imposed on America. Many liberals would like to
see the same kind of secularism established in the rest of the world,
including the Muslim world.

WHAT POSSIBLE JUSTIFICATION can there be for the liberal
campaign against public expressions of religion, both in America and
abroad? In the view of the cultural left, the policy of excluding religion from all institutions of government is necessary for historical,
constitutional, and sociological reasons. As many liberals see it, religion has been the source of most of the divisions and violence
throughout history. Liberals invoke the Inquisition, the religious
wars in Europe, and the Salem witch trials as proof of the horrors
produced by religious fanaticism. This is the historical justification
for secularism. Next, liberals, citing Jefferson, endorse his advocacy
of a "wall of separation" between church and state. The objective is
in part to protect religion from state interference, but also to protect
the government from the dangers of religious fanaticism, denominational conflict, and theocracy. This is the constitutional justification.
Finally, many liberals point to continuing religious diversity as a sociological reality. They insist that a strictly secular state is necessary
in order to be fair to all citizens and not privilege some people's religious beliefs over those of others.

How plausible are these concerns? Leading liberals are convinced
that religion represents, as author Sam Harris puts it in *The End of
Faith*, "the most potent source of human conflict, past and present."
Columnist Robert Kuttner gives the familiar litany: "The Crusades
slaughtered millions in the name of Jesus. The Inquisition brought
the torture and murder of millions more. After Luther, Christians did
bloody battle with other Christians for another three centuries."
Harris notes that most of the recent conflicts in the world—in Palestine, in the Balkans, in Northern Ireland, in Kashmir, in Sri Lanka—
show the continued vitality of the murderous impulse that seems
inherent in religion.[33]

The problem with this exposé of the crimes of religion is that it is narrowly ethnocentric, since the allegations made against Christianity could scarcely be made against other great religions, such as Hinduism or Buddhism. Liberals and even some conservatives like to speak of the "wars of religion" in the Muslim world, but they cannot name them, because there haven't been any. Historian Albert Hourani notes that in Islamic empires, mosques have generally served as a bulwark against tyranny. Even in the West, the crimes attributed to religion are exaggerated, while the greater crimes of secular fanaticism are ignored. The best example of religious persecution in America is the Salem witch trials. How many people were killed in those trials? Thousands? Hundreds? Actually, nineteen. Yet the event continues to haunt the liberal imagination. In his play *The Crucible*, Arthur Miller attempted to show the magnitude of the crimes of McCarthyism by comparing them to the Salem witch trials. Little did the hapless Miller realize that, to the degree the two historical episodes were even comparable, his analogy actually suggested that McCarthyism harmed a relatively small number of individuals.

It is strange to witness the passion with which some liberals rail against the Crusaders' and Inquisitors' misdeeds of more than five hundred years ago. Ironically these religious zealots did not come close to killing the number of people murdered by secular tyrants of our own era. How many people were killed in the Spanish Inquisition? The actual number sentenced to death appears to be around ten thousand. Some historians contend that an additional hundred thousand died in jail due to malnutrition or illness.[34] These figures are tragic, and of course population levels were much lower at the time. But even taking that difference into account, the death tolls of the Inquisition are minuscule compared to those produced by the secular despotisms of the twentieth century. In the name of creating their version of a secular utopia, Hitler, Stalin, and Mao produced the kind of mass slaughter that no Inquisitor could possibly match. Collectively these atheist tyrants murdered more than 100 million people.

Moreover, many of the conflicts that liberals count as "religious wars" were not fought over religion. They were fought mainly over rival claims to territory and power. Can the wars between England and France be counted as religious wars because the English were Protestants and the French were Catholics? Religious differences had very little to do with why the two countries were fighting. The same is true today. The clashes between Shia and Sunni Muslims in Iraq have nothing to do with religion: one group is the majority and now enjoys power, the other group has ruled the country for decades and is trying to restore its lost authority. Similarly, the conflict between the Israelis and the Palestinians is not, at its core, a religious one. It arises out of a dispute over self-determination and land. Hamas and the extreme Orthodox parties in Israel may advance theological claims—"God gave us this land" and so forth—but even without these religious motives the conflict would remain essentially the same. Ethnic rivalry, not religion, is the source of the tension in Northern Ireland and the Balkans.

"While the motivations of the Tamil Tigers are not explicitly religious," Harris informs us, "they are Hindus who undoubtedly believe many improbable things about the nature of life and death." In other words, while the Tigers see themselves as fighting for land and the right to rule themselves—as combatants in a secular political struggle—Harris detects a religious motive because these people happen to be Hindu and surely there must be some underlying religious craziness that explains their fanaticism. It's obvious that Harris can go on forever in this vein. Seeking to exonerate secularism and atheism from the horrors perpetrated in their name, he argues that Stalinism and Maoism were in reality "little more than a political religion." As for Nazism, "while the hatred of Jews in Germany expressed itself in a predominantly secular way, it was a direct inheritance from medieval Christianity." Indeed, "The holocaust marked the culmination of . . . two thousand years of Christian fulminating against the Jews."[35]

Is anyone fooled by this rhetorical legerdemain? For Harris to call twentieth-century atheist ideologies "religion" is to render the term meaningless. Should religion now be responsible not only for the sins of believers, but also those of atheists? Moreover, Harris does not explain why, if Nazism was directly descended from medieval

Christianity, medieval Christianity did not produce a Hitler. How can a self-proclaimed atheist ideology, advanced by Hitler as a repudiation of Christianity, be a "culmination" of two thousand years of Christianity? Harris is employing a transparent sleight-of-hand that holds Christianity responsible for the crimes committed in its name, while exonerating secularism and atheism for the greater crimes committed in their name.

What about the idea that separation of church and state was mandated by the American founders as the basis of a "new order for the ages"? In her book *Freethinkers*, Susan Jacoby argues that it was precisely to establish such a framework that the founders declined to make America a Christian nation and instead gave us "a nation founded on the separation of church and state." Jacoby credits the founders with "creating the first secular government in the world."[36] But consider this anomaly. The idea of separating religion and government was not an American idea, it was a Christian idea. It was Christ, not Jefferson, who said, "Render unto Caesar the things that are Caesar's, and to God the things that are God's." The American founders institutionalized this Christian idea—admittedly an idea ignored for much of medieval history—in the Constitution.

The framers' understanding of separation, however, was very different from that of today's ACLU. From the founding through the middle of the twentieth century, America had religious displays on public property, congressionally designated religious services and holidays, government-funded chaplains, and prayer in public schools. So entrenched was religion in American private and public life that, writing in the early nineteenth century, Tocqueville called it the first of America's political institutions. In a unanimous ruling in 1892, the Supreme Court declared that if one takes "a view of American life as expressed by its laws, its business, its customs, and its society, we find everywhere a clear recognition of the same truth . . . that this is a Christian nation."[37] Virtually all of the actions that secular liberals claim are forbidden by the nonestablishment clause of the First Amendment were permitted for most of American history. Thus liberals like Jacoby are in the peculiar position of claiming that the religion provisions of the Constitution were misunderstood by the founders and by everyone else for 150 years, until finally they were accurately comprehended by liberals. The arrogance of this claim is exceeded only by its implausibility.

Finally, some liberals defend secularism by pointing to the religious diversity in America. Historian Diana Eck has a recent book titled *A New Religious America: How a "Christian Country" Has Become the World's Most Religiously Diverse Nation.*[38] Since America no longer has the religious homogeneity it had in the eighteenth and nineteenth centuries, Eck insists, there is a pressing social need to adopt constitutional rules that do not violate the right of minorities to practice their own religion. We frequently hear that Nativity displays, monuments with the Ten Commandments, and prayers at public-school graduation all make the multitudes of American non-Christians feel extremely uncomfortable.

But where is the evidence for this? It is not the Hindu and Buddhist immigrants who press for secularism, it is the liberal activist groups. Muslims, Tariq Ramadan argues, would prefer more public recognition of religion in America so that they can be respected not just as individuals but as Muslims. The ACLU, of course, will have none of this. So the mantra of "diversity" seems to be a secular ruse to undermine all public religious expression. Moreover, the factual premise is unsound. Contrary to Eck, America is *not* the world's most religiously diverse nation. Surprising though it may seem, the total number of non-Christians in America adds up to less than 10 million people, which is around 3 percent of the population. Many Asian and African countries have religious minorities that make up 15–20 percent of the population. They are vastly more diverse than America. In terms of religious background, America is no more diverse today than it was in the eighteenth and nineteenth centuries. How is this possible? Because America currently draws its immigrants mostly from Mexico and Latin America, and virtually all of them are Christians. So not only does America remain a Christian country, but as historian Philip Jenkins points out, its Christian population relative to non-Christians is growing. Jenkins notes that the real story of America should be entitled "How This Christian Country Has Become an Even More Christian Country."[39]

Of course, religious minorities, however small their number, have the right to practice their religion free from government inter- ference. Nonbelievers should have the freedom to live secular lives. Several justices on the U.S. Supreme Court seem to believe that these rights are threatened every time a public school conducts a prayer service. In the 1992 *Lee v. Weisman* case, Justice Anthony Kennedy fretted that students who are exposed to prayers at public-school graduations are "psychologically coerced" to participate in religious exercises. Even if students are not required to participate, Kennedy worried that their respectful silence may be construed, against their will, as tacit endorsement of the religious message. No matter if the prayer was nondenominational, no matter if (as in this case) it was recited by a rabbi, Kennedy found that it violated the "no estab- lishment" clause.[40] Secular liberals cheered Kennedy's conclusion. The validity of his argument, however, is based on the questionable premise that any government support constitutes "establishment" of religion and thus a violation of the rights of others.

The logic can be tested by applying the premise to any area other than religion. If the government puts up a monument to Abraham Lincoln, is it violating the freedom of those who detest Lincoln? It would seem not. If the government decides to make a treaty with Pakistan, is it violating the rights of Americans who think the gov- ernment should instead be making a treaty with India? Certainly not. If a public school advocates one set of beliefs, is it infringing on the liberty of students who espouse a different set of beliefs? Absurd. If the government funds farm subsidies, is it "establishing" farming as a national occupation and discriminating against unemployed steel workers and travel agents? The notion is laughable. One's right to espouse a belief system does not require every institution of government—including every agency, every employee, every public- school program—to abstain from supporting a different set of views. And so it is with religion. No wonder that America's radical church- state doctrine, which defines "establishment" to cover virtually all public expressions of religion, is viewed by many people outside the United States as "establishing" an official posture of state hostility to religion.

* * *

SO FAR-FETCHED ARE the reasons given for secularism, and so intense is the ideological commitment to it, that there has to be a deeper explanation of why many liberals are so determined to eradicate all vestiges of religion from public life. Why are many liberals obsessed with whether there is a prayer at a school graduation or whether the local town hall has a Christmas crèche? What possible harm is being done by such things? Once the left-wing activists put aside the historical, constitutional, and sociological bunkum, they can speak candidly about what is really frightening them. The answer, it turns out, is the Christian right. As many liberals see it, the Christian fundamentalists are religious fanatics, just like bin Laden: they are "outside the mainstream." Operating by the dictates of faith rather than reason, they seek to "legislate their morality" and "impose their values" on the rest of society. Their goal, according to Lewis Lapham, the former editor of *Harper's,* is "to restructure the Supreme Court as an office of the Holy Inquisition." If they succeed in their agenda, Rob Boston of Americans United for Separation of Church and State warns, "We'd be close to a *de facto* theocracy."[41]

Now, it is possible to find in Christian fundamentalism tendencies that are illiberal and sometimes dangerous. I certainly do. There are some fundamentalists who want America to be governed by Old Testament law. These extremists should be resisted and marginalized, and they are. But when secular liberals say "fundamentalist," they usually don't really mean "fundamentalist." As George Marsden points out, fundamentalism is a tiny subset of American Protestantism.[42] Today liberals frequently use the term to try and discredit a much larger and quite different group—evangelicals. Many liberals routinely describe President Bush as a fundamentalist although he calls himself an evangelical. The term "evangelical" is not a denominational term. It refers to many different types of Protestants who share an emphasis on a personal experience of God and a desire to proclaim the teachings of Christ. In the nineteenth century, evangelicals were the ones who were in the forefront of the antislavery movement and the temperance movement. Evangelicals today include Northerners and Southerners, whites and blacks, Presbyterians, Baptists, and Methodists. According to pollster George Gallup, approximately one in four Americans fits the definition. These are the people that liberals want to dismiss as fanatics, theocrats, enemies of reason, and "outside the mainstream."

But these accusations are hard to sustain. Consider the charge that Christian conservatives pose a threat to democratic debate because they argue positions based on "blind faith" and are therefore immune to reason. Admittedly many Christian conservatives derive their social views about topics like abortion and homosexuality largely from the Bible. The fact that the Christian derives his position from faith, however, does not mean he cannot give reasons for his belief. If a Christian learns not to steal or murder or dishonor his parents from the Ten Commandments, it hardly follows that there is no rational basis for these precepts. The charge of irrationality seems to rely on using the term "rational" as a synonym for "liberal." In a recent book, appropriately titled *Reason,* former Clinton cabinet official Robert Reich thinks it is an obvious corollary of reason itself that government should regulate "public" conduct like insider trading and executive pay, but not "private" behavior like abortion and gay marriage.[43] Once you agree with Reich about his distinction between the private and public domain, his conclusion seems obvious. But Reich never stops to consider that his premise is hardly uncontroversial. Many conservatives would argue that abortion and gay marriage have public consequences no less significant—some would say far more significant—than insider trading and corporate pay scales. Thus there is no logical necessity, no mere operation of "reason," that propels one to Reich's conclusions. In identifying liberal policy with reason itself, Reich is either deluding himself or adopting the juvenile tactic of dismissing his opponents simply by labeling them "unreasonable." Reason, in this usage, comes down to "what I and my liberal friends think makes sense."

But aren't evangelicals, no less than fundamentalists, intolerant people who are trying to impose their values on the rest of society? Here it is necessary to clarify a widespread confusion about the term "tolerance." Tolerance does not mean approval. Indeed, the concept of tolerance implies disapproval. Tolerance means, "I don't like this, I find it reprehensible, my ordinary instinct is to suppress it, but I will put up with it." Thus for an evangelical Christian to say, "I consider adultery and homosexuality morally reprehensible, and I do not think society should condone such actions, but at the same time I do not wish society to interfere in the private lives of people," is a textbook demonstration of tolerance.

There is no valid basis for objecting to conservative Christians applying their religious and moral beliefs to politics. Every group—from evangelicals to civil rights activists to antiwar protesters—is trying to convert its moral principles into law. In a democratic society, no group can "impose" its values without winning a sufficient number of allies to its cause. Imposing values through popular assent is what democratic politics is all about. Don't laws that outlaw racial discrimination force people, whether they agree or not, to conform to a certain code of behavior? Conservative Christians who apply their religious beliefs to the causes they support are no more violating the Constitution than Martin Luther King did when he applied his religious beliefs to the cause of civil rights.

My conclusion is that the procedural objections to the political role played by evangelical Christians are a smokescreen. Indeed the whole liberal doctrine that seeks fairness and impartiality through "separation of church and state" is a fraud. The real objective of the secularists is to marginalize traditional morality. In one respect the Muslims are right—there is a war against Islam—but it is the secular liberals who are waging it. In another respect the Muslims are wrong: secularists don't hate Islam, they hate traditional religion in general. Karen Armstrong writes, "It is wonderful not to have to cower before a vengeful deity who threatens us with eternal damnation if we do not abide by his rules."[44] From this statement we can infer that religion is hated not because of its canonical teachings, such as the Christian doctrine of the resurrection or the Muslim injunction to go on a pilgrimage to Mecca. Rather, it is hated because it upholds the traditional moral code, which is upheld by God in the next world and (even more scary to secularists) by law and social stigma in this one.

The founders of classical liberalism advocated three types of freedom: economic freedom, political freedom, and freedom of thought and belief. These are the freedoms that are protected in the American Constitution. Many contemporary liberals want to add a new type of freedom to this list—moral freedom. Moral freedom means freedom from traditional morality. But this kind of freedom is controversial in America, and it is overwhelmingly rejected in the non-Western world. It is certainly not the kind of freedom that Muslims want. Traditional Muslims believe they have every right to maintain their religious societies, to keep religion as the basis of law, and to resist liberal efforts to impose bogus secular "reforms" on Islamic societies. The real culprits, in this case, are the Secular Warriors. Both in America and abroad, they are the ones who are trying to eradicate every public trace of the religious and moral values that most of the world lives by.

EIGHT

Emboldening the Enemy

How Liberal Foreign Policy
Produced American Vulnerability

It is one thing for radical Muslims to hate America for its role in undermining Muslim religious, cultural, and family values. It is quite another for this group to convert that hatred into violent attacks, such as the attack on 9/11. We have seen some of the ways the cultural left has exacerbated Muslim anger toward America and the West. Now I wish to show the left's role in emboldening Islamic fundamentalists to strike directly at America. Here it may be useful to distinguish conceptually between the "cultural left" and the "foreign policy left." Cultural leftists tend to march for abortion rights and homosexual rights, while foreign policy leftists march against the war in Iraq. In general, though, these are the same people. Their banners and placards say "Save *Roe v. Wade*" on one side and "Impeach Bush" on the other! In the next two chapters I will focus on the foreign policy activism of the left. I intend to show the left's continuing effort to undermine America's war against radical Islam. Iraq has become central to the objectives of the Islamic radicals, and here I explore how the left is working to defeat the democratic process there. Bizarre though it may seem, the left seeks America's most devastating foreign policy defeat, surpassing even America's loss in the Vietnam War.

None of these issues can be considered without understanding the goals of the Islamic radicals in this war. Remarkably, there is still great confusion about what these are. Years ago Sayyid Qutb wrote in *Milestones* that Muslims who are serious about the Islamic restoration cannot simply promulgate theories; they must seek to realize the Islamic state in "a concrete form." Since Islam in its authentic sense does not exist today, what is needed, according to Qutb, is "to initiate the movement of Islamic revival in some Muslim country."[1] In other words, the fundamentalists must take over a major state. This state would then provide a beachhead for launching the takeover of other Muslim countries. The ultimate objective, repeatedly stressed by bin Laden and others, is the unification of the Muslim community into a single Islamic nation, governed by Islamic holy law.

In 1979, Qutb's goal was achieved when the ayatollah Khomeini seized power in Iran and launched the first stage of the Islamic revival. Hamid Algar terms the Khomeini revolution "the most significant event in contemporary Islamic history."[2] It was an event comparable in significance to the French Revolution and the Russian Revolution. Virtually no one predicted it, yet it overturned the entire imperial structure and created a new order, even a new way of life. The mullahs restored the Islamic calendar, abolished Western languages from the schools, instituted an Islamic curriculum, declared a new set of religious holidays, stopped men from wearing ties, required women to cover their heads, changed the banking system to outlaw usury or interest, abolished Western-style criminal and civil laws, and placed the entire society under sharia.

The importance of the Khomeini revolution is that it demonstrated the viability of the Islamic theocracy in the modern age. Before Khomeini, the prospect of a large Muslim nation being ruled by clergy according to eighth-century precepts would have seemed far-fetched, even preposterous. Khomeini showed it could be done, and his successors have showed that it can last. To this day post-Khomeini Iran provides a viable model of what the Islamic radicals hope to achieve throughout the Muslim world. Khomeini also popularized the idea of America as a "Great Satan." Before Khomeini, no Muslim head of state had said this about America. Muslim leaders like Nasser might disagree with America, but they never identified America as the primary source of evil in the world. During the Khomeini era, there were large demonstrations by frenzied Muslims who cursed the United States and burned the American flag. For the first time, banners and posters began to appear all over Iran: DEATH TO AMERICA! THE GREAT SATAN WILL INCUR GOD'S PUNISHMENT! USA, GO TO HELL! AMERICA IS OUR NUMBER ONE ENEMY! These slogans have since become the mantra of Islamic radicalism. Khomeini was also the first Muslim leader in the modern era to advocate violence as a religious duty and to give special place to martyrdom.[3] Since Khomeini, Islamic radicalism has continued to attract aspiring martyrs ready to confront the Great Satan. In this sense, the seeds of 9/11 were sown a quarter of a century ago when Khomeini and his followers captured the government in Tehran.

Khomeini's ascent to power was aided by the policies of Jimmy Carter and his allies on the cultural left. The Carter administration's own expert on Iran, Gary Sick, provides the details in his memoirs.[4] It's a riveting story that has been largely erased from our national memory. Carter was elected president in 1976 by stressing his support for human rights. From the time he took office, the left contrasted Carter's rights doctrine with the shah's practices. The left denounced the shah as a vicious and corrupt dictator, highlighting and in some cases magnifying his misdeeds. Left-leaning officials such as Secretary of State Cyrus Vance, U.N. ambassador Andrew Young, and State Department human rights officer Patricia Derian pressed Carter to sever America's long-standing alliance with the shah. Eventually Carter came to agree with his liberal advisers that he could not in good conscience support the shah.

When the shah moved to arrest mullahs who called for his overthrow, leftists in America and Europe denounced these actions. Former diplomat George Ball called on the U.S. government to curtail the shah's exercise of power. Acceding to this pressure, Carter called for the release of political prisoners and warned the shah not to use force against the demonstrators in the streets. When the shah petitioned the Carter administration to purchase tear gas and riot control gear, the human rights office in the State Department held up the request. Some, like State Department official Henry Precht, urged the United States to prepare the way for the shah to make a "graceful exit" from power. William Miller, chief of staff on the Senate Intelligence Committee, said America had nothing to fear from Khomeini since he would be a progressive force for human rights. The U.S. ambassador to Iran, William Sullivan, even compared Khomeini to Mahatma Gandhi, and Andrew Young termed the ayatollah a "twentieth century saint."

As the resistance gained momentum and the shah's position weakened, he looked to the United States government to save him. Sick reports that the shah discovered he had many enemies, and few friends, in the Carter administration. Increasingly paranoid, the shah pleaded with the United States to help him stay in power. The Carter administration refused. Deprived of his last hope, with the Persian rug pulled out from under him, the shah decided to abdicate. The Carter administration encouraged him to do so, and the cultural left celebrated his departure. The result, of course, was Khomeini.

The Carter administration's role in assisting with the downfall of the shah is one of America's great foreign policy disasters of the twentieth century. In trying to get rid of the bad guy, Carter got the worse guy. His failure, as former Democratic senator Daniel Patrick Moynihan once said, was the result of being "unable to distinguish between America's friends and enemies." According to Moynihan, the Carter administration had essentially adopted "the enemy's view of the world."[5] Carter does not deserve sole discredit for these actions. The intellectual framework that shaped Carter's misguided strategy was supplied by the left.

Of course, the primary force behind the shah's fall was the fundamentalist movement led by Khomeini. But it is possible that the shah, with American support, could have defeated this resistance. Another option would have been for America to use its influence to press for democratic elections, an option unattractive both to the shah and to the Islamic militants. Even after the shah's departure, an

American force could have routed the Khomeini regime, an action that would have been fully justified given Iran's seizure of the U.S. embassy and the taking of American hostages. Determined at all costs to prevent these outcomes, the left sought not only to demonize the shah but also to favorably portray Khomeini and his radical cohorts. In Sick's words, Khomeini became "the instant darling of the Western media." The tone of American press coverage can be gleaned from *Time*'s cover story on February 12, 1979: "Now that the country's cry for the Ayatollah's return has been answered, Iranians will surely insist that the revolution live up to its democratic aims. Khomeini believes that Iran should become a parliamentary democracy. Those who know the Ayatollah expect that eventually he will settle in the holy city of Qom and resume a life of teaching and prayer."[6]

Immediately following Khomeini's seizure of power, leftist political scientist Richard Falk wrote in the *New York Times:* "To suppose that Ayatollah Khomeini is dissembling seems almost beyond belief. He has been depicted in a manner calculated to frighten. The depiction of him as fanatical, reactionary, and the bearer of crude prejudices seems certainly and happily false. His close advisers are uniformly composed of moderate, progressive individuals . . . who share a notable record of concern with human rights. What is distinctive about his vision is the concern with resisting oppression and promoting social justice. Many non-religious Iranians talk of this period as Islam's finest hour. Iran may yet provide us with a desperately needed model of humane governance for a third world country."[7]

The naïvety of Falk's essay is of such a magnitude as to be almost unbelievable. Falk should have known better, and I believe he did know better. Sick notes that in terms of the kind of regime he wanted to institute in Iran, "Khomeini was remarkably candid in describing his objectives."[8] As an expert on international relations, Falk was surely familiar with what Khomeini had been consistently saying for three decades. Along with Ramsey Clark, former attorney general in the Johnson administration, Falk met with Khomeini on his last day in Paris, before his triumphal return to Iran. Shortly after that meeting Clark held a press conference to champion Khomeini's cause. Falk, too, seems to have acted as a kind of unpaid public relations agent for the ayatollah's regime.

Upon consolidating his power, Khomeini launched a bloody campaign of wiping out his political opposition and reversing the liberties extended by the shah to student groups, women's groups, and religious minorities. In one year the Khomeini revolution killed more people than the shah had executed during his entire quarter century reign. Despite the fact that many progressive figures were imprisoned, tortured, and executed, Khomeini's actions produced a great yawn of indifference from America's cultural left. The same people who were shocked and outraged by the crimes of the shah showed no comparable outrage at the greater crimes of Khomeini. They knew, as well as everyone else, that liberty would be largely extinguished in Iran, and they greeted this prospect with equanimity.

Even when radical students overran the U.S. embassy on November 4, 1979, and took more than sixty American hostages, the left's sympathy was with the hostage takers. During this period three liberal clergymen—William Sloane Coffin of New York's Riverside Church, National Council of Churches executive director William Howard, and Catholic bishop Thomas Gumbleton—visited the hostages. They looked on with approval as the Iranian militants forced the hostages to record anti-American statements for use as propaganda. The American religious leaders did not seem embarrassed at being used by the hostage takers. Many of the allegations against the United States launched by the Iranian radicals corresponded exactly with the views of these liberal clergymen. Going beyond the expectations of the hostage takers, Coffin even faulted his fellow Americans for "self pity" and urged them to hold hands with their captors and sing.[9] In the hostage crisis, these men quite consciously contributed to America's humiliation.

By aiding the shah's ouster and with Khomeini's consolidation of power, the left collaborated in giving radical Islam its greatest victory in the modern era. Thanks in part to Jimmy Carter and the left, Muslim radicals got what they had been seeking for a long time—control of a major Islamic state.

HAVING SEEN HOW the Islamic radicals captured their first major country, let us now see why they decided to strike America on September 11, 2001. This is an important question because, for at least two decades prior to 9/11, radical Muslims were focused on fighting in their own countries. Khomeini had called for "Islam without borders" but what he meant by this was a single Islamic nation encompassing the entire Middle East. Khomeini's problem was twofold. First, Iranians are Persian and not Arab. Second, Iranian Muslims are Shia while the vast majority of Muslims are Sunni. Islamic radicals have fought hard since 1980 to replicate Khomeini's success by taking over an Arab country within the heartland of the Middle East. They have sought to demonstrate that Iran was not an isolated case, that further victories would follow, and that eventually the entire Muslim world would fall into the grasp of Islamic fundamentalism.

The strategy of radical Muslims during the 1980s and early 1990s was articulated by Abd al-Salaam al-Faraj, an engineering graduate of Cairo University who was implicated in the assassination of Egyptian president Anwar Sadat. Faraj's tract, *The Neglected Duty*, argued that Muslims were prevented from establishing an Islamic state by their corrupt and apostate rulers. Faraj made the case for Muslims to fight against their rulers, what he called "the near enemy," over distant countries like Israel or the United States, whom Faraj called "the far enemy." He reasoned that it was a waste of time to take on remote adversaries when the people betraying Islam and thwarting radical Muslims were the ones ruling the Muslim countries.

Faraj's strategy was adopted by virtually all the organizations of radical Islam, including Ayman al-Zawahiri's Islamic Jihad organization in Egypt, the Jamaat-i-Islami in Pakistan, and the Muslim Brotherhood. Zawahiri famously said, "The road to Jerusalem runs through Cairo."[10] What he meant by this is that radical Muslims must first take power in a Muslim country like Egypt, and then they would have a strong base to launch a war against Israel. Osama bin Laden also endorsed this strategy. His main emphasis during the 1980s was on driving the Soviets out of Afghanistan, so that it could become a Muslim fundamentalist state. When that was successful, bin Laden returned to Saudi Arabia and focused his efforts on changing the corrupt and insufficiently orthodox policies of the Saudi government.

In the two decades before 9/11, Islamic radicals launched a series of attacks aimed at weakening or overthrowing their regional leaders. In Syria, the Muslim Brotherhood sought to overthrow the dictatorship of Hafez Assad. In Saudi Arabia, a group of radical Muslims seized the Grand Mosque in Mecca. In 1981, a disciple of Faraj named Khalid Islambouli assassinated Sadat. In subsequent years, Islamic radicals killed other senior Egyptian officials, although their attempt on President Hosni Mubarak's life was unsuccessful. In 1995, a radical group firebombed the Egyptian embassy in Pakistan. Two years later, Islamic radicals detonated explosives at an archaeological site near the city of Luxor in Egypt. The blast killed between fifty and a hundred civilians, Egyptians as well as tourists. The radicals spilled a lot of blood during this period, but it was mostly Muslim blood.

Then, in the mid-to-late 1990s, a segment of the radical movement decided on a new strategy. In a fateful shift, Zawahiri abandoned the tactic of fighting the "near enemy" and decided to take the battle to the "far enemy," specifically the United States. According to Montasser al-Zayyat, a former associate, Zawahiri's decision astounded Muslim radicals and "surprised the whole world."[11] Groups like the Muslim Brotherhood disagreed so strongly with Zawahiri that its leaders publicly criticized him and severed ties with Islamic Jihad. But there were other radical Egyptians, such as Sheikh Omar Abd al-Rahman, who agreed with Zawahiri. In Afghanistan Zawahiri met Osama bin Laden, who was also shifting his sights from the near enemy to the far enemy. Soon Zawahiri's Islamic Jihad merged with bin Laden's group and a new organization, Al Qaeda, was born.

If Zawahiri and bin Laden had not changed course, 9/11 would not have happened. Why, then, did they do so? In his book *The Far Enemy*, Fawaz Gerges argues that the radical Muslims' strategy of fighting the near enemy proved unsuccessful, and so they decided to try something else. Gerges points out that by killing Muslim civilians the radical Muslims provoked a massive wellspring of protest from the community. (We saw this with the bombing in Amman, Jordan, on November 9, 2005.) This public reaction then provided a justification for the regimes to mount crackdowns on the radicals. In Saudi Arabia, the regime ousted and then beheaded the radical Muslims who took over the Grand Mosque. Egypt launched a systematic campaign to imprison or kill radical dissidents. Using its customary brutality, the Assad regime in Syria massacred thousands of Muslim Brotherhood members and sympathizers. "When jihadis met their Waterloo on home-front battles," Gerges writes, they "turned their guns against the West in an effort to stop the revolutionary ship from sinking."[12] This may be correct as far as it goes, but it does not go very far. Gerges fails to explain why Muslim radicals like Zawahiri and bin Laden, who apparently could not defeat their local governments, came to the conclusion that they could defeat the vastly more formidable United States.

Zawahiri and bin Laden themselves supply the answers to this question. In his book *Knights Under the Prophet's Banner*, Zawahiri writes, "The battle today cannot be fought on a regional level without taking into account the global hostility toward us." Infidel tyrants like Mubarak are simply "hired policemen who are faithfully serving the occupiers and enemies of the Muslim nation." Moreover, "It is clear that the Jewish-Crusader alliance, led by the United States, will not allow any Islamic force to reach power in any of the Muslim countries." In short, Zawahiri came to the conclusion that the near enemy could not be defeated because of the far enemy. "Therefore," he wrote, "we must move the battle to the enemy's grounds to burn the hands of those who ignite fire in our countries."[13] To rephrase his earlier slogan, Zawahiri now became convinced that the road to Cairo and Jerusalem ran through New York.

Even so, what would give radical Muslims the idea that they

could attack the United States without being decimated? From bin Laden we learn that the radical Muslims plotted the 9/11 attack after concluding that the far enemy was weaker than the near enemy. Despite the great wealth and power of the United States, bin Laden and his associates became convinced they could launch a devastating strike on American shores and win the ensuing battle. Bin Laden had witnessed a united force of Muslim fighters, the so-called Arab Afghans, drive the Soviet Union out of Afghanistan. The Arab Afghans, bin Laden notes, "managed to crush the greatest empire known to mankind. The so-called superpower vanished into thin air." Following the Soviet collapse, bin Laden began to devise a plan to inflict on America a fate "just like that of the Soviets—military defeat, political breakup, ideological downfall, and economic bankruptcy." Even though the demise of the Soviet Union left the United States as the world's only superpower, bin Laden decided that "America is very much weaker than Russia." Bin Laden based his opinion on America's military conduct in previous years. He saw that when America found itself in a drawn-out guerrilla war in Vietnam, it accepted defeat and withdrew. Americans, bin Laden concluded, love life so much that they are not willing to risk it. In short, they are cowards. When only eighteen American troops were killed in Somalia in 1993, bin Laden said, "America fled in the dark as fast as it could."[14]

It is important to recognize that bin Laden developed this theory of American weakness during the Clinton years. It was Clinton, after all, who ordered the withdrawal of American troops from Mogadishu. Islamic radicals had a very different view of the United States during the Reagan years. Although Reagan had ordered the pullout of American troops following the 1982 embassy bombing in Beirut, Muslim radicals recognized that Reagan was a strong leader. They witnessed this strength in Reagan's dealings with the Soviet Union, and a few of them experienced it when Reagan ordered a missile attack against Libyan strongman Muammar Qadafi. Qadafi had been implicated in a terrorist attack on American soldiers at a Berlin disco. America's retaliatory strike killed several of Qadafi's close associates as well as one of his sons. So persuasive was Reagan's military response that it seems to have convinced Qadafi to retire from the terrorism trade.

In Clinton, however, the Islamic radicals seem to have recognized that they were dealing with a different kind of leader. During Clinton's tenure bin Laden tested his theory of American weakness. He did this by launching a series of attacks on American targets and awaiting the response. These were massive attacks, unprecedented in the damage they inflicted. Yet in every case America reacted either by doing nothing or with desultory counterattacks that did not harm the perpetrators and actually made America look ridiculous in the eyes of the Muslim world. Consequently, bin Laden and Zawahiri concluded that the size and wealth of the American Sodom was no match for the will of the Muslim true believer. They resolved to strike the far enemy in its vital organs, the strike that occurred on 9/11.

Once again, it was the left that urged Clinton to adopt the course that he did. For years, the left's leading intellectuals had been warning that America's approach to the Muslim world was driven by hateful and deep-rooted prejudices about Muslims. While such prejudices seemed to be confirmed by the actions of the radical Muslims who tried to blow up the World Trade Center in 1993, liberal scholars like Edward Said and John Esposito ridiculed the stereotype of the fanatical Muslim terrorist. Shortly before 9/11, Esposito published a book titled *The Islamic Threat: Myth or Reality?* The general conclusion was that the threat was mostly a myth. Said warned that as a result of American ignorance, "The Islamic threat is made to seem disproportionately fearsome." He poured derision on the idea that "there is a worldwide conspiracy behind every explosion," a fantasy he attributed to "the menace theory of Islam."[15]

The response of Clinton and his advisers to Al Qaeda attacks on American targets was shaped by this left-wing analysis. Recall that many of Clinton's leading advisers—Warren Christopher, Anthony Lake, Richard Holbrooke, Sandy Berger—were retreads from the Carter administration. Their "experience" was largely in screwing up, and now they were going to be presented with another opportunity. In 1993, a group of radical Muslims tried to blow up the

World Trade Center. This was the first terrorist attack on American soil. Clinton at the time was preoccupied with his plan to integrate homosexuals into the military. His involvement with the CIA was primarily focused on increasing race and gender diversity in the top ranks of the organization. Consistent with an approach that treated foreign policy as an extension of domestic policy, Clinton treated the World Trade Center attack as an internal political problem. He portrayed the assault not as a hostile action against the United States, but as a kind of humanitarian disaster. Clinton commiserated with the victims—he felt their pain—but he did not say who was responsible for the attack, and he carefully avoided blaming the forces of radical Islam. In fact, he warned against "overreaction." His advisers persuaded him not to bolster anti-Muslim stereotypes.

In 1996 bin Laden declared war against America. The Clinton administration ignored this threat. That same year radical Muslims detonated a massive bomb at the Khobar Towers military installation in Saudi Arabia, killing nineteen U.S. soldiers. Clinton denounced the attack, but took no action to retaliate. On August 7, 1998, Al Qaeda escalated its operations once again, this time launching bomb attacks against the U.S. embassies in Kenya and Tanzania, causing more than two hundred deaths and wounding over four thousand. By this time Clinton was embroiled in the Lewinsky scandal. Interrupting his efforts to avoid impeachment proceedings, Clinton ordered a halfhearted counterstrike against what turned out to be a pharmaceutical plant in the Sudan, and against Al Qaeda facilities in Afghanistan that were largely unoccupied. As they witnessed the sorry spectacle of American timidity and incompetence, radical Muslims subjected the United States and its leaders to open derision. One Islamic activist told an Arab television station that he was sending a chastity belt to the White House because if President Clinton could get his sexual appetites under control, "perhaps his aim will improve when he decides to strike the next time."

But there would not be a next time, even though the attacks on America continued. On October 12, 2000, Al Qaeda orchestrated a suicide attack on the U.S.S. *Cole*, blasting a forty-foot hole in the ship's hull and killing seventeen sailors. Not since World War II had there been such a lethal assault on an American warship. Striking a heroic pose, Clinton said the attack would not deter America from its efforts to solve the Israeli-Palestinian conflict. The absurdity of Clinton's response can be seen when we recognize that the attack had nothing to do with the Israeli-Palestinian conflict.

In the last months of his administration, there were several occasions when Clinton was notified of intelligence reports locating bin Laden. Some Clinton officials argued that the United States should seek to arrest bin Laden but should not try to kill him. Clinton authorized a lethal attack if the opportunity presented itself, but in every case he and his advisers decided not to act. The Clinton team refused to provide arms to Ahmed Shah Massoud and his Northern Alliance to enable them to successfully attack bin Laden and his Taliban sponsors. Sandy Berger stressed the intelligence regarding bin Laden's whereabouts was never 100 percent reliable, and emphasized the high risk of civilian casualties. Janet Reno warned she would not support any attack that was inconsistent with international law. Madeleine Albright said an attack on Muslims might derail the Israeli-Palestinian peace process. The Clinton team was ever mindful of the risk of political embarrassment if the operation failed.

Clinton insists that he made every effort to get bin Laden. In a speech in October 2001 Clinton insisted, "I tried to take Bin Laden out the last four years I was in office." In his September 24, 2006, interview with Chris Wallace, Clinton angrily insisted, "I worked hard to try to kill him" and "came closer than anybody has since." Clinton cited his terrorism adviser Richard Clarke in support of his efforts. Yet Clarke himself wrote in his book that in the years leading up to 9/11, "I still do not understand why it was impossible to find a competent group . . . who could locate Bin Laden and kill him." Former CIA analyst Michael Scheuer estimates that the U.S. government missed "about ten chances to capture Bin Laden or kill him." This point becomes very clear once we recall that from 1996, when bin Laden moved from the Sudan to Afghanistan, until 2000, the year preceding the 9/11 attack, bin Laden was not in deep hiding. Author Steve Coll reports that he lived in a house provided by Mullah Omar near Kandahar. He moved freely through the territories of eastern Afghanistan that were under Taliban control. He talked openly on his satellite phone, calling media representatives in the Middle East and London to dictate statements and issue fatwas. His wives and children were routinely spotted in the local market. "On some Fridays," Coll writes, "he delivered sermons at Kandahar's largest mosque."[16] During this period he was interviewed by a number of journalists from around the world. The leftist writer Robert Fisk interviewed bin Laden in Afghanistan in 1996, as did a British journalist affiliated with the BBC. In late 1996 bin Laden met with the Pakistani reporter Abdel Bari Atwan in Kandahar. Fisk secured another interview with bin Laden in early 1997. In March 1997, bin Laden spoke in person to Peter Arnett of CNN. In early 1998 bin Laden met with John Miller of ABC News. In May 1998 bin Laden held a press conference near Khost in southeastern Afghanistan. Several Pakistani journalists and a Chinese reporter were present. In January 1999 bin Laden granted a personal interview to a journalist affiliated with *Time* magazine. Isn't it strange that all these people could find bin Laden but not the Clinton administration?

The obvious reason for Clinton's failure is that his administration simply did not make the bin Laden mission a top priority. After all, there were other objectives to focus on. Madeleine Albright and Hillary Clinton were promoting a petition drive organized by the Feminist Majority Foundation to pressure the Taliban to liberalize its position on women's rights. For others in the administration, the prize target wasn't bin Laden, it was special prosecutor Kenneth Starr. Starr was the political foe the Clinton team really wanted to "get," and they largely succeeded in discrediting him. Bin Laden was left to concoct other schemes. The conclusion seems unavoidable. The radical Muslims made the decision to attack America on 9/11 because they decided that America was weak. They came to this conclusion as a result of the actions—and inaction—of the Clinton administration and its allies on the left.

SINCE SEPTEMBER 11, 2001, there has been a strange and almost fanciful debate about measures taken by the Bush administration to prevent another such attack. The 9/11 attacks confirmed America's extreme vulnerability. From the moment they occurred, it has been evident that such an attack could happen again, with even worse consequences. America is a big, open, and porous society. Every year some 60 million people enter the country on flights, and more than 100 million people come by land or sea. America offers a virtually limitless supply of potential targets: population centers, sports arenas, theme parks, power plants, water supply systems, electricity grids, tunnels, bridges, and computer networks. Virtually any group of determined people possessing weapons and skills, and willing to give their lives, could wreak havoc. One might expect all Americans to rally behind a concentrated effort to protect the homeland by locating the bad guys, arresting them, holding them, and extracting information from them. One might expect this, but one would be wrong.

From the outset, the left has led a campaign to oppose the administration's most important measures to avoid another terrorist attack. The left's campaign has been spearheaded by radical groups like the National Lawyers Guild and the Center for Constitutional Rights. Listening to the left, one almost gets the impression that September 11 never happened. Indeed many on the left portray the United States government, not Al Qaeda, as the gravest threat to American citizens. In this view, bin Laden might detonate an occasional explosion, but Bush is plotting to deprive all Americans of their basic liberties. Author Gore Vidal even suggests that the Bush administration has largely concocted its terror warnings as part of a scheme to establish martial control over America. The same note is struck by Joe Conason, who claims that America is now operating under "a nascent military regime." Writing in *Harper's*, Lewis Lapham detects nothing less than "the hallmarks of fascist sentiment in the character of the American government."[17]

So powerful is the left's solicitude for civil liberties that Democratic Party chairman Howard Dean even suggested that the United States should not presume bin Laden's guilt until he had been given the opportunity to have a fair trial. Radical lawyer Ramsey Clark agreed to defend Saddam Hussein in court on the grounds that the

U.S. government had "demonized" him before giving him an impartial hearing. Activist lawyer Lynne Stewart, a veteran of militant causes in America, chose to represent the blind sheikh Omar Abd al-Rahman. Although Stewart portrayed Rahman as a noble soul exercising his free speech rights and the U.S. government as a malevolent institution motivated by anti-Muslim prejudice, Rahman was found guilty of plotting several terrorist bombings in America. Stewart herself was arrested and convicted of conspiracy when she was caught transmitting clandestine messages from the blind sheikh to his radical acolytes. Apparently moved by her plight, philanthropist George Soros contributed $20,000 to Stewart's defense.[18]

The Stewart case illustrates the symbiotic relationship between liberals and the far left. Leftists like Stewart stake out the extreme position and their allies like Soros provide political cover. This is not to say that liberal concerns about civil liberties are insincere. They are not, and in some cases they may be valid. Many libertarians and some conservatives have raised similar concerns. The critics stress that Bush should go after the bad guys only in a way that protects their constitutional rights. If not, the rights of all Americans are jeopardized. We have here an echo of the ACLU's credo that rights are best protected at their extreme. If the Bush administration is forced to release a man accused of building a "dirty bomb" on the grounds that he was denied access to a lawyer, then the rest of us are more secure in our liberties. Whether this is true or not, it is based on the assumption that the freed suspect would not proceed to build and then detonate such a bomb. In that case many thousands of Americans would be manifestly less secure in life and liberty.

The issue here is an old one, and it was raised during the Civil War when President Lincoln suspended habeas corpus and took other measures that his critics said violated constitutional rights. Lincoln—like Bush today—denied that he violated those rights. But Lincoln went on to argue that even if he had violated the rights, he would be justified in doing so. Lincoln's argument was that the integrity of the government was fundamental to upholding the Constitution and protecting all rights. Lincoln contended that it makes no sense to endanger the ship of state in the name of protecting this right or that right, because if the ship sinks then no rights can be protected. The point applies to 9/11 in this way. If there are further terrorist attacks, the sense of public danger would be so great that many of the liberties we take for granted today would be curtailed. America would become like Israel, a state under martial supervision. To avoid this, it is better to relinquish conveniences and even some liberties in order to permit reasonable measures to protect both security and liberty.

Let us examine some of the left's criticisms of the Bush administration to see if the government has been acting reasonably. One of the earliest concerns raised by the left concerned racial profiling. From this point of view, the government should not pursue terrorism by singling out any particular group. Recently Al Gore went to Saudi Arabia to apologize for the U.S. government's "terrible abuses" inflicted against Muslims who were "indiscriminately rounded up" after 9/11. Human Rights Watch and the ACLU jointly issued a report warning that "Muslim men were arrested for little more than attending the same mosque as a September 11 hijacker or owning a box cutter."[19] It is hard to disagree with the report's conclusion that the experience for innocent Muslim detainees was Kafkaesque. But then the country had just been through a Kafkaesque experience. Neither Gore nor the human rights report acknowledged that the detainees were released as soon as it became clear that they had nothing to do with the 9/11 attacks.

The irony of the racial profiling debate was that the 9/11 terrorists seemed right out of central casting—they fit every stereotype of the fanatical Muslim terrorist, right down to their nose hairs. Given the fact that the terrorists were Muslims who claimed to be acting in the name of Islam, it would seem rational for the government to focus its surveillance on mosques rather than, say, yoga conventions, blues bars, or Knights of Columbus meetings. It is true that not all Muslims are Islamic terrorists, but it is equally true that all Islamic terrorists are Muslims. To forgo racial profiling is to expose the entire population to the scrutiny that would otherwise be focused on high-risk groups. Even Gore found himself being searched, as if the country needed to be secured against the threat of one of its leading presidential candidates carrying out terrorist attacks on his own country! As a consequence of liberal pressure, terrorism screening has become an equal-opportunity business.

Strangely, though, the government's effort at comprehensive scrutiny has encountered the same left-wing resistance as racial profiling. The provisions of the Patriot Act are not limited to any particular group but cover all Americans. The act includes a provision that permits government surveillance of terrorist suspects' bank records, hotel bills, phone records, computer databases, and library borrowings. The inclusion of libraries infuriates Senator Russell Feingold, who thinks it is outrageous that the government can intrude on privacy in this way. Feingold raises the prospect of Americans "afraid to read books, terrified into silence." But imagine a group of FBI agents who are tracking an Al Qaeda cell member who is plotting an attack. He goes to a public library and checks out a book on electronic circuitry. Shouldn't law enforcement be able to examine what he is reading? Liberal fears about innocent Americans having their literary pursuits placed under government scrutiny would be justified if there were cases in which the Patriot Act had been abused in this way. But there has been no such case.

Soros warns that the Bush administration's entire security apparatus—the Patriot Act, the Department of Homeland Security—is frightening Americans and silencing their criticism of the government's policies. "When I heard President Bush say either you are with us or you are with the terrorists, I hear alarm bells. This is not the America I chose as my home . . . where disagreement is not tolerated."[20] But when President Bush made that statement in the immediate aftermath of 9/11 he was insisting that other countries needed to make a decision either to stand with America or to stand with the terrorists. The context of Bush's remarks makes it clear that he was not speaking about American citizens. Soros's claim that the Bush administration won't tolerate disagreement is bizarre in view of the fact that he has been an outspoken critic—to the point of investing millions of dollars in a publicly announced campaign to defeat Bush—and he has suffered no government sanction or retaliation of any kind.

Groups on the left have expressed outrage over the fact that the U.S. government holds foreign insurgents captive at Guantánamo Bay and other facilities without charging them or granting them access to lawyers. Legal scholar Laurence Tribe fulminates that thousands of captives are denied constitutional protections "simply because they are not U.S. citizens." Columnist Bob Herbert argues that "the fundamental right in the case of the Guantánamo detainees is the right not to be deprived of liberty without due process of law."[21] It has long been understood, however, that the rights in the U.S. Constitution only apply to U.S. citizens. In a moral sense, all human beings have natural rights, but there is an important distinction between natural rights and civil rights. The constitution is a social compact between citizens. Through mutual consent, citizens give to their government the power to protect certain rights. These rights do not extend to those who stand outside the social contract. Americans have no obligation to extend them to aliens, and they are most certainly inapplicable to those who are apprehended in foreign jihads against America.

The ACLU and other groups have demanded that U.S. courts supervise the detention of foreign combatants both at home and abroad. In one of its reports Human Rights Watch faulted the U.S. government for holding Khalid Sheikh Mohammed, the chief architect of 9/11, in an undisclosed foreign location.[22] The left's contention that such men are entitled to court supervision to ensure protection of their civil rights is quite remarkable. Courts have never previously interfered in this way in the treatment of foreign captives. Left-wing groups routinely file lawsuits to force the government either to charge its foreign prisoners or to free them. Although the Bush administration's determination to hold such captives without trial is presented as outrageous, it is hardly bizarre for countries at war to detain the enemy. It is not customary for nations to provide enemy captives with lawyers, except when they are tried for war crimes. It is normal practice to keep enemy fighters in detention until the war is over or the government determines that they are no longer a threat.

Obviously the government has to be much more careful when it is dealing with American citizens who are suspected of collaborating with Al Qaeda or conspiring to commit terrorism. American citizens do have constitutional rights and they should not be violated. It is no violation of constitutional rights, however, for the government to hold without trial a citizen who has enlisted in a foreign military struggle against the United States. While affirming that even accused terrorists who are American citizens must be granted due process, the Supreme Court has said, both in the *Hamdi* and *Padilla* cases, that those rights can be met by military tribunals.

In December 2005, the *New York Times* disclosed that the Bush administration had been secretly listening to the phone conversations of Americans who were calling abroad to speak to figures connected with Al Qaeda. Bush's authorization of this surveillance brought a storm of criticism from the left and even from some civil libertarians on the right. John Dean of Watergate fame was on hand to make the obvious Nixon comparison. Congressmen John Conyers and John Lewis said they would support a bill of impeachment against President Bush. Critics said that Bush had violated a law requiring the federal government to get a court warrant before subjecting American citizens to surveillance. These allegations have emboldened lawyers in some of the nation's biggest terrorism cases to file claims to get their clients released. The *Times* reports that defense lawyers for Lyman Faris, who admitted plotting to blow up the Brooklyn Bridge, and Mohammed Junaid Babar, convicted of involvement in a plot to set off fertilizer bombs, are seeking to establish that their clients' phone conversations were illegally taped and therefore their convictions are invalid.[23] If the left is worried that dangerous men may be set free to devise further schemes to harm Americans, it never publicly expresses such concerns.

Is there any merit to the charge of illegal wiretapping? Actually, there is, but the issue is not clear-cut. The Foreign Intelligence Surveillance Act was passed in 1978 when an enemy like Al Qaeda was not even contemplated. Moreover, Congress had authorized Bush to use all necessary force to respond to the 9/11 attacks, and the Bush administration argued that this authority extends to its measures to trace Al Qaeda's American connections. I am skeptical of the Bush administration's logic here. I think it would have been better for Bush to have sought a change in the old law, or to have secured specific congressional authority to act. But the administration did notify leading members of Congress, both Republican and Democrat, of its surveillance practices, so the legislative branch was at least aware of the executive's actions. While this legal debate is important, it camouflages the simple reality that the U.S. government should be listening to conversations involving terrorist suspects, just as it should be monitoring their financial transactions. Two of the 9/11 hijackers made overseas calls to Al Qaeda operatives; if those conversations had been intercepted, 9/11 may have been prevented. When situations like this arise, it may not always be possible to secure court approval for surveillance in advance. If the law says otherwise, the solution is not to impeach the president but to change the law.

Another statute frequently invoked on the left is the Geneva Convention. Critics have bitterly protested the Bush administration's view that the Geneva Convention does not apply to Al Qaeda captives. Yet the terms of the convention apply only to signatories or parties observing the rules. The Al Qaeda fighters do not represent a state. They are not soldiers in the conventional sense that they wear uniforms and operate in accordance with the laws of war. They ignore the distinction between military and civilian targets. They extend to their captives no protections whatsoever. Consequently they have placed themselves outside the orbit of the Geneva Convention rules.

The most serious charge leveled against the Bush administration in this context is the charge of torturing foreign prisoners to obtain information. Reports of torture have brought forth a torrent of liberal indignation. Columnists like Anthony Lewis and Jonathan Schell are apoplectic on the subject. The *New York Times* gravely warns that torture clearly "doesn't work" because "centuries of experience show that people will tell their tormentors what they want to hear."[24] This may be generally true, but (with due respect to the *Times*'s extensive experience on this subject) is it always true? The Israeli government seems to have used torture quite effectively to locate Palestinian hideouts where hostages have been held. Is it not at least possible that torturing Khalid Sheikh Mohammed could provide useful information about future attacks? It seems dangerously smug to make lofty pronouncements about torture when many lives could be at stake.

Undoubtedly torture can be misused, but then the criticism should focus on those misuses. Moreover, there are some forms of torture that no decent community can sanction, no matter what its effectiveness. But this is an issue not of whether torture should be allowed but of what kind of torture should be allowed. Perusing through reports from Human Rights Watch, I list what the group considers to be America's most egregious forms of torture: sleep deprivation, force-feeding of detainees who refuse to eat, incessant hard rock and rap music, long periods of darkness and isolation, "stress positions" such as being forced to stand with arms outstretched, exposure to very warm and very cold temperatures, and (most controversially) immersion into water to create a sensation of drowning. While I support the idea of congressional oversight of these measures, I don't find myself shuddering over them. Most are scarcely rougher than what millions of American soldiers suffer in boot camp. Given the forms of coercion that have been used historically, and that are still used throughout the world, the interrogation techniques used by America's military agencies seem warranted under the circumstances.

It is possible to have a reasonable debate over what powers the government should possess to effectively fight the war and at the same time minimize the threat to civil liberties. What is striking about the left's position is how obstructionist it is. Kenneth Roth of Human Rights Watch argues that the U.S. government should "formally abandon all forms of coercive interrogation."[25] This is another way of saying that it should content itself with information that captured terrorists and insurgents choose to share. Clearly if the Bush administration were to adopt the left's agenda, it would find itself incapacitated in fighting the war. This does not seem to be a prospect that frightens or deters the left. At every stage the left seems to support the policy that most endangers American security. Considering that America is at war, the restrictions on liberty to date have been minimal. Apply the left's arguments to World War II and their ridiculousness becomes apparent. "Nazi Captives Being Held in Detention Centers Without Trial." "German Prisoners Refused Fifth Amendment Protections." "Government Found Taping Phone Conversations Between U.S. Citizens and Hitler Staff." I am quite sure there were no such front-page headlines in the *New York Times*.

Why then does the left hamper America's homeland security in this way? In the following chapter, I will offer a theory to explain the strange behavior of the left. Here I simply note that what liberals consider fine points of principle, the enemy interprets as weakness. The 9/11 attacks were the direct result of bin Laden viewing the United States as a feeble giant, all tied up in knots and waiting to be struck. Whatever its motivations, the left through its actions is increasing America's vulnerability. Having emboldened the enemy to attack us once, the actions of the left are now emboldening the enemy to attack us once again.

NINE

The War Against the War

Decoding bin Laden's Message to America

In 2004, a leading critic of the Bush administration published a stinging critique of the U.S. government's war on terror. He
found Bush's conduct objectionable from the very time the president
was informed about the 9/11 attacks. He charged that notwithstanding the gravity of the occasion, Bush continued reading to children
"a little girl's story about a goat and its butting." The critic proceeded
to fault Bush's motives for the war on terror. Bush made the decision to invade Iraq, he said, because of "oil and more business for his
private companies." Bush knew that Iraq posed no security threat
but "the black gold blinded him and he put his own private interests
ahead of the American public interest." As a consequence, the critic
charged, "Bush's hands are covered with blood" and Iraq has become a "quagmire." Yet the president refuses to change course because, after all, "the Bush administration has profited" from the
destruction of Iraq, as shown by "the enormity of the contracts won
by large corporations like Halliburton." While Bush pretends to promote liberty abroad, "he has brought tyranny and the suppression of

liberties to his own country" through "the Patriot Act, implemented under the pretext of fighting terrorism."

Michael Moore? Al Franken? Nancy Pelosi? Actually, the speaker is Osama bin Laden, in an address to the American people on the eve of the 2004 election. Not only do bin Laden's more recent statements seem plagiarized from Moore's Web site and Pelosi's speeches, but in addition bin Laden seems to have adopted the practice of explicitly citing and commending the works of the left. In his 2004 missive, bin Laden said his message could be better understood if Americans read the works of Robert Fisk, "who is a fellow Westerner . . . but one whom I consider unbiased." Bin Laden called on people to pay more attention to Fisk "so that he could explain to the American people everything he has learned from us."[1] In his January 2006 videotape bin Laden informed Americans that "if Bush carries on with his lies and oppression, then it would be useful to read the book *Rogue State.*" Bin Laden went on to cite a passage by the author, William Blum, who calls on America to withdraw from the Middle East and "give an apology to all of the widows and orphans and those who were tortured" by American troops. Bin Laden proposed such steps as part of a "truce" between Al Qaeda and the United States.

Who are these people singled out for praise by bin Laden? A British leftist who covers the Middle East for London's *Independent* newspaper, Fisk is the author of several books that blame America for inflicting conquest and unending war on the Middle East. Fisk's books receive enthusiastic reviews in America's left-leaning magazines like *The Nation.* Blum is a former Vietnam War protester who posts his articles on leftist Web sites and writes for magazines like the *Progressive.* Noam Chomsky has praised his work, and in 2002 Blum joined Jane Fonda, Barbara Ehrenreich, and a host of other prominent liberals in denouncing Bush's preparation for the invasion of Iraq. Blum describes his life's mission as "slowing down the American empire—injuring the beast."[2] One can see how bin Laden might see his own mission in those same terms.

Blum's reaction to bin Laden's endorsement? "I'm not repulsed and I'm not going to pretend that I am," he told the *Washington Post.*

Blum compared bin Laden's blurb to being listed on Oprah's Book Club. While Blum admitted he would not like to live in bin Laden's model society, he said he agreed with bin Laden about America's role in the Middle East. "If he shares with me a deep dislike for certain aspects of U.S. foreign policy . . . I think it's good that he shares those views."[3]

The mystery of bin Laden praising American leftists deepens when we realize that bin Laden is not accustomed to speaking this way. Bin Laden's earlier statements are delivered in a lofty Islamic rhetoric, with multiple references to the Koran and the battles of early Islam. Now, however, bin Laden seems to be speaking in a kind of American lingo, making arguments that seem very odd for him to make. How unnatural it is to hear bin Laden discuss the Florida recount or Bush's supposed misreading of U.S. opinion polls. Even more telling, a review of bin Laden's statements prior to 2004 shows that he always referred to America as a single entity. Never previously did he distinguish between good Americans and bad Americans. Bin Laden's view of the United States used to be one of undifferentiated evil. But starting in his October 2004 statement, bin Laden insinuates that not all Americans are so evil.

To see how bizarre this is, imagine if Hitler had issued regular missives during World War II in which he praised a group of Americans and cited from their writings. Imagine if he repeated their arguments and rhetoric with such precision that it would be hard to tell his words from theirs. Imagine further that one of Hitler's favorite American authors embraced the Hitler endorsement, noting that Hitler and he felt pretty much the same way about American foreign policy and praising Hitler for holding such strong anti-American sentiments. The reaction throughout the country would have been one of unmitigated outrage! The reason there was no comparable outrage in this case is because one side, the left, was able to divert attention from the content of bin Laden's political message, and the other side, the right, totally missed the significance of bin Laden's actions.

Conservatives have reacted with cocktail-party bemusement to bin Laden's professions of ideological intimacy with the left. There have been lots of quips about bin Laden being appointed to the board of directors of moveon.org or to a senior editorial position at *The Nation*. The typical conservative analysis concludes with a solemn attempt to dissuade liberal Democrats from giving in to bin Laden's demands. As David Gartenstein-Ross wrote in frontpage magazine.com, "Accommodation is a trap. Those who favor negotiation and appeasement err in believing that mollifying Bin Laden's immediate grievances will bring us peace. Ultimately, a strategy of accommodation and negotiation with Al Qaeda is the road to national suicide."[4] This approach completely misses the point of what bin Laden is trying to do, which is not to convince his enemy to capitulate but to convince his allies in America to coordinate their actions more closely with his.

Some on the left have shrewdly recognized this, which is why they make supreme efforts to deny any connection between bin Laden and the left-wing cause. Commenting on bin Laden's 2004 videotape, David Wallechinsky informed the readers of huffington-post.com: "My guess is that he wasn't trying to help either side. It is more likely that he was tired of being ignored. He saw the world was focused on the American election, and he released his video at that time in order to capture the most possible attention." If this notion of bin Laden as frustrated attention seeker seems implausible, even more farfetched is Robert Fisk's claim that bin Laden released his 2004 videotape to help Bush win the election. As Fisk told the left-wing radio program *Democracy Now,* "I'm sure Bin Laden realizes that further threats are more likely to help Bush than Kerry. What he wants now, of course, is a president who will further mire the country in the Middle East swamp. So I think that this is probably Bin Laden's vote for George Bush."[5] Consider the absurdity of this analysis. Bin Laden and Bush are deadly enemies. Bin Laden calls Bush an apostle of Satan, the murderer of the Muslim people. Why would bin Laden seek to secure the electoral victory of a person he views as the great slayer of Muslims? If bin Laden seeks to defeat Bush's war on terror, wouldn't the easiest way to do that be to defeat Bush's bid for reelection?

When bin Laden released his 2006 videotape, the left once again sought to steer public attention away from his political endorsement of left-wing sources. A few days after the tape's release, two former Clinton officials, Daniel Benjamin and Steven Simon, rushed to the *New York Times* to interpret what bin Laden might be signaling to the world. Many speculations later, they conclude on an inconclusive note: "It is too early to say how the tape will affect Muslim opinion."[6] But this analysis is a diversion, because bin Laden's tape was not addressed to Muslim opinion. It was manifestly addressed to the American people. If bin Laden was signaling anyone, it was not Muslims but Americans. It is very important that we understand what he was trying to say.

TO UNDERSTAND BIN Laden's American strategy, we need to re-examine with fresh eyes the reaction to 9/11 and the debate over the war on terror. Earlier in this book I spoke of a short period of national unity following 9/11, but there was one group that did not join in these sentiments. This was the left. According to the left, 9/11 was not a uniquely tragic event. "As atrocities go," Noam Chomsky remarked, "it doesn't rank very high." Historian Eric Hobsbawm adds, "It was an appalling human tragedy. But it didn't change anything in the world situation." In the left's view, the event was of little consequence and paled before the terror that America had long inflicted on Muslims and the rest of the world. Shortly after 9/11, Chomsky traveled to Islamabad to inform a Muslim audience that for centuries America had been killing colossal numbers of people, far more than the few thousand killed in bin Laden's attack. The only significance of 9/11, Chomsky added, is that "for the first time, the guns have been directed the other way. That is a dramatic change."[7]

In this sense, 9/11 represented for the left a kind of equalization or political justice. To put it bluntly, America deserved it. "Given the constant belligerence and destructiveness of U.S. foreign policy," wrote William Blum, "retaliation has to be expected." Author and future Nobel laureate Harold Pinter termed America a "rogue state" that "knows only one language—bombs and death." Political scientist Robert Jensen said that 9/11 was "no more despicable than the massive acts of terrorism that the U.S. government has committed during my lifetime." Some on the left took immense symbolic satisfaction in the destruction of the World Trade Center. Author Norman Mailer wrote that "everything wrong with America led to the point where the country built that Tower of Babel which consequently had to be destroyed."[8]

In addition to viewing 9/11 as predictable and overdue, some on the left even admitted fantasizing about it. "They did it," the French critic Jean Baudrillard wrote, "but we wished for it." Political scientist Richard Berthold said that "anyone who can blow up the Pentagon would get my vote." There were calls for an encore. Referring to American soldiers killed in Somalia in 1993, anthropologist Nicholas De Genova expressed his hope that bin Laden and his allies would inflict on America "a million Mogadishus." Political scientist Ward Churchill said that in order to compensate for the mass murder that America has inflicted throughout the globe, bin Laden would have to kill several million more Americans.[9]

From the beginning, the left derived from 9/11 the lesson that American foreign policy was to blame and therefore America was the enemy. Historian Glenda Gilmore said, "We have met the enemy, and it is us." Since America's war against terrorism is evil, Joel Stein wrote in the *Los Angeles Times*, "I don't support our troops. We shouldn't be celebrating people for doing something we don't think was a good idea." In an argument that echoed bin Laden's own justification for killing American civilians, Churchill argued that by refusing to "effectively oppose" their government's genocidal policies, U.S. citizens were guilty of "endorsing official criminality."[10]

If 9/11 wasn't very significant for the left, what was significant was President Bush's reaction to 9/11. It is this reaction, Hobsbawm writes, "that did change the world." The left argued that the Bush administration's response to terrorism itself constituted terrorism— indeed a worse terrorism than that of 9/11. Howard Zinn wrote that in the name of a war on terror, "We are terrorizing other people." Cindy Sheehan routinely calls Bush "the biggest terrorist in the world." Robert Fisk said Bush was using 9/11 to invade "a country which had nothing to do with those atrocities."[11]

Iraq? No, Fisk is talking about Afghanistan. Today, in the context of the Iraq debate, many liberal Democrats seek to enhance their political credibility by noting that they supported Bush's invasion of Afghanistan. Some liberals were indeed supportive of Bush's action there. Others—especially elected leaders—acquiesced in it because they did not want to be perceived as "soft on terrorism." But the left was opposed to Bush's war on terror from the outset, and mobilized to stop Bush from bombing Afghanistan to overthrow the Taliban. Even the prospect appalled historian Eric Foner, who said, "I am not sure which is more frightening—the horror that engulfed New York City or the apocalyptic rhetoric emanating daily from the White House." The same note of moral equivalence was struck by historian Howard Zinn, who wrote that just like the 9/11 attacks, "The U.S. bombing of Afghanistan is also a crime which cannot be justified." To invade Afghanistan, Richard Falk wrote, shows an obstinate American "refusal to negotiate with the Taliban" and represents a "frontal denial of that country's sovereign rights."[12]

On September 19, 2001, leading figures on the left published an ad in the New York Times under the banner headline "Not in Our Name." The ad condemned Bush's war on terror as a "war without limit." The signers of the ad were an interesting mix of cultural leftists and foreign policy activists. The list included authors Edward Said and Howard Zinn, novelists Kurt Vonnegut and Toni Morrison, playwright and gay rights activist Tony Kushner, civil rights leaders Jesse Jackson and Al Sharpton, feminists Gloria Steinem, Barbara Ehrenreich, and Katha Pollitt, former Vietnam War protesters Jane Fonda and Tom Hayden, movie directors Spike Lee and Oliver Stone, actors Susan Sarandon, Martin Sheen, and Danny Glover, death row inmate Mumia Abu-Jamal, and Democratic congressman Jim McDermott.[13] The activist group MoveOn.org circulated a petition to its supporters warning that if America invaded Afghanistan, "We become like the terrorists we oppose."[14] The left, by its own count, organized more than a hundred demonstrations across the country to stop the United States from overthrowing the Taliban regime.

If the left had gotten its way, Bush would never have invaded Afghanistan and the Taliban would still be in power. Islamic radicals would still be in control of two states, Iran and Afghanistan. Al Qaeda would still have an official state sponsor, so that its future attacks could be more effectively planned, funded, and executed. One can see why bin Laden might be pleasantly surprised to find, in the very nation he attacked, a group of people seeking to minimize the prospect of retaliation and to keep his Taliban supporters in power. If he was furious about rulers in the Muslim world who inexplicably promoted America's cause, bin Laden could be expected to be exhilarated to see a group in America—secular infidels no less—who surprisingly promoted the Islamic fundamentalist cause.

On the issue of Afghanistan, however, the left remained on the margin of political discourse. Its position of vocal opposition to the war on terror was generally shunned by the Democratic leadership in Congress. But the left did succeed in mobilizing an energetic and powerful political movement. This movement, led by groups like Act Now to Stop War and End Racism (ANSWER), is frequently termed "antiwar," although it is more accurately termed "anti-Bush," because its opposition is not to war per se but to Bush's war. From the left fringe, this movement has over the past few years migrated into the political mainstream. In the 2004 primaries, it won over the leading Democratic contenders. It now defines the position of the mainstream of the Democratic Party.

IT IS THE Iraq war that has provided the rallying point for liberal Democratic opposition to Bush's war on terror. Even some libertarians and conservatives have joined the coalition to defeat Bush's Iraq policy. Some of this opposition is principled and derives from genuine and legitimate concerns that Bush is not fighting the war in the most effective way. A good deal of it is opportunistic, as left-leaning Democrats who opposed Bush's war on terror from the outset found in Iraq a convenient occasion to go public with their opposition. It is the left, however, that provides the most coherent opposition to Bush's war on terror. Moreover, with Iraq becoming the centerpiece of this war, the left has become the leader of the broad-based movement against America's presence in that country.

The left's position on Iraq has been clear from the outset: prevent Bush from getting into the war, and if this proves unsuccessful, then make sure that he loses the war. Having failed to achieve the first goal, the left is now explicitly promoting the second goal. Susan Watkins, editor of the *New Left Review*, affirms that "U.S.-led forces have no business in Iraq" and that "the Iraqi people have every right to drive them out." Political scientist Robert Jensen claims the U.S. is losing the war in Iraq "and that's a good thing. I welcome the U.S. defeat." Leia Petty of the Campus Antiwar Network explains the purpose of her group's demonstrations: "We're here as part of a growing counter-recruitment movement that has the potential to stop Bush's ability to carry out his agenda of war and terror." Author James Carroll writes that the United States should not only "accept the humiliation" of withdrawal but "renounce any claim to power or even influence over Iraq." Social scientist Nicholas De Genova argues that in Iraq and elsewhere, "The only true heroes are those who find ways that help defeat the U.S. military."[15] In a sense the left's position flows directly from its premise: since America is the leading terrorist force in the world, the real war against terrorism is a war against America.

Again, one can see the benefits of the left's position from Al Qaeda's point of view. Bin Laden has said that a "third World War is now raging in Iraq," where the outcome for both sides is "either victory and glory, or misery and humiliation." Ayman al-Zawahiri has declared Iraq the location of "the greatest battle of Islam in this era." Why is Iraq so important to these Islamic radicals? Because since the Khomeini revolution in 1979, Muslim fundamentalists have not captured a single Middle Eastern state. True, the Taliban seized power in Afghanistan, but Afghanistan has always been peripheral to the Muslim world. Moreover, the Taliban was rudely ousted by American forces in the aftermath of 9/11.

Right now there is only one success story for radical Muslims, and that is Shia Iran. The problem is that Shia Muslims are a small minority in the Islamic world. More than 80 percent of Muslims are Sunni. Islamic radicals badly need a second success in the Middle East so that they can show that the Khomeini revolution was not an aberration. Moreover, they need to demonstrate the viability of a Sunni Islamic state that can serve as a model for most of the world's Muslims. Although Iraq's population is majority Shia, it is through the success of a Sunni insurgency that bin Laden and his allies seek to establish in that country their revolutionary model. That is why bin Laden sent Abu Musab al-Zarqawi into Iraq in the fall of 2002, before the American invasion. In a 2005 letter to insurgents, Ayman al-Zawahiri laid out the Al Qaeda strategy: "Expel the Americans from Iraq. Then establish an Islamic authority or emirate. Then extend the jihad wave to the secular countries neighboring Iraq."[16] With Iran and Iraq in their control, the Islamic radicals plan to wage war in the other Muslim states. First Jordan. Then Egypt. Then Saudi Arabia. Then Pakistan. Then Indonesia and Malaysia. Then Turkey.

If Iraq is vitally important to Islamic radicals, it is no less critical for President Bush. His success or failure there will largely determine his two-term legacy. Why, then, did Bush make Iraq a focal point of his war on terror? Today there is widespread liberal derision about Bush's motives. Many liberals triumphantly note that there were no weapons of mass destruction in Iraq. So Bush must have misled the American people about this. The left goes even further, asserting that "Bush lied." *The Nation* claims that Bush went to war based on "falsehoods and deceptions." Writing in *Dissent*, Jeff Faux refers to "the liar in the White House." Al Franken goes so far as to say that "the President loves to lie." Author Joe Conason insists that Bush's deceptions on Iraq "will someday fill many volumes." Activist Cindy Sheehan insists, "My son died for lies. George Bush lied to us and he knew he was lying." The theme of Bush as a devious prevaricator has become absolutely central to the left-wing understanding. Of late even mainstream Democrats have started to talk this way. Zbigniew Brzezinski, national security adviser in the Carter administration, faults Bush for going to war on "false pretenses."[17]

Moreover, critics on the left charge that Bush lied by claiming a link between Saddam Hussein and Al Qaeda. In fact, Senator Barbara Boxer points out there is "absolutely no connection" between Iraq and the 9/11 attacks. Columnist Bob Herbert joins the chorus, reminding us that "the United States was attacked on September 11, 2001 by Al Qaeda, not Iraq."[18] Bush, however, never claimed that Saddam Hussein was responsible for 9/11. He did suggest that the war against Saddam Hussein was part of the war against terror. We have here two conflicting views of that war. Many on the left want the war to be confined to getting "the guys who did 9/11." But Bush never viewed the war on terror in this narrow way. For Bush, 9/11 was symptomatic of a new Islamic radicalism that threatened not only American lives but also vital American interests in the Middle East. From Bush's perspective, Islamic radicalism and terrorism thrive because of the toxic political climate in the region, and that climate is fostered by the vicious and dysfunctional regimes in the Middle East. Iraq and Iran were part of what Bush called an "axis of evil" threatening the peace of the world. The solution, therefore, is to attempt to change the conditions in the Muslim world that give rise to terrorism.

Why Iraq? One reason is that after 9/11, a number of leading figures in the Bush administration came to the conclusion that, in the face of a catastrophe of this magnitude, it would not be sufficient to go to Afghanistan and shoot some people on the monkey bars. Rather, America needed to take action in the heart of the Middle East. Remember the old Western movies where John Wayne is called into town as the new sheriff to apprehend a bunch of cattle stealers? He goes into the bar, where the bad guys are shouting and jeering at him. He doesn't know who the culprits are, but he finds a couple of obstreperous hoodlums and slams their head together, or pistol-whips them, and then he walks out of the bar. The message is that there is a new sheriff in town. After 9/11, I believe, the Bush administration wanted to convey this message to the Islamic radicals. In Saddam Hussein, Bush located an especially egregious hoodlum who would become the demonstration project for America's seriousness and resolve.

The Bush administration also chose Iraq because of its strategic importance. Iraq borders on Iran, Syria, Kuwait, Jordan, Turkey, and Saudi Arabia. Thus an American military presence in Iraq could be vital in preventing Islamic radicalism from overrunning the Middle East. Moreover, Iraq is an oil-rich country. By conquering Iraq, America would convince the entire oil-producing world that it has vital interests in the region and is willing to act to protect them. In addition, there was a legal pretext to invade Iraq. Saddam Hussein was openly violating his Gulf War commitments. The United States could invoke his treaty violations as a justification for action. So these were some of the unspoken reasons for the invasion. They were unspoken because in democratic societies nations frequently act on the basis of realpolitik but they cannot always defend their actions in these terms. Consequently democratic leaders have to give idealistic reasons for actions that frequently have both idealistic and Machiavellian motives.

Of course, the stated justification—the belief that Saddam Hussein was seeking to acquire weapons of mass destruction—was also a genuine reason for the invasion. It is easy, with the benefit of hindsight, to fault Bush for being wrong about WMDs. But unlike pundits and rival presidential candidates, statesmen do not have the benefit of hindsight. They must act in the moving current of events, using information that is available to them. At the time there was little doubt across the political spectrum that Saddam Hussein was pursuing WMDs. Hussein himself acted as if he had such weapons, constantly evading the efforts of United Nations inspectors to monitor Iraqi weapons facilities. Bush had to weigh the risk of invading Iraq and being wrong, against the risk of not invading Iraq and being wrong. In the first case, he would be risking American troops in an unpopular war that would, nevertheless, result in the removal of a vicious dictator. In the second case, he would be risking Hussein acquiring a deadly weapon, which could end up in the hands of terrorists. If as a consequence a massive bomb exploded in Chicago killing half a million Americans, then who would take the responsibility? Weighing the risks, Bush decided it would be better to take preventive action and invade Iraq. Given what he knew at the time, it was the right decision.

In retrospect, Bush was wrong to invade Iraq at the time that he did, in the way that he did. With the benefit of hindsight, I think Bush might have done better to focus on Iran, which had nuclear aspirations of its own and was pursuing them—it turns out—with greater effectiveness. Statesmen, however, do not have the luxury of making decisions in retrospect. Consider a similar decision made by President Roosevelt. In the period leading up to World War II, a group of émigré German scientists warned Albert Einstein that the Germans were building an atomic bomb. The émigrés told Einstein that the German project was headed by that country's greatest scientist, Werner Heisenberg. Acutely aware of the dangers of Hitler possessing an atomic bomb, Einstein took this information in the fall of 1939 to President Roosevelt, who commissioned the Manhattan Project. The United States built the bomb, and later dropped two of them on Japan. Many years later, Americans discovered that the Germans were nowhere close to building an atomic bomb. Their project was on the wrong track, and it seems to have stalled in its infancy. Some historians believe that Heisenberg was trying to thwart the project from the inside. Be that as it may, in retrospect we now know that the intelligence that led to the Manhattan Project was wrong. But no one goes around saying, "Einstein lied," or, "FDR lied." They didn't lie; they used the information they had to make a tough decision in a very dangerous situation. The same is true of Bush. Acting against the somber backdrop of 9/11, he may have acted in haste, and he might have acted in error, but he did not act in bad faith. Therefore the claim that "Bush lied" is itself a lie.

IN THE DEBATE leading up to the Iraq invasion, hardly anyone objected to the war on the grounds that Hussein was not trying to make weapons of mass destruction. Leading Democrats agreed with Bill Clinton's 1998 assessment that Iraq had become "a rogue state with weapons of mass destruction, ready to use them or provide

them to terrorists." During the Iraq debate, former presidential candidate Wesley Clark took it for granted that Saddam Hussein pos-
sessed WMDs but argued that this fact did not justify an American
invasion. "After all," he said, "other nations have weapons of mass
destruction. Are we going to invade them?" Others opposed Bush's
plan because of their fear that Saddam Hussein would use WMDs.
Historian Arthur Schlesinger said, "The one thing that would very
probably lead Hussein to resort to his ghastly weapons would be just
this invasion of Iraq by the U.S."[19] This record is important because
many liberals today fault Bush for his erroneous judgments while
conveniently forgetting their own.

If we review the debate leading up to Bush's invasion of Iraq, there
was the leftist objection to the war and there was the mainstream liberal objection. Cindy Sheehan expressed the leftist view when she
said, "Our country has been taken over by murderous thugs . . . war
criminals . . . a pack of cowards and murderers who lust after for-
tunes and power . . . by spreading the cancer of imperialism in the
Middle East." In this view Bush didn't really care about Saddam Hussein, any more than he really cared about bin Laden. In fact, Katha
Pollitt and Chalmers Johnson pointed out, America used to support
Saddam Hussein, just as America once supported bin Laden. I attended one rally in which a speaker said, "We probably sold Saddam
those weapons of mass destruction." More broadly, the left sensed
the Iraq invasion was part of a larger plot, what Edward Said termed
"an old-fashioned colonial occupation" of Iraq. Many on the left
cheered Arundhati Roy's claim that "Bush is far more dangerous
than Saddam Hussein." Writing in salon.com, Michelle Goldberg
quoted anti-Bush activists predicting, "If bombs start falling on Iraq,
expect insurgency at home."[20] The objective of the left was evidently
to keep Saddam Hussein in power.

Contrary to popular perception, America never supported bin
Laden. Yes, bin Laden was part of the Arab Afghan resistance to Soviet occupation of Afghanistan. In order to maintain "deniability" in
its diplomatic dealings with the Soviets, however, America's aid was
channeled through Pakistan. Author Steve Coll reports that never
did America directly deal with or fund bin Laden.[21] Bin Laden denies

he received any U.S. aid, and clearly he didn't need it. His faction never lacked for money, partly because of his own fortune and also because of the financial support that came from Saudi Arabia and other oil-rich Muslim countries. What about the charge that America created Saddam Hussein and sold him dangerous weapons? Pure fantasy. America sided with Hussein during the 1980s, but that was during the period of the Iran-Iraq war, when Hussein was battling the ayatollah Khomeini. In that contest, it was not unreasonable for America to tilt toward Hussein, at least to prevent an Iranian victory. Even so, at no time did America sell any weapons to Hussein.

Despite its fundamental flaws, the leftist view of the war has been taken up by leading Democrats. Former presidential candidate Al Gore now alleges that Bush's Iraq invasion "was preordained and planned before 9/11." Senator Kennedy claims that Bush concocted the scheme to invade Iraq and then "announced to the Republican leadership that the war was going to take place and was going to be good politically."[22] In the debate leading up to the invasion, however, this was not the view of most Democrats or even of most liberals. The liberal position was not opposed to force, it was opposed to force in the absence of collective action and the support of the United Nations. Leading critics like Senator Robert Byrd and former president Carter demanded that George W. Bush do what his father, George H. W. Bush, did in the Gulf War of 1991: assemble a broad international coalition of countries and then act with the authorization of a United Nations resolution. Ironically when George H. W. Bush did this—line up the U.N., bring in the Europeans, even win the support of many Muslim countries—a majority of liberal Democrats opposed his action to expel Saddam Hussein from Kuwait. In the House of Representatives only 86 Democrats supported the Gulf War, while 179 voted against it. In the Senate, 10 Democrats voted to liberate Kuwait by force, while 45 Democrats opposed the plan.

It is true, as liberals say, that multilateral action is usually preferable to unilateral action. But even collective action has its limitations. Many people today express regret that in the Gulf War of 1991 American troops didn't go all the way to Baghdad. Certainly Operation Desert Storm could have been extended to overthrow Hussein, which would have saved America enormous expense, both in money and in lives. So why didn't American troops, having ejected Hussein's forces from Kuwait, pursue them as they retreated into Iraq? The reason is that America was part of a multilateral coalition. The coalition decided in advance that it would repel Hussein from Kuwait, and then stop. If America had gone further it would risk the shattering of the coalition and the opposition of its own allies. Therefore Hussein was permitted to stay in power.

Moreover, the question facing George W. Bush in 2002 was not whether to act with or without international backing. Germany and France were from the outset strongly opposed to U.S. military action. The United Nations was generally uncooperative. Bush had to decide whether to act without this support or not to act at all. Recognizing this, many Democrats insisted on Bush's obtaining broad international support—support that they knew was not there—as a tactical device to constrain Bush's options and prevent him from using force to overthrow Saddam Hussein.

So what about the United Nations? Liberal scholars fault Bush with foolishly ignoring the U.N. As a consequence of America's disregard for international law, the United States has, in the words of political scientists Robert Tucker and David Hendrickson, "assumed many of the features of the rogue nations against which it has done battle over the years."[23] Liberals like to refer problems to the United Nations because it carries the aura of legitimacy. But there is a problem, and it goes beyond the membership of the U.N.'s human rights committee or the corrupt windbags who make up the U.N.'s bureaucracy. Actually, the problem is with international law itself. The core principle of international law is sovereignty. Sovereignty means that the borders of a country are legally and morally inviolable. You cannot trespass across a nation's boundaries or you will be violating its sovereignty.

Now consider the dictators that have inhabited the world over the past half century, from Pol Pot to Idi Amin to Mobutu to Bokassa to Kim Jong-Il to Saddam Hussein. Ask yourself: by what right do such men rule their countries? The obvious answer is none. So what is the moral objection to some other power stepping across the border and pushing the dictator out? None. Yet the hallowed principle of sovereignty says that this is prohibited. The conclusion is that international law, in its current form, gives legal and moral protection to many of the bad guys in the world, allowing them to oppress their people and preventing any outside force from displacing them. Thus for Bush to accede to his liberal critics and refer Iraq to the United Nations would have produced the same outcome as if Bush had adopted the left's recommendation to leave Saddam Hussein alone. Either way, the murderous dictator would still be the sovereign head of Iraq.

BY ITSELF, AMERICA'S military operation against Iraq was a magnificent success. One of the largest land armies in the world was defeated in a matter of days. American casualties were minimal. Saddam Hussein went into hiding. America's victory, however, brought a strange reaction from some in the leftist camp. "Our government has declared a military victory," columnist Howard Zinn wrote following the fall of Baghdad. "As a patriot, I will not celebrate." In a later column, Zinn went on to challenge the "unexamined premise that military victory would constitute success." Clearly he was hoping for a different outcome, and so were others on the left. "It's scary for Democrats, I have to say," former Clinton official Nancy Soderberg said on Jon Stewart's *Daily Show*. "There's always hope that this might not work." Equally revealing was Gary Kamiya's comment on salon.com. "I have a confession," he wrote. "I have at times secretly wished for things to go wrong, wished for the Iraqis to resist longer. Wished for the Arab world to rise up in rage."[24]

America's victory, however, brought two unexpected outcomes. The first was a deadly and resourceful insurgency against American occupation. The resistance was largely made up of former Hussein loyalists who were used to running the country but now found themselves rudely ejected from power. The insurgents were supported in their efforts by Islamic radicals, some of them Iraqi, some from other countries. As is now widely recognized, the Bush administration blundered in failing to anticipate this resistance. Bush's dismay, however, was not shared on the American left. On the contrary, leftists welcomed the insurgency as the legitimate voice of the people of Iraq. We can see this by consulting our two bin Laden Book Club authors. According to William Blum, "The resistance is composed of Iraqi citizens who are simply demonstrating their resentment about being bombed, invaded, occupied, tortured, slain, and subjected to daily humiliations." Robert Fisk exulted, "America's war of 'liberation' is over. Iraq's war of liberation from the Americans is about to begin."[25]

From the outset, the left sought to portray America's military campaign against the insurgency as barbaric and immoral, while ignoring the barbarity and immorality of the insurgents' actions. Since the left had to be careful about praising men who chop off the heads of innocent civilians and exhibit their handiwork on the Internet, the focus of the left's outrage was on innocent Iraqi civilians who were killed in America's military campaigns. Arundhati Roy terms America's civilian casualties "the new genocide." George Soros argued that "the war on terrorism has claimed more innocent civilians in Afghanistan and Iraq than have the attacks on the World Trade Center."[26] Of course, the left is entirely aware that unlike the 9/11 assassins and the insurgents in Afghanistan and Iraq, American troops do not target civilians for attack. With rare exceptions, they have been careful to minimize civilian casualties.

Even so, the left points to civilian casualties as evidence of American immorality. A favorite figure is 100,000 civilian casualties in Iraq. This figure was published in the British journal *Lancet*. It turns out to be highly exaggerated. The journal conducted a very small survey, and then extrapolated its results to cover the whole country. It did not actually count bodies. Iraq Body Count has produced more reliable estimates, which are in the range of 30,000.[27] This is still a high number. But it pales before the 300,000 people whom Saddam Hussein deposited in his mass graves. Hussein's bloody rampage was halted by the dictator's overthrow. The 30,000 figure also pales before the 500,000 Iraqi children who reportedly died as a result of United Nations–imposed economic sanctions against Iraq. The effect of Bush's invasion of Iraq was to end the cruel and ineffective sanctions policy and thus prevent more Iraqi deaths from malnutrition and starvation. In view of these preceding conditions, it seems obvious that America's war in Iraq has ended up *saving* innumerable Iraqi lives that would otherwise have been lost.

For the left, however, the purpose of emphasizing civilian casualties was candidly given by former CNN reporter Peter Arnett. Speaking on Iraqi state television in the early days of the Iraq invasion, Arnett said, "It is clear that within the United States there is a growing challenge to President Bush about the conduct of the war. So our reports of civilian casualties here are going back to the United States. It helps those who oppose the war."[28] Arnett was fired for those remarks, although his expulsion may have been based less on the fear that political bias would infect his reporting and more on his candor in revealing his motives.

Following the capture of Baghdad, a further surprise awaited the Bush administration: no weapons of mass destruction! Immediately the left seized on this fact as a stunning confirmation of its long-standing charge that there was no justification for the war, Bush had acted on false premises, and therefore America should cut its losses and get out of Iraq. Bush responded with a bold and surprising rationale for why America should stay—to bring democracy to Iraq and to the Middle East. From the outset, leading liberals expressed skepticism and even ridicule. Gary Hart expressed the common view among Democrats that democracy cannot be imposed "at the point of a bayonet." George Soros wrote that "with all the experience I have gained . . . I would consider Iraq the last place to choose for a demonstration project" in democracy.[29]

These objections were premature. With due respect to Soros's experience, it seems odd to suggest that countries should postpone their bid for democracy until he considers them eligible. We know that after World War II the United States did impose democracy at the point of a bayonet in Germany and Japan, with excellent results. The deeper point being made by some of the critics seemed to be that it was somehow wrong to use force to establish freedom. How can coercion be used to create liberty? This argument seems plausible, until we realize from history that where freedom has come to a country, it has usually come by force. America got its freedom as a result of a Revolutionary War. How did African Americans get freedom? It took the invasion of a Northern army to secure for the slaves a liberty that they were in no position to secure for themselves. Regrettably, force is often required to establish freedom because tyrants rarely relinquish power voluntarily.

Even so, liberal critics ridiculed the idea that Bush was really sincere about implementing democracy in Iraq. Applying her characteristic sarcasm, columnist Maureen Dowd wrote, "In Bushworld, we can create an exciting Iraqi democracy as long as it doesn't control its own military, pass any laws, or have any power." Writing in *Foreign Affairs*, political scientist Tony Smith claimed that "the call for democratic change was an integral part of a power play by Washington to control the entire Middle East."[30] These are good examples of how mainstream liberals routinely endorse the leftist view that Bush's democratic rhetoric conceals a naked imperial ambition.

Bush has proved this criticism wrong, however, by allowing democracy to take its course in Iraq. The Bush administration had its own schedule for elections, but the Iraqis pushed for elections to be held sooner, and they were. The Bush team wanted the secular liberal fellow, Iyad Allawi, who had been appointed interim prime minister, to win the election. The Iraqis chose religious figures, first Ibrahim al-Jaafari and then Nouri al-Maliki, and the Bush administration accepted these outcomes. The Bush team wanted an Iraqi constitution with equal rights for women. The Iraqis produced a constitution that gives special place to Islam and includes sharia provisions that treat women unequally than men. The Bush administration has accepted the verdict of Iraq's elected representatives on this issue. Moreover, Bush has proved the left wrong by handing over the oil fields to Iraq's new government, demonstrating that America had no desire to steal Iraq's oil. Contrary to Maureen Dowd, Iraq now has an elected government that does control its own military, pass its own laws, and exercise all the power provided by the constitution. Even more impressive, Bush has agreed that U.S. troops will leave Iraq when the Iraqi government decides they are no longer needed.

* * *

IGNORING THESE REMARKABLE signs, Bush's liberal critics have raised two questions: What if the Iraqis don't want democracy? What if the Iraqis don't want American troops in their country? The first question is extremely odd because it presumes that there is a group of people that has no intention of controlling its own destiny. If there is any evidence for this, in Iraq or anywhere else, it has never been produced. On the contrary, I turn on my television and see Hajem al-Hassani, the Sunni Arab speaker of the National Assembly, say, "My dream is to be the Tip O'Neill of Iraq."[31] Recalling O'Neill's resemblance to our federal government—big, fat, and out of control—I am not ordinarily excited to find a man who wants to emulate Tip O'Neill. But I wish al-Hassani good luck. They need more rotund, jovial wheeler-dealers in Baghdad today.

What if the Iraqis don't want us there? Columnist Bob Herbert argues that "the occupation is perceived by ordinary Iraqis as a confrontation and a humiliation." James Dobbins writes, "The beginning of wisdom is to recognize that Washington has lost the Iraqi people's confidence and consent." Robert Byrd laments that "we are now the occupiers, despised by the people of Iraq."[32] The interesting question is how all these people have become so knowledgeable about what the Iraqi people want. Their conclusions seem to be drawn solely from the existence of an insurgency that is made up of less than 2 percent of the Iraqi people and draws its support almost exclusively from the minority Sunni population. In fact, the composition of the insurgency by itself refutes the idea of a broad-based resistance of American occupation. If the Iraqi people opposed America's presence, *all* segments of the population would rebel. In fact the rebellion derives its support entirely from the one group that was rudely ejected from power.

Congressman John Murtha points to an opinion poll showing that more than half of Iraqis "want us out and almost half of them think we're the enemy." Put aside the fact that the poll was ambiguously worded, and other polls find Iraqis want American troops to stay for at least another two years.[33] Even if Murtha's preferred pollsters were correct in their findings, what do those results really prove? Polls change because people change their minds. The way that democratic countries express the people's will is not through shifting poll results but through the decisions and policies made by their elected representatives. If the Iraqi people don't want American troops there, they can vote for a government that will demand that the troops leave. Murtha's conclusion that "we've lost the hearts and minds of the people" seems to be largely a product of wishful thinking.

For a group that is supposed to be committed to democracy, liberals seem strangely drawn to a cornucopia of explanations for why democracy isn't working in Iraq. Columnist Bob Herbert discounted the Iraqi election because "a real democracy requires an informed electorate," whereas the Iraqi electorate is "woefully uninformed." For Arianna Huffington, Iraq had a democratic election "in name only" since "most of the candidates lacked name recognition." Jonathan Steele found Iraq's election defective because many Sunnis didn't vote and therefore "voters had only a limited choice." Robert Dreyfuss found the process flawed because "the Sunni community was tricked into voting" and moreover "the Sunnis who were elected to the parliament do not represent the resistance." Writing in the *American Prospect*, Ivan Eland speculated, on no historical evidence in particular, that "spreading democracy doesn't reduce terrorism and, if anything, actually makes it worse."[34]

Even in Afghanistan, after that country held its first free election in history, leading liberals complained about the inadequacy of the democratic process. "At least a third of Afghanistan is still so dicey that voters there cannot be registered." Due to the influence of warlords, "voters had to choose between the unknown and the notorious." "Afghanistan remains unstable." The elected leader, Hamid Karzai, "has not managed to extend his authority beyond Kabul." "Opium production is at a record level."[35] When evaluating these criticisms, let us remember that, in Iraq as in Afghanistan, we are witnessing fledgling democracies. Think of how imperfect and unsteady America's first steps toward democracy were. The important point is that 50 million Afghans and Iraqis are free, and for the first time in their history, they have a chance to control their own destiny.

Finally, we must confront the argument—first advanced by the left, but now popular among all Bush's critics—that the war in Iraq has only succeeded in creating more terrorists. Ted Kennedy argues that Iraq has now become "a fertile new breeding ground for terrorists."[36] Richard Clarke argues that as a result of the American presence in Iraq, "President Bush has sowed the seeds of current and future terrorism against the United States." This argument is based on a paradox: the war against terrorism is producing more terrorists. The basis for the claim is the increased number of terrorist and insurgent attacks following the Iraq invasion. Jimmy Carter cites these attacks as "direct evidence that the Iraqi war has actually increased the terrorist threat."[37] Carter's argument was supported in the fall of 2006 by an intelligence report that called Iraq a cause celebre for terrorists.

But there is an alternative explanation for the increased violence. The radical Muslims have upped the ante in Iraq because they have realized how much they stand to lose if Iraq becomes a functioning, pro-American democracy. Iraq is a grand experiment by America to see if the alien seed of democracy can take root in the Middle East. The past few decades have witnessed a great democratic tide sweep the world. Latin America, once run by dictators and strongmen, is now largely democratic. Africa, once the province of Big Daddy despots, has seen a burst of popular self-government. Despite some backsliding, Russia is on the stumbling road to democracy. Many of the "Oriental despotisms" of Asia have been transformed into democracies. Who would have thought any of this possible a century ago? Countries like Japan and India, with no history of self-government, have become functioning democracies.

Yet with the exception of Israel, until recently there were no democracies in the Arab Middle East. To find Muslim democracy you have to go to Turkey, Indonesia, or Malaysia—in the Arab world, democracy does not exist and has not existed. America is trying to change that, and to establish a new model that traditional Muslims might wish to emulate. Already the effects are being felt. Egypt held a parliamentary election in November 2005 in which all groups, even the candidates affiliated with the Muslim Brotherhood, were allowed to participate. "Now everybody in Egypt is talking about democracy," says Negad El Borai, director of the Cairo-based Center for Democratic Development. "Nothing would have happened without U.S. pressure." In 2005, Lebanon held its first parliamentary election in three decades. It, too, was the result of a popular movement inspired by Iraq. Walid Jumblatt, leader of the Druze in Lebanon and longtime critic of the United States, said, "When I saw the Iraqi people voting, it was the start of a new Arab world. The Berlin Wall has fallen. We can see it."[38] If a democratic wind blows through Iraq, and then spreads to other countries, we could see the beginning of an historical transformation no less momentous than the transformation of the former Soviet Union.

The Islamic radicals are terrified at this prospect. This is why they will do anything to subvert Iraqi democracy, even to the point of provoking a civil war that would surely produce untold numbers of Muslim deaths. Not that the radicals abhor democracy per se. As we saw with the victory of Hamas in the Palestinian territories and the advances of the Muslim Brotherhood in Egypt, the radicals are likely to do pretty well in free elections. What truly frightens them is pro-American democracy. This is something entirely new in the Arab world. Until now the Islamic radicals have had to face only America-backed dictators who are typically secular tyrants with little support from the people. Given a choice between secular tyranny and Islamic tyranny, many Muslims might prefer Islamic tyranny. But what if the choice were between Islamic tyranny and Islamic democracy? Then traditional Muslims would have a serious alternative to consider, and the outcome could well be different.

The Bush administration has made costly blunders in Iraq. Some of these could have been avoided, others are in the nature of war. There were also catastrophic blunders in World War II—errors in planning, training casualties, bad intelligence, battles lost that should have been won. Even so, the fight went on because the whole country recognized the importance of defeating Hitler. The difference now is that the United States is no longer united: one side seems dedicated not to defeating the Islamic radicals but to defeating the United States. There is a war against the war, and it is being waged by the left with mainstream liberal encouragement. The reason for this home-grown resistance is political. A few years from now, if Iraq is a stand-ing—even if somewhat fragile—democracy, this result will be a magnificent triumph for Bush's policy and assure his place in history. It will also consolidate the claim of the Republican Party to be the party that can be trusted over the long term with national security. The implications for the Muslim world, and for America, are huge. Therefore two groups are making supreme efforts to defeat Bush in Iraq. The first group is the Islamic radicals and insurgents, who are indeed fighting harder because they have a great deal to lose. The other group is the American left, which is also fighting harder be-cause it too has a great deal to lose. Although these two groups do not speak a word to each other, they have in Bush a common enemy, and therefore, whether they fully realize it or not, they are allies in the war against the war on terror.

WE ARE NOW in a position to better understand the real message contained in bin Laden's 2004 and 2006 videotapes. Bin Laden of-fers a vital clue when he informs Americans in his 2004 statement that "in truth, your security lies not in the hands of Kerry, Bush, or Al Qaeda. It lies in your own hands, and whichever state does not encroach upon our security thereby ensures its own."[39] Clearly bin Laden was proposing some sort of a deal. But to whom? And what deal? Many interpreted bin Laden to be offering America the same terms that he seems to have offered European countries: stop sup-porting the war on terror and we will stop targeting your country.

This interpretation rested upon reading the word "state" to mean "country." But bin Laden didn't say "country." This was a letter ad-dressed to Americans, and its subject was the upcoming choice in the 2004 election. Clearly bin Laden was saying that American states that vote against Bush's war on terror would be spared future at-tacks. In a sense bin Laden was taking up a complaint that Michael Moore issued immediately after 9/11. Moore protested that bin

Laden had picked the wrong targets, because he had concentrated his attacks in states that did not vote for Bush. In his 2004 statement, bin Laden seems to be telling blue America: I know you may be scared of me because of what I did on 9/11, but if you vote against Bush, I will not target your states the next time.

In other words, bin Laden's signaling can be understood as an effort to establish a broader political alliance. Speaking to Americans in his 2006 videotape, bin Laden called for a "truce." Again, a truce with whom? Bin Laden recognizes, of course, that no truce is possible with Bush. His truce is obviously directed to a different group, Bush's political opposition. More than once in the videotape, bin Laden refers to polls showing that a majority of Americans oppose America's involvement in Iraq. While scorning Bush for ignoring these polls, bin Laden goes on to praise "the sensible people" in America who protest the Iraq war and who have helped to produce declining public support for it. Bin Laden calls on these "sensible people" to recognize that wars are not won based on "strength and modern arms" alone but also through the kind of "patience and steadfastness" that America does not seem to have but the Islamic radicals do.[40]

It is now possible to discern bin Laden's message to the American left, which I express in my own words: "Your group and my group have very different ultimate goals. You want a permissive society, and I want sharia. Even so, the remarkable thing is that our strategic objectives at the current time are very similar. You want to destroy President Bush, and to do this you have to discredit Bush's war on terror. I too need to defeat Bush's war on terror. Neither one of us can succeed on our own. We in Al Qaeda are too weak to defeat the U.S. military. You are not strong enough politically to defeat Bush in your country. We need each other. So let us coordinate our efforts. I want you, the sensible people, to accept a silent truce between Al Qaeda and the American left. You may be reluctant to do this because of a fear of terrorism. But if you work with me I will make sure that I don't target your states in any future attacks. Here is how our collaboration can be most effective. I will intensify jihad against Bush abroad, and you fight against him in your political battle at home. My insurgents and martyrs will continue to increase the body count of American casualties in Iraq and elsewhere, and you can use my efforts to undermine the will of the American people to continue Bush's war on terror. This way, the patience and steadfastness of the Muslim fighters can outlast America's enormous military might. I win, and you win also. It will be the greatest victory, fought by the two most improbable allies, in history."

TEN

The Left's Hidden Agenda

Unmasking the Liberal-Islamic Alliance

FOR THE PAST five years we have been debating the war on terror, yet there is something surreal about this debate. The premise of the debate is that both sides want the United States to win the war, and the disagreement is over the best way to fight Islamic radicalism and terrorism. But is this premise really true? Consider this. When there is good news for American foreign policy, it is ignored or downplayed by liberals in the press. For all Iraq's problems, there has been remarkable progress there since Hussein's removal from power. The country has seen the holding of free elections, restoration of sovereignty, formation of a new government, ratification of a constitution, introduction of a sound currency, revival of oil production, a newly established stock market, a surge of new businesses, training of new police and military, rebuilding of roads, opening of schools, new fire stations, an improved computer network, and the increased availability of clean water. Per capita income in Iraq has doubled since 2003 and is now higher than before the invasion. There are now more than a hundred independent newspapers and TV stations in the country.

How often do you see reports about any of this on TV or in the newspapers? Typically there is no coverage, and when there is, it is minimal. Good news in the war on terror is assiduously down-played. Recently the U.S. government released documents seized from Al Qaeda safehouses in Iraq. The documents conveyed the Al Qaeda leaders' desperation that the insurgents were losing their ability to destabilize the country. Each month, they confessed, the Iraqi government grows stronger. Suicide attacks had been reduced to ineffective "hit and run" operations. Indeed, according to Al Qaeda, its best hope at this point was a "media strategy" aimed at disguising the failing insurgency. One might think all of this would be front-page news in America, but typically the stories reporting the documents were minimized. A typical example was the *New York Times*, which did a small back-page report on the subject.[1]

When victories in the war on terror are too obvious for the press to ignore, they are greeted by leftists in the media with silent dismay or open ridicule. Matthew Rothschild, editor of the *Progressive*, was unimpressed by America's killing of Iraq's terrorist mastermind Abu Musab al-Zarqawi. Rothschild predicted that Zarqawi's demise would have "virtually no effect" since "Zarqawi was losing popularity even among Sunni insurgents." The leftist blogger Juan Cole scoffed that in portraying Zarqawi as a terrorist mastermind the U.S. government had "overestimated his importance." *The Nation* insisted that Zarqawi had become "something of a sideshow" and that by killing him Bush may have succeeded only in creating a "martyr." Consequently Zarqawi's death "remains part of a larger and tragic story of miscalculation."[2]

By contrast, when there is bad news for American foreign policy, leftists in the media become visibly excited and cannot stop talking about it. Years after Abu Ghraib, the *New York Times* continues to report on it, and liberal outlets like salon.com titillate their viewers with "new photographs" aimed at further humiliating the U.S. government. Similarly leftists reacted with undisguised glee to civil strife in Iraq following the destruction of the Shia mosque in Samarra. At the first sign that marines may have killed some two dozen Iraqi civilians in Haditha, the liberal press began daily front-page coverage of the allegations, and John Murtha and his leftist admirers quickly proclaimed the scandal "worse than Abu Ghraib."[3] There is a pattern here: the left reacts to events as if America were the enemy and toward the Islamic radicals and insurgents as if they were the good guys. This is the most troubling consequence of a divided America: one side now cheers for the enemy and labors for its success. With the help of the left, Al Qaeda's "media strategy" appears to be working.

But why would the left take the side of America's sworn enemies, while treating the American government as the adversary? The issue of the left's motives is the great unanswered question among conservatives. So far, there are several theories to explain the left's behavior. Perhaps the most common theory is that the left is weak and does not understand the threat. The right-wing pundit Mark Steyn has made valiant attempts to show the left that Islamic fundamentalists are really illiberal and don't care for people like Barney Frank and Maureen Dowd. Since leftists refuse to become exercised over the threat posed by "crazy mullahs," Steyn concludes that they are "unserious" about foreign policy. Another conservative theory is that the left hates America. As Jeane Kirkpatrick once put it, the left always blames America first. David Horowitz and others insist that this is because the left is made up of "neo-Communists" in a new garb.[4] Radio host Michael Savage has a different theory, conveyed by the title of his recent book *Liberalism Is a Mental Disorder*.

In reality, the left understands the threat of Islamic fundamentalism very well. Contrary to Mark Steyn, it is very serious about foreign policy. Nor is the left weak in promoting the values it believes in. As we have seen, the left has an aggressive global campaign to undermine patriarchy and traditional religion, and to promote secularism, feminism, and the corruptions of American popular culture. This campaign is far more comprehensive than anything contemplated on the right. Its centerpiece is a battle against traditional Islamic morality, which is viewed by the left as the greatest barrier to achieving the triumph of liberal morality worldwide. So the Muslims who say America is "against Islam" are partly right. Of course, it is not America that is against Islam, it is the cultural left. The left does not want to acknowledge its hostility to Islam, so it accuses the right of fighting a religious war. The left charges the Bush administration with political imperialism to distract attention from its own campaign of cultural imperialism.

Yet, oddly enough, the left does not want this campaign of social transformation to be extended to the war on terror, even though military conquest would be an obvious way to transform illiberal societies like Afghanistan and Iraq into more liberal ones. The left's reluctance is not due to weakness but due to calculation. Instead of fighting a war, the left seeks a kind of global law enforcement campaign against bin Laden and "the guys who did 9/11." The left would prefer the narrowest possible fight against the most illiberal forces in the world. Again, the critical question is why.

One reason is that Bush is fighting Islamic radicalism with democracy. The left frequently poses as the champion of democracy. It has to, because liberals are generally committed to the democratic idea, and the left relies on liberal support to secure mainstream legitimacy for its agenda. Recall, however, that the left has won virtually all of its victories in America not through the democratic process but by going around it. How did abortion become legal? How did the left get its radical doctrine of secularism adopted? How has the left managed to overturn virtually all laws against pornography? How is gay marriage being pushed today? In every case, the left has relied on the courts to declare a "right" and then enforce that right against the will of the American people and their elected representatives. In this sense, the biggest victories of the cultural left in the past few decades have all been achieved undemocratically.

The left knows it is imperative to circumvent democracy in the Muslim world. Notice how the left never calls for democratization in Syria or Iran. The left may fault America for being "hypocritical" in supporting Pakistan, Egypt, or Saudi Arabia, but it rarely presses for democratization in those countries either. In the 1980s the left constantly pressured the United States to compel its allies, like Pinochet in Chile, Marcos in the Philippines, and the Afrikaner government in South Africa, to democratize. So why has the left lost its appetite for democracy in the Middle East? The reason is that leftists have figured out that in that region the tyrants are relatively liberal, and the Muslim people are socially and religiously conservative. The Gulf kingdoms are the most liberal regimes in the Middle East today— there is a parliament and a relatively free press, and women enjoy a wide array of liberties—but all of them are ruled by kings and oligarchs. When Kuwait recently gave women the vote, it was the hereditary ruler, the emir, who had to pressure the elected parliament to adopt the measure. The most liberal regime in the Middle East in the past half century was Iran under the shah. As long as you didn't protest against the government, you could dress as you liked, believe as you liked, and live as you liked. Eventually the shah was overthrown, not so much because he was a tyrant as because he was a liberal!

The notion of "liberal tyranny" is surprising because Americans are accustomed to thinking of "liberal democracy." We often use the terms "liberal" and "democratic" synonymously, presuming that liberalism leads to democracy and that democracy is an expression of liberalism. In reality, liberalism and democracy are quite different. Liberalism means individual rights. Democracy means majority rule. Liberalism refers to the right of individuals to shape their lives. Democracy refers to the right of a people to collective self-determination. One may say that, in America, we have exercised our democratic choice for a liberal society. We have chosen liberalism from within democracy. But this is not an inevitable choice. Other societies can vote differently. In Algeria during the early 1990s, the Islamic Salvation Front campaigned on a platform of ending women's employment, enforcing the veil, and making sex outside of marriage punishable by death. The party won resounding victories at the polls. The electoral success of Hamas in the Palestinian territories and of the Muslim Brotherhood in Egypt confirms the pattern of Muslims voting for illiberal outcomes.

For the left, Iraq is a frightening example of what happens when a tyrant like Saddam Hussein is replaced by an elected government. Repressive though he was, Saddam Hussein was also something of an egalitarian. He treated men and women with brutality, but (from the left's point of view) at least he treated them with equal brutality.

Although rights didn't count for much under Hussein, men and women had the same rights in court. Conceding that Iraq was "no feminist paradise" under Hussein, the *New York Times* praised him for granting women "access to educational, professional and personal opportunities." Moreover, Hussein was a secular ruler who kept the mullahs under strict control. By contrast, Iraq's democratic constitution declares Islam the official state religion, makes Islam a valid source of law, and permits no law that contravenes the clear teachings of Islam. Iraqi elected officials seek to implement some form of sharia, at least in domestic or family law. What makes these rules even more appalling from the left's perspective is that they have been enacted through popular consent. It is the Iraqi people who have rejected feminism and secularism. Women can vote in Iraq and they too supported the regime that is in power. Having seen what Muslims do when they get democracy, the American left seems to have secretly given up hope for democracy in the Middle East. As a consequence of Iraqi democracy, the *Times* warns, "the future of women's freedom is in serious question." The new leaders "could be consigning Iraqi women to a life of subjugation" and secular Iraqis to "a bleak, Iran-like future." In the same vein, columnist Maureen Dowd fretted that "the Iraqi election may actually be making things worse" because it "is going to expand the control of the Shia theocrats."[5] This, by the way, is the same Maureen Dowd who earlier complained that the United States would never let the Iraqis choose their own leaders and rule their own society.

Author Sam Harris draws the logical conclusion: America should not encourage democracy in the Muslim world. "It would be like opening the polls to the Christians of the fourteenth century." Harris's candor is exceptional. Most people on the left won't admit that they consider Muslims too backward and fanatical to entrust them with the ballot. So leftists subject democracy in the Muslim world to impossible standards. Here is a classic statement from the liberal Jewish magazine *Tikkun:* "There can be no democracy in Iraq without a fundamental redistribution of legal, economic, political and social power toward women and their equal representation throughout the region's economies and governments."[6] By this measure democracy is impossible in the world today, since nowhere do women have equal representation in economic and political life. A kind of utopianism, in this way, is deployed as a weapon against progress.

THE LEFT WOULD rather use the United Nations and other international groups that it dominates to promote its agenda. Liberal enthusiasm for the U.N. seems rooted in a belief in ethical universalism. "The emphasis on patriotic pride is morally dangerous," the philosopher Martha Nussbaum writes. "We should give our first allegiance to . . . the moral community made up of all human beings." Another prominent thinker, Richard Rorty, pines for what he terms "the parliament of man, the federation of the world."[7] But do not for a moment think that Nussbaum, Rorty, or anyone on the left would trust the world community with genuine legislative power. The main problem with "world government" is that it would place a chastity belt on the left's social agenda. By Western standards, most people in Asia, Africa, Latin America, and the Middle East are very conservative. On issues like feminism and homosexuality, they are to the right of Pat Robertson! They are likely to impose far more restrictions than now exist in the West on birth control, divorce, homosexuality, and abortion. I doubt Nussbaum and Rorty would want to live under the moral rules enacted by a truly representative world government. For these reasons the left should be very relieved to be spared world government and to have the United Nations instead. As a self-styled surrogate for the global community, the U.N. enables the left to espouse the ideal of world government without having to actually live by that ideal.

To many conservatives, the level of trust the left places in the United Nations seems ridiculously naïve. How can the U.N., which does not command an effective fighting force, resolve conflicts that may require the use of force? What good is the U.N. in stopping rogue states from acquiring dangerous weapons? Is it credible to expect this international agency, half of whose member countries are governed by dictators, to be an effective instrument for the promotion of democratic values? This criticism of the left is itself naïve. It presumes that leftists expect the U.N. to do these things. In reality, the left has entirely different goals for the United Nations. From this point of view, the U.N. and its various agencies function well as an international leftist legislature, proclaiming ever-new "rights" and then enforcing them in countries that would never themselves consider passing such laws.

We have seen how this process works. The left relies on multilateral treaties and international conferences to adopt leftist priorities and declare them universal rights. Then human rights groups like Amnesty International and other leftist NGOs use leverage against liberal tyrants to force them to comply with the left's agenda or be found in violation of international law. Recently, the left won a big victory in Morocco when, after a decade of pressure from international NGOs, King Mohammed VI agreed to replace the country's Islamic family law with a Western-style code. In one sweep, Morocco abolished polygamy and established something close to no-fault divorce. The left was jubilant: here was an obliging tyrant taking his orders not from the Moroccan people but from Human Rights Watch. Now Regan Ralph, executive director of Human Rights Watch, says the "true test" for the king is to abolish the country's personal status code, which stipulates that the husband is the head of the family.[8] In a similar vein, the European Union is pressuring Turkey to liberalize its divorce laws and adopt a nondiscrimination provision on homosexuality as a condition for being admitted into the European Union. The EU demonstrates how political and financial leverage can be used to armtwist Muslims into setting aside their religion as the basis of law and adopting secular and liberal laws instead.

The left has a second major problem with democracy in the Muslim world. If democracy succeeds there, the result is a big win for George Bush and his conservative allies. Recall the left's seething hatred for Bush, a man whom Sean Wilentz terms "the very worst president in all of American history." Let us also remember that the left is still reeling from its loss in the Cold War. Despite the rhetorical bravado with which liberals continue to say, "We won the cold war," the left knows very well that it lost the Cold War. It's easy to forget now that for at least two decades leftists commonly used the term "cold warrior" as an epithet. Some continue to mourn the collapse of the Soviet empire. "To this day," historian Eric Hobsbawm recently admitted, "I notice myself treating the memory of the Soviet Union with indulgence and tenderness." A leading critic of the Iraq war, the British leftist George Galloway, says, "Yes, I did support the Soviet Union, and the disappearance of the Soviet Union is the biggest catastrophe of my life."[9]

The outcome of the Cold War helped to consolidate the image of the Republican Party as the party that could be trusted with national security. The left recognizes that if Bush's policies succeed in the Middle East, this result would solidify patriotic sentiments and may even boost traditional values generally. The left recognizes the military is a conservative institution with a large number of Southerners and evangelical Christians. Military values are right-wing values. The left despises these values, but it cannot openly attack the military for fear of being called unpatriotic. Learning from its past mistakes, the left has adopted a wily new strategy: it now seeks defeat for America on behalf of the American military. Even though military personnel strongly support Bush's mission in Iraq, the left solicitously urges: "Let's bring our troops home." "Let's keep them out of harm's way." "Iraq is not worth the life of one more American soldier."

The left is fighting a high-stakes battle in which its identity as a viable political movement is at stake. As Paul Starr admits, "Liberalism is at greater risk now than at any time in recent American history. The risk is of political marginality, even irrelevance."[10] His remarks can be understood in this way: America has a one-party system of government. This means that one party tends to dominate American politics in a given era. The major party sets the agenda, and the other party has the choice of reactively opposing its ideas or of sounding a feeble cry of "me too." During the Andrew Jackson era, the Democrats were the majority party. This dominance lasted half a century, until the Civil War. After the war, the Republicans became the majority, a position they held until the Great Depression.

Since 1932, the Democrats assumed the majority position, which continued through the Roosevelt, Kennedy, and Johnson administrations.

Since 1980, the Republican Party has been in the ascendancy. First there was Reagan, then the GOP sweep of Congress in 1994, and then George W. Bush's election and reelection. Despite short-term reversals, the broader pattern is one of Republican success. And now the party of conservatism is looking to solidify its hold on American politics for the next several decades—a nightmarish prospect for liberal Democrats. In addition, the Supreme Court seems ready to tip decisively to the right. If this happens, it would endanger the left's entire social agenda. As long as the left dominated the courts, it retained the power to achieve its most important objectives, in many cases by invalidating laws passed by representative bodies. A conservative court would deprive cultural liberalism of its most valuable political institution. No wonder the left is desperate to reverse the conservative tide.

Even so, it may seem paradoxical for the party of autonomy and secularism to risk an important country like Iraq falling into the clutches of Islamic radicals who would execute homosexuals and impose strict forms of sharia. It appears even more incredible that the left would consider allying with groups that proclaim themselves the sworn enemies of America. The mystery disappears, however, when we realize that the left is simply applying the doctrine of the lesser evil. From its point of view, the left is allying with the bad guys in order to defeat the worse guys. Obviously leftists do not wish to live in the kind of society that bin Laden seeks to establish. But the left also knows that bin Laden wants to establish sharia in Baghdad, not Boston. The left is willing to risk an Islamic fundamentalist state in Iraq in order to improve its prospects of defeating conservative government here in America.

Another way to put it is that the left is more than willing to partner with foreign enemies it doesn't like in order to vanquish a domestic enemy it rabidly hates and fears. Columnist Ellen Willis warns that "what used to be the right-wing lunatic fringe is now the Republican mainstream. . . . The radical right feels entitled to dominate not only government but all social institutions." Bill Moyers charges that Bush and the right are causing nothing less than the "intentional destruction of the United States of America."[11] From the left's point of view, an Iraq ruled by bin Laden and his successors is troubling, but an America ruled by Bush and the conservatives is intolerable. So the left fears Bush more than bin Laden, and from its perspective, it is right to do so. The entire social agenda of the left, which was advancing without serious opposition, is now existentially jeopardized by Bush and his supporters. It is Bush, not bin Laden, who threatens to marginalize the cultural left and discredit its most cherished values.

Once again—this cannot be emphasized often enough—I am not suggesting that the left hates America. Nor does the left always "blame America first." The left doesn't blame America for undermining the shah of Iran, getting rid of Ferdinand Marcos, or imposing economic sanctions against South Africa. The left doesn't fault America for its global support of contraception, liberal divorce laws, and the legalization of prostitution. The left is entirely in favor of Hollywood and the music companies spreading decadent cultural values through movies, television, and songs. The left would like to have Mapplethorpe's photographs and *Brokeback Mountain* seen in every country. In short, the left wants America to be a shining beacon of global depravity, a kind of Gomorrah on a Hill.

CONTRARY TO DAVID Horowitz and others, the left in America doesn't want communism or full-scale socialism but for America to become more like Europe. Whether they mean it or not, Hollywood leftists are always threatening to move to Europe if Republicans are elected one more time. Liberals like Felix Rohatyn routinely call for American courts to adopt European precedents.[12] There has been a spate of left-leaning books extolling the old continent. Consciously seeking to contrast Europe with America, these books have titles like *The European Dream, Why Europe Will Run the Twenty First Century*, and *The United States of Europe*. Author Tony Judt terms Europe a "model for universal emulation."[13]

Part of the appeal is economic. Europe has a short work week and a generous welfare state. While many Americans take pride in how much the country's welfare rolls have been reduced, author T. R. Reid reports that "in Norway the government takes pride in showing that the number of recipients has been growing rapidly." The main appeal of Europe, however, is its cultural politics. "It is in Europe," Jeremy Rifkin writes, "where the feeling of the sixties generation has given rise to a bold new experiment in living." If many Muslims criticize America for moral decadence, many Europeans criticize America for not being decadent enough. Unlike America, Europe is completely secular. France is so systematically hostile to all religion that one of its leading politicians, Nicolas Sarkozy, speaks of the nation's "secular fundamentalism." Flag waving is not considered respectable in Europe. "The open display of patriotism," Reid writes, "is widely sneered at in Europe."[14]

Europeans also despise traditional America, which is why Bush is the object of pathological derision and why Michael Moore's books have broken publishing records across the continent. Appealing to a nondiscrimination provision in its charter, the European Union has forced all member nations to admit homosexuals into the military. Many European countries have legalized gay unions. Meanwhile, traditional marriage has declined to the point where it is now a minority lifestyle. Reports of adultery do not harm a European politician's reputation, and in France they sometimes enhance it. Childlessness has become a common phenomenon in European households, with the result that the population of Western Europe is shrinking. Of the women who do have children, few devote themselves to full-time motherhood. In France, all children between the ages of three and five are placed in full-time, government-funded day care, a system that Hillary Clinton enthusiastically recommends for this country.[15] Many Europeans find nothing controversial in assisted suicide or recreational cocaine use. European countries generally permit abortion but are horrified by the idea of capital punishment.

Many Europeans regard cultural depravity as a mark of their sophistication. In many cases the government gives its blessing, as in

Amsterdam, where drugs are legal and you can walk into a coffee-house and order hashish or marijuana with your cappuccino. The Dutch government provides users with free needles and "treatment"—often consisting of more drugs. Prostitution is also legal, and the only government regulation of it is to ensure that the facilities are sanitary, condoms are used, and taxes are collected. The government even conducts tours of the red light district, and official maps helpfully designate the locations of brothels. Best of all, there are no pesky religious conservatives to object to any of this. The "conservative" reaction to Islamic radicalism in Europe is mainly to take a firm stance on behalf of liberal decadence. The general tone of the European right is, "We won't stand for any fanatical immigrants questioning the secular basis of our society or telling us to pull our pants up."

Finally, Europe provides an operational demonstration of the alliance between left-wing radicals and Islamic radicals. In several European countries, radical imams celebrated 9/11 and called for the destruction of America while leftist academics and civil rights groups demanded the imams' "right to be heard" and defended the legitimacy of their "dissent." In Britain, secular leftists and Muslim fundamentalists jointly formed the Stop the War Coalition and worked together to discredit Tony Blair for supporting America's Iraq policy. For the American left, Europe is politically far ahead of the United States and provides a blueprint for the direction in which this country should move.

SINCE EUROPEAN DECADENCE stands at the opposite pole to the traditional values of non-Western cultures, the left is faced with a problem: how to impose the liberal values of Europe on those conservative cultures? Here we see why the left does not want to dismantle American power. The left needs American power to promote its agenda. What the left seeks is a transformation in the use of American power. This explains why many on the left frequently call for the United States to intervene militarily in countries where no American self-interest is involved. The same people who oppose

American action in Iraq or Iran insist that America should intervene in Haiti, Liberia, Rwanda, Kosovo, or Sudan. While Bush is preoccupied with Iraq, George Soros complains that "already the United States has been reluctant to get engaged in Liberia."[16] Columnist Nicholas Kristof has repeatedly urged America to intervene, if necessary with military force, in Darfur. At first glance such rhetoric seems simply bizarre. The reason people such as Soros and Kristof advocate apparently pointless intervention is that, from their perspective, it is not pointless. Indeed, it provides an excellent opportunity to promote the values of contemporary liberalism.

The left would like America's military to become more like Europe's peacekeeping forces that engage in so-called humanitarian intervention. Traditionally, such intervention has been limited to extreme cases, such as stopping genocide. The left would like to expand the scope so that force is used, as Rifkin puts it, "to protect people's universal human rights." In this view, rather than promote democracy, America's military would be more like a "nanny state" with guns. In a recent article in *Foreign Affairs*, Isobel Coleman calls on the United States to use its power to "champion female education in Iraq." The U.S. should also "do everything it can to aid Iraqi women's groups and programs designed to help women leaders there." In particular, "Washington should consider establishing a women's college in Baghdad." Also, "The U.S. should start channeling a significant portion of its reconstruction dollars to Iraqi business women." Moreover, the U.S. mission should have "an adviser on gender issues" to implement these various initiatives.[17]

At the risk of being a spoiler at the feminist picnic, one might stop and ask: why should the United States do any of this? Shouldn't these decisions be made by the Iraqi people through their elected representatives? If the cultural left has its way, the U.S. military would become the enforcement arm of the left's social agenda. The left seeks to stop parents who use corporal punishment on their children, lock up patriarchal husbands who rule over their families, prosecute people who are intolerant toward homosexuals, take down religious monuments that have been erected with public funds, block the efforts of citizens who object to pornography displays and abortion clinics, and distribute condoms and sex kits in schools and communities around the world. These measures are likely to stir up opposition, so the left needs American power abroad to quell the resistance. Thus the left has an important role in its scheme for the U.S. military. Call it the Immorality Police. Rather than suppress immorality, the unique role of the armed forces would be to enforce it.

To achieve a fundamental transformation of American foreign policy, the left needs America's current policy to suffer a loss from which it cannot recover. The left seeks to engineer this defeat by imposing so many restraints on Bush that he can neither win the war abroad nor effectively defend against terrorist attacks at home. This strategy sets up a no-lose situation: it is the liberals who encumber the president, yet it is Bush who will be blamed if there is another attack. The left also seeks to demoralize the American people so that they demand immediate withdrawal from Iraq. This is where bin Laden and the Iraqi insurgents come in. The terror they produce is the propaganda the left needs in order to convince the American people that the war is imposing an unacceptably high toll. Even decapitations broadcast over the Internet serve the purpose of disheartening Americans, which is why the left shows no indignation over Al Qaeda's use of such tactics. When Islamic radicals kidnapped and then brutally murdered four American contractors working in Iraq, the leftist blogger Markos Moulitsas was unmoved. Writing on his Web site, dailykos.com, Moulitsas confessed, "I feel nothing over the death of the mercenaries. They are there to wage war for profit."[18]

The left's model for Iraq is its successful campaign a generation ago to sway public opinion against the Vietnam War. Just as liberals in the press were able to turn military victories like the Tet offensive into political defeats, today's left-leaning journalists are working overtime to turn military and political gains in Iraq into political liabilities. While the military destroys insurgent strongholds in Fallujah, the headlines focus entirely on civilian casualties. As part of this technique, leftists in the press can be counted on to highlight casualty figures: "Death Toll Reaches 2,000!" and so on. As the left knows, the American people don't like casualties, but what they dislike even more is a cause that cannot succeed. That is why leftist politicians and pundits continually harp on this theme. "The idea that we are going to win the war in Iraq," declares Democratic national chairman Howard Dean, "is just plain wrong." Senator Patrick Leahy declares that "it has become increasingly apparent that the most powerful army in the world cannot stop a determined insurgency." So insistent are these leftist refrains that even mainstream liberals now echo these themes. Zbigniew Brzezinski calls for America to cut its losses and retreat from Iraq rather than following the counsel of "those who mindlessly seek an unattainable victory."[19]

Although the left cannot say this, it is vital from its point of view for America to withdraw before Iraqi forces are adequately trained to fight the insurgency. To advance the prospects of the left, Bush must lose, and therefore the insurgents must win. Leading leftists seem determined to settle for nothing less than total defeat. In order for this to happen, the left must keep the Iraqi people constantly guessing about whether America will pull out. As long as ordinary Iraqis fear a hasty withdrawal, they will never report insurgent activity to the government or to the Americans. Iraqis know that if American troops withdraw, the informants they leave behind will be the first ones targeted for assassination by the insurgents. Consequently America is deprived of one of its vital tools for winning the war, which is the information provided by law-abiding Iraqi citizens.

If the United States fails in Iraq, then the nation's infant democracy will be strangled in its crib. More than this, America's democracy initiative in the Middle East will collapse. This is precisely what the left wants. Not that the left is happy about the prospect of an Al Qaeda–run fundamentalist state in Iraq. It is a worthwhile price to pay, however, for inflicting a devastating defeat on Bush. This will ensure that the Democrats win back the presidency, the Congress, and the Supreme Court, restoring the supremacy the Democrats enjoyed for much of the twentieth century.

Islamic radicals like bin Laden, who once considered "America" the enemy, have come to recognize the left as a crucial ally. The radical Muslims know what military strategists from Sun Tzu to Clausewitz have pointed out—the strength of a country is determined by the sum of its military force and its will to fight. When the will is absent, then all the force in the world is useless. Contrary to the relentless propaganda from left-leaning media outlets, in reality there is no way that America can lose the ground war in Iraq. The Shia majority, which makes up 60 percent of the Iraqi population, and the Kurdish minority, which makes up 20 percent, both have a strong vested interest in supporting democracy. They are the de facto allies of America. The Kurds also happen to be one of the most pro-American people in the world. The insurgency is drawing almost exclusively from the Sunni population, which numbers 20 percent. Not that the insurgency makes up one-fifth of the Iraqi population. It is composed of a small fraction of the Sunnis, perhaps twenty to thirty thousand people. So this is not Vietnam, where there were a million men on the other side. The insurgents are ruthless, as shown by their willingness to kill fellow Muslims and attack religious sites in the hope of fomenting social chaos and civil war. So far, this desperation strategy has provoked a good deal of sectarian violence, but as Al Qaeda documents acknowledge, it has little chance to dislodge the existing government. It does not take a degree in military tactics to discover what the insurgents already know: no resistance made up of a few thousand guerrillas can win a war against the Iraqi majority backed up by the resources, training, and might of the U.S. military.

There is one way, however, for the Islamic radicals to win. They can win the war in the American mind. This is where the left fits into bin Laden's tactical scheme. Bin Laden recognizes that Al Qaeda by itself cannot destroy America's will to resist. It is impossible for bin Laden to persuade the American people to get out of Iraq. He relies on other Americans to undertake this psychological mission. To bin Laden's unbelievable good fortune, there is a group in the United States dedicated to precisely this task. The left is Al Qaeda's secret weapon in the campaign for American public opinion. As bin Laden knows, the left has already succeeded once, in Vietnam. Here again, in Iraq, the left is laboring for a similar outcome, a Saigon-style evacuation by the U.S. military.

Remember that Vietnam was a defeat for the American armed forces, but it was a victory for the political left. It was a victory in the sense that the left demanded that America accept humiliation and withdraw, and America accepted humiliation and withdrew. The left sought the "liberation" of Vietnam, and Vietnam was "liberated." This outcome turned out to be very bad for the people of Indochina, who suffered unimaginable horrors following the U.S. pullout. At the same time, the Vietnam disgrace helped to advance the leftist agenda in America. First, the antiwar cause unified the left. As we discover from histories of the period, opposition to Vietnam brought together the foreign policy left and the cultural left, so that devotees of Ho Chi Minh and devotees of hallucinogenic drugs all marched together against the war. Second, the outcome in Vietnam decimated the political influence of the right. Not only did America's defeat corrode the morale of the American military, but it also undermined patriotism and traditional values in America. The Nixon presidency was further crippled, and a new generation of liberal Democrats was elected to Congress in 1974. Finally, as historian David Allyn shows, the left's triumph in Vietnam paid handsome social dividends.[20] It greatly bolstered the counterculture, giving added impetus to women's liberation, gay rights, and the sexual revolution. So, from the left's point of view, Vietnam was not only a foreign policy success but also a cultural success. Therefore, for this group, the prospect of "another Vietnam" is an outcome that is eagerly anticipated.

Since the left is determined for its own reasons to ensure that America loses the war on terror, it becomes a natural ally for bin Laden. Together they form what may be termed the liberal-Islamic alliance against American foreign policy. Like the left, the Islamic radicals realize they are teaming up with "infidels," and they have no qualms about doing so. In Iraq, for example, Al Qaeda has shown no hesitation in making common cause with Saddam Hussein's Baathist infidels. Bin Laden calls it a "convergence of interests."[21] Both are fighting against the Americans, and so they find themselves on the same side. By the same token, bin Laden and his followers believe they can work together with America's left. Both are fighting against Bush's war on terror, and so there is another "convergence of interests."

The left's de facto alliance with Islamic fundamentalism places decent liberals and Democrats in a difficult position. Liberal Democrats have never been entirely comfortable with the left's extreme positions, and most of them would not condone working with the enemy to defeat America's war on terror. On the other hand, liberal Democrats recognize that most of the ideas and activist energy in their party come from the left. While liberal Democrats may publicly distance themselves from leftists at election time, they are reluctant to wholly reject them.

Now, however, the stakes are higher. First, the left has carried the liberal doctrine of autonomy so far that it is virtually indistinguishable from the promotion of vice and decadence. Freedom has come to be defined by its grossest abuses, and "progress" for the left has come to mean progress in moral degeneracy. As a result, the ideas of "freedom" and "liberalism" have become repellent to many traditional people around the world, especially in the Muslim world. Liberals should not allow their good name to be corrupted in this way. Liberal Democrats should articulate a vision of autonomy that promotes self-fulfillment while recognizing that there are higher and lower forms of autonomy. Moreover, liberals know that there are certain things—like genocide and racial bigotry—that are wrong, quite apart from our subjective impulses. It is time for liberals to integrate autonomy into a framework that restores the traditional distinction between right and wrong.

Second, liberal Democrats who take their cues from the left are generally hoping to improve their prospects for winning elections. In the process, however, they are making an unconscionable "pact with the devil" and gravely harming the security interests of the United States. Is it worth risking the loss of the Middle East, not to mention the chance of further 9/11-style attacks, to improve the electoral chances for Hillary? Abraham Lincoln said that if America were ever destroyed, it would be from within. The left is the internal enemy that is helping the external enemy achieve its goal of the destruction of America.

Decent liberals and Democrats have every right to oppose the current administration, but they should do so without succumbing to the dangerous and irresponsible tactics of the left. Like Joseph Lieberman, Thomas Friedman, Peter Beinart, and others, the good liberal can make his case for how the war on terror could be fought better, with a view to improving the chances of defeating Islamic radicalism, protecting America's vital interests, and securing the safety of American citizens. The only choice for decent liberals and Democrats is to repudiate the left and consign it to the margins of political respectability where it came from, and where it has always belonged.

ELEVEN

Battle Plan for the Right

How to Defeat the Enemy at
Home and Abroad

CONSERVATIVES NEED A new direction in the war on terror, and a new strategy in the culture war. So far the right is fighting the two wars separately and also unwisely, courting the wrong people while alienating its most important allies. No wonder the outcome of the war on terror remains uncertain, and conservatives face the prospect of being routed in the 2008 elections. What is required is a novel approach based on the recognition that the war on terror and the culture war are related. Indeed they are two different arenas of the same struggle. Given this fact, we need to pose two questions. How can we use the culture war to win the war on terror? How can we use the war on terror to win the culture war? In this concluding chapter I offer foreign and domestic policy strategies that will help conservatives win both wars.

The danger now facing the right is obvious. The consequences of losing the debate over Iraq may be the loss of Iraq itself. Such an outcome would not only imperil America's vital stake in the Middle East; Bush's Iraq failure would be used to discredit conservative foreign policy for a generation. Are we ready for Vietnam all over again? If the left can convert national security—usually a source of political strength for the right—into a liability, then it has vastly improved its chances for winning future elections. If conservatives lose badly, all three branches of government—the presidency, the Congress, and the Supreme Court—could end up in the grip of the opposition. The entire conservative agenda, from tax cuts to school choice to restricting abortion, would be stalled. Moreover, the right's political loss would be followed by a cultural assault seeking to demonize Bush as another Nixon and conservatives as dangerous fanatics who cannot again be trusted with power. At a time when the right is within sight of complete victory, it risks losing everything and returning to the minority status it held in the years before Reagan.

So far conservatives and Republicans seem eerily blind to the prospect of political annihilation. Their political strategy can be described as looking for friends in all the wrong places. First, many conservatives attempt to persuade leftists to wake up to the threat of the radical Muslims and join a united American war on terror. Call this the "One America" strategy. Second, the right intends to rebuild ties with Europe so that the West can generate the kind of alliance it had against the Soviet Union during the Cold War. Call this the "One West" strategy. Finally, the right is on a quest to locate liberals in the Islamic world who can be recruited in the cause of "civilization" against "barbarism." Call this the "Don Quixote" strategy.

None of these approaches is working. We have found the liberals in the Muslim world, and it hasn't made a bit of difference, even though all eight of them have agreed to support us. The Europeans don't share our conservative principles, and now that the Cold War is over, they have realized that their interests diverge from ours. The stereotypes of European anti-Americanism (Bush the mad cowboy, Bush the Christian fundamentalist) are largely based on hostility to American conservatism. Even more remote is the prospect of persuading the left to join Bush and the conservatives in the war against Islamic radicalism. Has this approach to date produced a single convert? Nor will it, since the basic strategy of the left is to work with the Islamic radicals in order to defeat Bush and the right.

It's time for conservatives to jettison these self-defeating strategies. They are rooted in nostalgic beliefs about a common Western
heritage and common American culture, as well as erroneous assumptions about Islam. Instead, we need a multicultural strategy
based upon the firmer foundation of common beliefs and values. So
far Bush has been fighting his war against Islamic radicalism mainly
on the military front. Such a campaign is indispensable, but it can
never succeed, no matter how many insurgents it kills, if the supply
of radical Muslims is continually replenished from the ranks of the
traditional Muslims. The traditional Muslims are the only people
who are capable of stopping radical Islam. Thus victory in the war on
terror depends on America's ability to create divisions between traditional Muslims and radical Muslims. America can decisively win
this war by allying with traditional Muslims, and working with them
to defeat the Islamic radicals.

The best way for the right to make such an alliance is to convey
to Muslims that we share common ground with them on traditional
values. Conservatives can communicate this message by challenging
and attacking the left and the Europeans on the international stage.
Instead of trying to unify America and the West, the right should
highlight the division between red America and blue America, and
also between traditional America and decadent Europe. By resisting
the depravity of the left and the Europeans, conservatives can win
friends among Muslims and other traditional people around the
world.

On the domestic front, the right must stop its petty infighting and
engage in a concerted political campaign to expose the left as the
enemy at home. In order to achieve its own objectives, the left is
serving as bin Laden's public relations team in America, and conservatives should not be afraid to say this. Conservatives must show the
de facto alliance between the Islamic radicals and the American radicals, and demand that mainstream liberals and Democrats expel this
faction from their camp. In short, the right should force liberals to
banish the left from the precincts of political respectability. In this
way conservatives can turn the tide both at home and abroad, and

improve their chances for winning both the war on terror and the culture war.

LET US EXPLORE these themes in greater detail. First I want to examine how conservatives can use the culture war to win the war against Islamic radicalism. If the American left is covertly allied with the radical Muslims, the American right should openly ally with traditional Muslims. Former CIA analyst Reuel Marc Gerecht is one of the few people to recognize that "these religious traditionalists—and not the liberal secularists—are the most valuable allies the United States has."[1]

Traditional Muslims are in a difficult position. Numerous surveys such as the Pew Research study have shown that the vast majority reject terrorism. At the same time they don't want their condemnations of terrorism to sound like an endorsement of Western secularism and moral depravity. In general the traditional Muslims also reject violence, although some will approve violence that is used in what they consider "wars of national liberation." Moreover, the Pew survey shows that very few Muslims consider democracy a "Western way of things that would not work here." The World Values Survey shows that in most Muslim nations support for self-government is just as high as in the West. In some countries more than 90 percent of Muslims endorse democracy—a higher percentage than in the United States.[2] Muslims want democracy, but at the same time they want real democracy. They want governments that reflect Muslim interests, not American or Israeli interests.

For traditional Muslims, self-rule also means the right to establish a society under God's rule and governed, at least in some aspects, by Islamic law. This is not to say that traditional Muslims are enemies of individual freedom. They support basic freedoms, such as the right to own property, the right to assembly, the right to one's religious beliefs, the right to vote, and the right to criticize the government. At the same time, they reject contemporary liberalism. Traditional Muslims do not support the right to blaspheme against

Islam, the right to sex before marriage, the right to no-fault divorce, the right to abort one's offspring, or homosexual rights. Nothing discredits freedom in the eyes of traditional Muslims so much as the equation of freedom with what they perceive as gross immorality and licentiousness. For many Muslims, it is not freedom but moral depravity that is today the distinguishing feature—and leading export—of American civilization. When traditional Muslims see how freedom is used in America, they become increasingly convinced that the Islamic world is better off without this kind of freedom.

What traditional Muslims identify as the sins of the United States, however, are really the sins of the cultural left. Traditional Muslims don't see the Americans who work hard, go to church, and look after their families. Instead they turn on their TV sets and witness the perverted lifestyles that Hollywood presents as sophisticated, admirable, and typical of "the American way." In the United Nations and elsewhere, Muslims confront feminists, zero-population-growth activists, and sexual libertines who present themselves as champions of American and indeed universal values. This is America's face to the non-Western world as portrayed by the left. As a consequence of the left's prominent role in international activism and popular culture, traditional Muslims see one America and do not realize that there are two Americas. They see the immorality of blue America and take it to be representative of all of America. The Turkish journalist Mustafa Akyol points out that this ignorance is exploited by bin Laden and his allies. "The masterminds of Islamic radicalism work hard to mask the religiosity and decency of average Americans."[3]

In order to build alliances with traditional Muslims, the right must take three critical steps. First, stop attacking Islam. Conservatives have to cease blaming Islam for the behavior of the radical Muslims. Recently the right has produced a spate of Islamophobic tracts with titles like *Islam Unveiled, Sword of the Prophet,* and *The Myth of Islamic Tolerance*. There is probably no better way to repel traditional Muslims, and push them into the radical camp, than to attack their religion and their prophet. Conservatives should also reject Huntington's doctrine of a "clash of civilizations." This, too, sets up a false division between the Islamic world and the West, placing traditional Muslims and radical Muslims in the same camp, which is exactly where bin Laden wants them. Moreover, Huntington ignores the clash of civilizations within the West, and he wrongly assumes that a social or religious conservative in America would have more in common with an American or European leftist than with a traditional Muslim. Admittedly some on the right may feel uncomfortable about teaming up with Muslims. Yes, I would rather go to a baseball game or have a drink with Michael Moore than with the grand mufti of Egypt. But when it comes to core beliefs, I'd have to confess that I'm closer to the dignified fellow in the long robe and prayer beads than to the slovenly fellow with the baseball cap.

As much as possible, conservatives need to enlist traditional Muslims in the war against radical Islam. For this reason the 2005 ports controversy involving the small country of Dubai was particularly harmful. With unerring opportunism, the left seized on the issue. Leftists pretended to be outraged at the prospect of Muslims administering America's ports, even though the security of the ports would have continued to be the responsibility of U.S. government agencies. The left also saw a chance to subvert the Bush administration's effort to build ties with friendly Muslims. Partly as a result of liberal political pressure, but also as a consequence of foolish prejudice, many conservatives in the House and Senate joined the chorus demanding cancellation of the ports deal. Finally the government of Dubai chivalrously stepped aside, but the whole episode left many traditional Muslims jaded and frustrated.

If conservatives hope to make friends in the Muslim world, they must stop holding silly seminars on whether Islam is compatible with democracy. In reality, a majority of the world's Muslims today live under democratic governments—in Indonesia, Malaysia, India, Bangladesh, Nigeria, and Turkey, not to mention Muslims living in Western countries. There is nothing in the Koran or the Islamic tradition that forbids democracy. Islam calls for the Muslim community to be governed by a caliph who is God's viceregent on earth, but no procedure is specified for who should be the leader or how he should be chosen. The Koran does call for governance to be done by *shura*, or consultation, and as the Muslim historian Hamid Algar writes, "An election is nothing more than a mechanism for the implementation of this general Koranic principle." Even Islamic radicals like Qutb and Mawdudi admit this. The only caveat, as Khaled Abou El Fadl points out, is that "a case for democracy presented from within Islam must accept the idea of God's sovereignty. It cannot substitute popular sovereignty for divine sovereignty but must instead show how popular sovereignty . . . expresses God's authority, properly understood."[4] This mirrors the Declaration of Independence's argument that it is the Creator who endows us with our inalienable rights, and thus it is a perfect expression of the conservative understanding of American democracy.

A SECOND WAY for conservatives to build ties with traditional Muslims is to let them govern their own societies. This is the meaning of Islamic democracy—Muslims must choose their own way. Iraq is the test case for this. If the people of Iraq want Islam to be the state religion, we should allow it to happen. If they want sharia, let them have it. But wouldn't all this be a violation of true democracy? Not at all. As Noah Feldman points out, England has an established church, so religious establishment is not incompatible with religious toleration. Israel is simultaneously a democracy and a Jewish state. Moreover, most European countries have democratically chosen to relinquish some of their economic liberties in the interest of economic security. So why can't Muslim countries choose to give up some of their civil liberties in order to promote civic morality? Just as democracy has enabled Japan to establish a very different kind of society than France or America, so democracy will enable Muslims to define their own civilization. As philosopher Charles Taylor says, we should recognize the concept of "multiple modernities."[5] This is multiculturalism in its truest and best sense, and it deserves conservative support. The right should recognize, as the left does not, that democratization does not mean Westernization.

In this context, it is time for conservatives to retire the tiresome invocation of Turkey as a model for Islamic society. No Muslim country is going the way of Turkey, and even Turkey is no longer going the way of Turkey. Atatürk thought of himself as a European, and what he did in Turkey was anomalous and, in all candor, ridiculous. Atatürk abolished the religious courts in favor of the Swiss legal code, ended religious education in schools, legalized gambling and alcohol, replaced existing commercial laws with the German commercial law, outlawed Islamic dress in public buildings, abolished the Islamic calendar, changed the alphabet, and converted the great mosque of the Hagia Sofia into a museum. As the liberator of Turkey—a kind of Turkish Gandhi—Atatürk could in his lifetime get away with these extreme measures. But now his militant secularization of Turkey is being reversed, and on balance it is a good thing. Muslims have the right to live in Islamic states under Muslim law if they wish.

Support for democracy does not mean that conservatives need a worldwide campaign to overthrow unelected regimes. While democracy is desirable as a long-term goal, it is not always in America's interest to have democracy now. Foreign policy is not philanthropy, but rather a way for the United States to promote its interests worldwide. America is not obliged to use its resources to produce anti-American outcomes. There are hereditary monarchs in the Middle East, as in the Gulf kingdoms, who are pro-American and enjoy fairly high levels of popular esteem. It would be imprudent under current circumstances to pressure these kingdoms to democratize or liberalize. (They are already quite liberal by Middle Eastern standards.) Nor should America seek to coerce tyrants like Musharraf, Mubarak, and the Saudi royal family to become more liberal or secular. If they do, they will become further alienated from their people and become more vulnerable to being overthrown. When there are democratic results, as with the election victories of Hamas or the Muslim Brotherhood, America must recognize the legitimacy of the people's choice. But this imposes no obligation on the United States to provide aid or support to governments that oppose American interests and threaten American allies.

It is necessary to show that democracy works in the Middle East, and then to let the traditional Muslims pursue it for themselves. Iraq represents America's initiative not to establish democracy everywhere but to establish democracy somewhere. This is a good time for conservatives to revive a new form of the Reagan doctrine, which held that people should fight for their own freedom, and if they do, then America will help. In Iraq, of course, there was no prospect of the Iraqi people overthrowing Hussein on their own. But even in Iraq American policy is moving toward the Reagan doctrine. Increasingly Iraqis are protecting their own freedom while America moves into a supporting role. An updated Reagan doctrine would also be a good policy for the United States to employ in Iran. As Iran continues to pursue nuclear weapons and promote Islamic radicalism on the world stage, diplomacy and the threat of sanctions cannot in the long term deter the mullahs from doing what they are clearly determined to do. Consequently the best option for America is to work with pro-democracy forces to overthrow the existing regime. Such forces do exist, but until now they have lacked organization, confidence, and most of all opportunity. This could change rapidly. If Iranians are willing to challenge the authority of the ruling mullahs, America should stand ready to assist them with material, financial, and if necessary military support. Replacing the mullahs' regime in Iran should be an important priority for America because Iran is the one major country that the Islamic radicals now control.

Traditional Muslims have numerous concerns about American foreign policy, and most stem from the belief that America is prejudiced or unfairly hostile to Muslims. I believe these concerns are largely erroneous, and many of them could be dispelled if the administration clearly articulated its strategic concerns and made the moral case for America. This is the area in which the Bush administration has failed abysmally. Presidents have to recognize that deeds must be backed up with words. Bush seems incapable of taking on the critics of American foreign policy, and no one else in the government seems up to the task.

So my third recommendation is for the Bush administration, and conservatives generally, to level with traditional Muslims and talk sense to them. Currently Muslims who raise difficult questions about U.S. foreign policy are met with uneasy equivocations. Many traditional Muslims who do not support Hamas or Hezbollah nevertheless question the role of America as an honest broker in the Middle East.

They note that while the United States poses as a neutral peace-maker, its politicians routinely assure their home constituencies they are unequivocally on the side of Israel. Muslims demand to know if America is an umpire or a player. America's diplomats make supreme efforts to dodge this question, hoping that the Muslims will stop posing it. This hope is unrealistic, and moreover, there is no reason for the United States to equivocate in this way. Instead, the Bush administration should say, "Yes, we are on Israel's side, and there are reasons for it. There is a religious affinity between Jews and Christians. Israel is a democratic society like the United States. Many Americans are much more comfortable with Jews, whom they know, than with Muslims, whom they don't know. Older Americans remember that during the Cold War many Arab countries were allied with the Soviet Union, while Israel has been a reliable American ally. Memories of the Holocaust remain strong, and there is a lot of guilt about what happened to the Jews, in part because they had no place of their own to go to. Finally, Jews exert effective political influence in both of America's major parties, and Muslims have not developed that." The advantage of such candor with traditional Muslims is that it wins their respect, even when they find themselves on a different side. Muslims, who understand the language of political self-interest, might oppose America's actions in a given situation, but they cannot deny that if they were in America's position they would act in the same way.

IN THE SOCIAL domain, the right is perfectly poised to forge an alliance with traditional Muslims. The natural basis for this alliance is the moral framework shared by Christianity, Judaism, and Islam. Conservatives need to discover what several thoughtful Muslims have already recognized. The attitude of the ordinary Muslims to the liberal assault on the family, Seyyed Hossein Nasr writes, "is not much different from those of traditional Jews and Christians in the West." As Nasr puts it, "Secularism is the common enemy. . . . Men and women in the West who are still devoted to the life of faith should know that those closest to them in this world are Muslims."

Mustafa Akyol makes the same point. "From the Muslim point of view, Christians are the closest friends and allies in the world." He offers conservatives some sage advice: "America must help Muslims see that it is indeed a nation under God. The culture it exports should celebrate more than materialism, disbelief, selfishness, and hedonism. America must do a better job of portraying its principles of decency. Otherwise it will be despised by devout Muslims throughout the world, and the radicals will channel that contempt into violence."[6]

The implication of this counsel is that conservatives must support rather than condemn Muslims when they defend their traditional values. The right must stop its ridiculous preening as the champion of secularism and feminism—a pose that does not fool the left and only alienates traditional people around the world. Nor should the right make the disastrous mistake of defending moral depravity as it did at Abu Ghraib. Moreover, the right must strive to prevent the cultural left from exporting bogus rights and cultural debauchery abroad. One way conservatives can convey their seriousness about this is by choosing appropriate occasions to attack Hollywood. Of course, the right-wing media does protest the debauched values of the movie and music industry. But this time we must do it in the full recognition that the domestic culture war has international ramifications. So the conservative critique of Hollywood must be launched with the global audience in mind. The right should organize an international conference on the effects of Hollywood and American popular culture on non-Western cultures. It would be fascinating to hear from Muslims and other traditional people about how their local cultures are being affected by Hollywood movies and TV shows. Besides, on what basis would self-styled American liberals object to a proposal so open-minded and multicultural?

Conservatives can also work with traditional Muslims, and with traditional people from around the world, to promote shared values at the United Nations. At the very least the right can lead a global coalition to thwart U.N. resolutions undermining the family. A hint of how this might succeed can be seen from the 1994 U.N. Population Conference in Cairo, where Catholic groups from Western and non-Western countries teamed up with Muslim groups to exclude any reference to abortion as a legitimate form of birth control. More recently, the Bush administration took a bold step in the U.N. when it supported a resolution introduced by Iran to deny consulting status to a group of homosexual organizations led by the International Lesbian and Gay Association. This group is so outlandish that until a few years ago it included as affiliates pedophile clubs like the North American Man-Boy Love Association. Predictably, leftist groups were incensed by the Bush administration's stance. Imagine siding with the Iranians! Congressman Tom Lantos, a California Democrat who serves on the Congressional Human Rights Caucus, warned that Bush's decision was a "major setback" for a "core component of our nation's human rights diplomacy."[7] If so, our nation's human rights diplomacy is way off track and more such "setbacks" are needed.

Conservatives usually criticize the U.N. for its financial corruption and shameless anti-Americanism. But the U.N. has also become an instrument of left-wing cultural imperialism, and this part of its agenda has been completely overlooked on the right. Conservatives typically call for America to withdraw from the U.N. or stop funding it. The right's hostility is understandable, and was no doubt heightened by the U.N.'s refusal to authorize the Iraq invasion. Conservatives pay a price, however, for their rejectionist attitude. The left is able to portray the right as a group of isolationist cranks. Moreover, the left is able to implement its global agenda at the U.N. without being challenged in that forum by the American right.

Conservatives should recall that during the Cold War, the U.N. had the same flawed structure it does now, but the right was able to use the organization to choreograph symbolic confrontations with the Soviet Union. A series of high-profile diplomats, from Daniel Patrick Moynihan to Jeane Kirkpatrick, made the U.N. an international stage on which to successfully dramatize the differences between the totalitarian state and the free society. If the Bush administration took the U.N. seriously, it could better bend the organization to its purpose. Rather than surrender the U.N. to the left, conservatives should become more involved, not merely in the Security Council but also in the General Assembly, where American influence has been weak. Not that we need the U.N. to highlight the crimes of Islamic radicalism. It is much more important for the right to make the U.N. the international theater to expose the depravity of the left, and thereby build ties with traditional people around the world. The right can restore American influence in the U.N. by working cooperatively with non-Western cultures to stop the liberal cultural aggression that operates under the pretext of "human rights" and "international law."

None of this is to deny that there are universal human rights. These are the rights affirmed in the United Nations charter. There is the right to human dignity, the prohibition of genocide, the right to practice one's religion, and the right to marry and to form a family. These rights are the product of the old liberalism—of classical liberalism—and they are rights that traditional Muslims and traditional people around the world generally support. There is a crucial distinction, however, between the legitimate rights of classical liberalism and the bogus rights of the cultural left. Conservatives should feel no qualms about allying with traditional people around the world to disband this regime of bogus rights. In this way, the right can deliver a major blow to the international left and undermine the left's domestic claim to be the party promoting "universal rights." In reality, the left is promoting a parochial Western agenda that is morally repulsive to, and emphatically rejected by, most of the world.

Conservatives must strive to convince traditional Muslims that there are two Americas, and that one of these has a lot in common with them. To the degree that conservatives highlight the traditional morality of red America, they risk further alienating many Europeans. Let them be alienated. Despite the ancestral attachment that many on the right have for Europe, conservatives gain nothing by courting people who do not share their basic values, either on foreign policy or on social issues. Conservatives should pay less attention to Europe and more to their real allies in the rest of the world. During the Danish cartoon controversy, for example, the American right made a huge tactical blunder in viewing the entire matter through the prism of free speech. Yes, we support free speech, but that wasn't the only issue here. As the Danish, French, and German newspapers that reprinted the cartoons understood, what was also at stake was blasphemy as a social virtue, what one newspaper arrogantly termed "the right to blaspheme against God." So this would have been the perfect opportunity for conservatives to distinguish the United States from Europe, and declare that in this country we do not consider ridiculing other people's religion to be a sign of virtue or enlightenment. So how should American conservatives have responded to the cartoons? With the same distaste that American liberals would react to cartoons mocking Martin Luther King! The general lesson is that while Europeans cozy up to the radical Muslims, conservatives must move closer to the traditional Muslims, and one way to do this is to seize every opportunity to repudiate European decadence.

Here is the message that conservatives should convey to traditional Muslims around the world: "We know that America has some serious cultural problems. We consider these our problems, and we are taking responsibility for addressing them. Our biggest task is not one of nation building abroad but of nation building in America. Leave this project to us. Do not support the radical Muslims who attack America. This is an intolerable strategy that gives Islam a bad name, and we will resist it with all our power. It is also unnecessary because you have allies in America who are doing what we can to make our country better. There are healthy and wholesome aspects of American culture that enrich our lives, and we would be happy to export these to you, if indeed you want them. At the same time, we are determined to reverse the tide of liberal immorality in the United States, and we pledge to do what we can to stop the export of cultural depravity to your society. When we are unable to do this, we will speak out and clarify that this part of America makes us ashamed. In this way you will see that we, like you, are working not merely toward the free society but also the decent society." On this basis the right can establish its own truce with traditional Islam, mirroring the truce that bin Laden seeks with the American left.

WE HAVE SEEN how conservatives can win the war on terror by more effectively fighting the culture war at home and on the international stage. I now want to explore the other side of the equation by raising an issue pertinent to the next presidential election. Our elections have become global media events, giving conservatives a unique opportunity not only to address the American people but also the rest of the world. So, how can the right use the war on terror to win the culture war? This is a crucial question because the war on terror has never been solely about the future of the Islamic world. It is also about the future of America, about what kind of people we are and about which values we want to project abroad.

Now conservatives need to inquire whether there is a way to harness the foreign policy debate over terrorism in such a way as to redefine, and reinvigorate, the domestic culture war. It is impossible to overstate the importance for the right to win the culture war. More than anything else, it is the culture war that has been the reason for the right's electoral success in the last decade and a half. Conservatives, having fallen into a kind of governing lassitude, sorely need some of the bold confrontational strategies of the kind they employed when they were in the minority. In order to give the culture war a new thrust, I propose that conservatives adopt a two-part strategy.

Expose the domestic insurgency. Oddly enough, many conservatives continue to treat the cultural left as a kind of well-meaning opposition that is deluded or simply hasn't come up with its own effective strategy for fighting the Islamic radicals. In reality, the left already has a foreign policy and a strategy, and it is called working in tandem with bin Laden to defeat Bush. As we have seen, the left and the Islamic radicals operate like the two sides of a scissors, each prong working separately, but toward the same end. Conservatives need to identify the enemy at home and show its tacit relationship with the foreign enemy. Not only is there a close parallel between the rhetoric of the two groups, but they have the same goal of defeating Bush in Iraq, and they need each other to accomplish this goal. In short, the left is the domestic insurgency that provides a counterpart to the Iraq insurgency. It is at least as dangerous as any of bin Laden's American sleeper cells.

Conservatives need to expose the alliance between the left and Islamic radicals. Once they do this, the leftist chorus in the media will let out a banshee-like howl of indignation. In order to silence the right, the domestic insurgents will no doubt hurl the charge of "McCarthyism." Conservatives should not be intimidated by this accusation. Although McCarthy was vilified for claiming that there were communists and Soviet sympathizers in the U.S. government, the files of the former Soviet Union reveal that he was largely right, even if he made some of his points in a reckless and buffoonish way. Moreover, the charge of McCarthyism is a diversion because (as I have repeatedly pointed out throughout this book) I am not accusing anyone of treason or even of anti-Americanism. At any rate, with the end of the Cold War, the weight of the accusation will be greatly diminished. At the same time, the left's shrieks of outrage will confirm that the right has finally come close to accurately describing the strategy of the enemy at home.

Unlike McCarthy, who never disclosed the identities of the communists and Soviet sympathizers in high places, I intend to name the enemy at home. Recognizing that list making is a tenuous business, I provide mine solely for the purpose of truth in advertising. Drawing from the various species of leftists portrayed in this book, I offer this roster of people and groups that deserve the label of domestic insurgents. Here is the litmus test that confirms their eligibility. If you presume that these individuals want Bush to win and bin Laden to lose the war on terror, their rhetoric and actions are utterly baffling. By contrast, if you presume that they want bin Laden to win and Bush to lose the war, then their statements and actions make perfect sense.

The Congressional Left: Ted Kennedy, Patrick Leahy, Barbara Boxer, Russ Feingold, Hillary Clinton, Robert Byrd, Patty Murray, Barbara Mikulski, Nancy Pelosi, Charles Rangel, Carl Levin, Tom Lantos, Maxine Waters, Ed Markey, John Conyers, Dennis Kucinich, Cynthia McKinney, Barney Frank, Jim McDermott, and Jack Reed

The Intellectual Left: Noam Chomsky, Howard Zinn, Edward Said (deceased, but his influence is very much alive), Richard Rorty, Martha Nussbaum, Rashid Khalidi, Eric Hobsbawm,

Cornel West, Sean Wilentz, Paul Starr, Robert Reich, Eric
Foner, Laurence Tribe, Henry Louis Gates, Tony Judt, Thomas
Frank, and Garry Wills

The Hollywood Left: Martin Sheen, Barbra Streisand, Tim
Robbins, Susan Sarandon, Sean Penn, Harry Belafonte, Rob
Reiner, Rosie O'Donnell, Oliver Stone, Danny Glover, Jane
Fonda, Spike Lee, Alec Baldwin, Norman Lear, Cameron
Diaz, Sharon Stone, Ed Asner, and Janeane Garofalo

The Activist Left: Howard Dean, Michael Moore, George
Soros, Cindy Sheehan, Ramsey Clark, Nicholas De Genova,
Markos Moulitsas, Nan Aron, Ralph Neas, Paul Begala, Amy
Goodman, Ward Churchill, Jim Wallis, Mumia Abu-Jamal,
Gary Kamiya, and Arundhati Roy

The Foreign Policy Left: Chalmers Johnson, Robert Fisk,
David Cole, Gore Vidal, Jonathan Schell, William Blum,
James Carroll, Seymour Hersh, Jimmy Carter, Bob Herbert,
George Galloway, Mark Danner, Robert Scheer, Juan Cole,
Anthony Lewis, and Richard Falk

The Cultural Left: Frank Rich, Al Franken, Maureen Dowd,
Salman Rushdie, Tony Kushner, Toni Morrison, Jane Smiley,
Arianna Huffington, Eve Ensler, Kurt Vonnegut, Norman
Mailer, Katha Pollitt, Eric Alterman, Karen Armstrong, Bill
Moyers, Ellen Willis, Barbara Ehrenreich, Molly Ivins, Mari
Matsuda, Thomas Frank, Joe Conason, and Wendy Kaminer

Leftist Organizations: Act Now to Stop War and End Racism
(ANSWER), United for Peace and Justice, Peaceful Tomorrow,
Open Society Institute, National Lawyers Guild, Human
Rights Watch, Center for Constitutional Rights, Amnesty
International, Ford Foundation, Code Pink, Planned
Parenthood, American Civil Liberties Union (ACLU), National
Abortion Rights Action League (NARAL), People for the
American Way, and moveon.org

Split liberal Democrats from the left. Since 9/11 President Bush has
made it clear that America's war will be waged not only against ter-

rorists and insurgents but also against those who sponsor and support them. This logic has a domestic equivalent. Should conservatives do political battle with the domestic insurgency while ignoring the intellectual movement and the political party that sponsors it? We know who the domestic insurgents are, and we know who is sheltering and supporting them. There is a symbiotic relationship between mainstream Democrats and the left that conservatives simply cannot ignore. Typically the Democratic Party looks to its left wing for ideas, activism, and money. When Democratic candidates need funds, they turn to the music industry and Hollywood. When they need advice on judicial nominations, they bring in activist groups like NARAL, the ACLU, and People for the American Way. During the election season, Democrats count on left-wing blogs and groups like moveon.org to rally their activist base.

Leftists, for their part, benefit from the political cover provided by mainstream liberalism. The leftist fantasies of Michael Moore became respectable when leading Democrats began to fawn over him, and when he was invited to share Jimmy Carter's box at the 2004 Democratic Convention. (You are unlikely to see David Duke in Nancy Reagan's box at the Republican Convention.) Not only do liberal Democrats propel domestic insurgents like Moore and Cindy Sheehan to national prominence, but the left is also able to deploy "useful idiots" from the Democratic camp in order to advance its ideological agenda. A perfect example is Congressman John Murtha, whose great value to the left is that he endorses leftist propositions while sporting war medals on his chest. Every time Murtha makes ethnocentric and ignorant proclamations about Iraq and about Muslims, two subjects on which he knows virtually nothing, the left parades his military credentials to immunize him from criticism. Hey, this man served his country! Don't question *his* loyalty, even when he makes the same arguments as Noam Chomsky and Osama bin Laden.

Conservatives should force liberal Democrats either to embrace the domestic insurgency or to repudiate it. This is a choice that liberal Democrats will make supreme efforts to avoid. They do not wish to disavow the left because they rely so heavily on its ideas and activism. Conservatives must pressure liberal Democrats to decide how they want to be perceived by the American people. Do liberal Democrats agree with Cindy Sheehan and Arundhati Roy that Bush is more dangerous than bin Laden? Do they support the claims of Howard Zinn and other leftist pundits that the Iraqi insurgents are freedom fighters who represent the true voice of the Iraqi people? Will they echo Howard Dean's insistence that there is no way America can win in Iraq? Are they, like Nancy Soderberg and Gary Kamiya, waiting and hoping that things go wrong for America in Iraq? Are they unmoved, like Markos Moulitsas of dailykos.com, when U.S. civilians are murdered by Islamic fanatics? Would they, like William Blum, welcome bin Laden's endorsement of their foreign policy views? Do they applaud Michael Moore's plaintive wish that bin Laden's 9/11 attack should have been directed at red America instead of blue America? By driving a wedge between liberal Democrats and the left, and forcing the liberals to spurn the domestic insurgency or be tarred by it, conservatives can strengthen their political prospects and at the same time weaken bin Laden's allies in the United States.

None of the strategies outlined here is easy, but each of them needs careful consideration in view of the peculiarity of our situation. It's a two-front war in which conservatives are embroiled, a military fight against the radical Muslims abroad and a political battle against the radical left at home. These two forces have formed a strange coalition—a kind of alliance of the vicious and the immoral—and they are now working together against us. We have to recognize this, and take them on simultaneously. There is no way to restore the culture without winning the war on terror. Conversely, the only way to win the war on terror is to win the culture war. Thus we arrive at a sobering truth. In order to crush the Islamic radicals abroad, we must defeat the enemy at home.

NOTES

INTRODUCTION

1. Michael Moore, "Death, Downtown," September 12, 2001, michael-moore.com.

2. "You Helped This Happen," transcript of remarks by Jerry Falwell on the September 13 edition of the *700 Club;* "Falwell Apologizes to Gays, Feminists, Lesbians," CNN.com, posted September 14, 2001.

3. Ahmed Rashid, *Taliban,* Yale University Press, New Haven, 2001, p. 115.

4. Paul Berman, *Terror and Liberalism,* W. W. Norton, New York, 2000, p. 7.

5. Kristine Holmgren, "Nightmare of Fascism Seems Too Real Since Sept. 11 Attacks," *St. Paul Pioneer Press,* November 20, 2001.

6. Robert Byrd, *Losing America,* W. W. Norton, New York, 2004, p. 91.

7. Ibid., pp. 129, 178.

8. Salman Rushdie, *Imaginary Homelands,* Viking, New York, 1991, p. 389. Maureen Dowd, "Rove's Revenge," *New York Times,* November 7, 2004. Nina Siegal, "The Progressive Interview: Art Spiegelman," *Progressive,* January 2005, p. 37. Wendy Kaminer, "Our Very Own Taliban," *American Prospect,* online edition, September 17, 2001.

9. Transcript of Cindy Sheehan remarks, rally in support of Lynne Stewart, San Francisco State University, April 27, 2005, discoverthenetworks.org. Edward Said, *From Oslo to Iraq,* Pantheon Books, New York, 2004, p. 229. Jonathan Raban, "September 11: The View from the West," *New York Review of Books,* September 22, 2005, p. 8. Jane Smiley, "Why Americans Hate Democrats," November 4, 2004, slate.msn.com. Eric Alterman, "Corrupt, Incompetent and Off-Center," *The Nation,* November 7, 2005, p. 12. Jonathan Schell, "The Hidden State Steps Forward," *The Nation,* January 9, 2006. Garry Wills, "Fringe Government," *New York Review of Books,* October 6, 2005, p. 48.

10. Statement of Senator Edward Kennedy on the Federal Marriage

Amendment, July 13, 2004; statement of Senator Edward Kennedy on Iraq, September 10, 2004. Clinton cited by Kate O'Beirne, "Hillary Prepares," *National Review,* October 10, 2005, p. 34. Markey cited by Lewis Lapham, "Democracyland," *Harper's,* March 2005, p. 8.

11.   Graffito in "Iraq 182," collected and translated by Amir Nayef al-Sayegh, *Harper's,* November 2004, p. 19. Zawahiri cited in "Al Qaeda Number Two Hits Out at U.S. in New Audiotape," Agence France-Presse, February 11, 2005.

12.   Bernard Lewis, *Islam and the West,* Oxford University Press, N.Y., 1993, p. 35.

13.   "Interview: Osama Bin Laden," *Frontline,* May 1998, pbs.org.

14.   Benazir Bhutto, "Western Media: The Prism of Immorality," *New Perspectives Quarterly,* fall 1998, p. 32. Bernard Lewis, *The Crisis of Islam,* Modern Library Press, New York, 2003, pp. 80–81.

15.   Fareed Zakaria, "Culture Is Destiny: A Conversation with Lee Kuan Yew," *Foreign Affairs,* March-April 1994.

16.   Neil MacFarquhar, "Bin Laden Denounces Muslim Infidels," *San Diego Union-Tribune,* November 4, 2001, p. A-3.

17.   Eve Ensler, *The Vagina Monologues,* Villard, New York, 2001, pp. xxviii–xxix.

18.   Bin Laden cited in *The 9/11 Commission Report,* W. W. Norton, New York, 2004, p. 54. "Bin Laden's Statement: The Sword Fell," *New York Times,* October 8, 2001, p. B-7.

19.   Anne Norton, *Leo Strauss and the Politics of American Empire,* Yale University Press, New Haven, 2004, p. 216. Mari Matsuda, "A Dangerous Place," *Boston Review,* December 2002–January 2003. Rashid Khalidi, *Resurrecting Empire,* Beacon Press, Boston, 2004, p. xi. Reprinted in Edward Said, *The Politics of Dispossession,* Vintage, New York, 1995, p. 298.

20.   Transcript of Osama bin Laden speech, October 30, 2004, aljazeera.net.

21.   Michael Moore, "Heads Up," April 14, 2004, michaelmoore.com. James Carroll, *Crusade,* Metropolitan Books, New York, 2004, p. 3. Joe Conason, "Bush's Ideological Quagmire," September 24, 2005, salon.com. Gwynne Dyer, *Future Tense,* McClelland & Stewart, Toronto, 2004, p. 9. Arundhati Roy, *An Ordinary Person's Guide to Empire,* South End Press, Boston, 2004, p. 94.

ONE

1. *The 9/11 Commission Report,* W. W. Norton, New York, 2004, p. 154.

2. Early on the report offers this explanation of the motives of the enemy: "Its purpose is to rid the world of religious and political pluralism, the plebiscite, and equal rights for women." This is one of the few unsupported statements in an otherwise expertly documented report. As I will show later in this book, it is completely wrong to suggest that the political goal of the 9/11 attackers or their sponsors is global elimination of voting rights or women's rights or religious diversity. The report gives no evidence for this claim because there is no evidence for it. Fortunately the report does not continue this line of unfounded speculation. See p. xvi.

3. *Al-Risala* in Bernard Lewis, *The Crisis of Islam,* Modern Library, New York, 2003, p. 157. *Al-Maydan* in Lance Morrow, "Who's More Arrogant?" *Time,* December 10, 2001. Sheikh Omar in Peter Bergen and Paul Cruickshank, "Clerical Error," *The New Republic,* August 8, 2005.

4. Thomas Friedman, "The Land of Denial," *New York Times,* June 5, 2002, reprinted in *Longitudes and Attitudes,* Anchor Books, New York, 2003, p. 183. Edward Said, "Islam and the West Are Inadequate Banners," *Guardian,* September 16, 2001. Stanley Hoffman, "On the War," *New York Review of Books,* November 1, 2001, p. 6. George Bush, Address to Joint Session of Congress, September 20, 2001. Barbara Ehrenreich, "The Empire Strikes Back," *Village Voice,* October 9, 2001. Hendrik Hertzberg and David Remnick, "The Trap," *The New Yorker,* October 1, 2001, p. 38.

5. *The 9/11 Commission Report,* p. 169.

6. "Terrorism of the rich" is from Jean Baudrillard, *The Spirit of Terrorism and Requiem for the Twin Towers,* Verso, London, 2002, p. 23. "Notes Found After the Hijackings," *New York Times,* September 29, 2001, p. B-3.

7. "In for the Long Haul," *New York Times,* September 16, 2001.

8. George Bush, Address to the U.N. General Assembly, November 10, 2001.

9. George Bush, Address to the Nation, September 11, 2001. Bush, Address to Joint Session of Congress. Victor Davis Hanson, *An Autumn of War,* Anchor Books, New York, 2002, p. 170.

10. Bush, Address to Joint Session of Congress. Norman Podhoretz, "De-

fending and Advancing Freedom," *Commentary,* November 2005, p. 56. "The Week," *National Review,* August 29, 2005. Mustafa Akyol, "Bolshevism in a Headdress," *American Enterprise,* April-May 2005, p. 29. George Bush, State of the Union Address, January 29, 2002.

11.   Daniel Pipes, *In the Path of God,* Transaction Publishers, New Brunswick, 2003, p. xi. Francis Fukuyama, "Their Target: The Modern World," *Newsweek,* January 2002, special issue. John Gibson, *Hating America,* Regan Books, New York, 2004, p. 88. Bush, Address to Joint Session of Congress.

12.   Tony Blair, speech to the Labor Party Conference, October 1, 2001.

13.   Pipes, *In the Path of God,* p. xii. George Bush, Second Inaugural Address, January 20, 2005.

14.   George Bush, speech at the National Endowment for Democracy, Washington, D.C., October 6, 2005.

15.   Dexter Filkins, "Foreign Fighters Captured in Iraq Come from 27, Mostly Arab, Lands," *New York Times,* October 21, 2005, p. A-10.

16.   Khaled Abou El Fadl, *The Place of Tolerance in Islam,* Beacon Press, Boston, 2002, p. 11.

17.   Maxime Rodinson, *Islam and Capitalism,* University of Texas Press, Austin, 1978, pp. 14, 16. Gilles Kepel, *The War for Muslim Minds,* Harvard University Press, Cambridge, Massachusetts, 2004, pp. 6, 141.

18.   Noah Feldman, *After Jihad,* Farrar, Straus & Giroux, New York, 2003, p. 7. Madani cited by John Esposito, *The Islamic Threat,* Oxford University Press, N.Y., 1992, p. 184.

19.   See, e.g., Mona El-Naggar, "Banned Group Urges Egyptians to Vote on Sept. 7," *New York Times,* August 22, 2005, p. A-7. Joshua Hammer and Christine Spolar, "Ballot Initiative," *The New Republic,* September 26, 2005, p. 16. Megan Stack and Tyler Marshall, "Islamists Ride Wave of Freedom," *Los Angeles Times,* December 18, 2005, p. A-22. Najoub in David Remnick, "The Democracy Game," *The New Yorker,* February 27, 2006, p. 63.

20.   Fareed Zakaria, *The Future of Freedom,* W. W. Norton, New York, 2004, p. 18.

TWO

1. The actual vote in the Senate was 29 Democrats for and 21 against. The vote in the House was 81 Democrats for and 126 against. Ruth Conniff, "The Progressive Interview: Barbara Boxer," *Progressive*, July 2005, p. 41.

2. "10 Questions for Al Franken," *New York Times Magazine*, April 4, 2004. Stephen Applebaum, "Interview with Michael Moore," BBC-TV, June 30, 2004.

3. Patrick Buchanan, *The Death of the West*, St. Martin's Press, New York, 2001, p. 6.

4. Robert Jensen, "Saying Goodbye to Patriotism," counterpunch.org, November 12, 2001. Katha Pollitt, "Put Out No Flags," *The Nation*, October 8, 2001.

5. Bill Clinton, speech at Georgetown University, November 7, 2001.

6. See, e.g., Peter Bergen and Alec Reynolds, "Blowback Revisited," *Foreign Affairs*, November-December 2005. Noam Chomsky, *9–11*, Seven Stories Press, New York, 2002, pp. 12, 40.

7. Arundhati Roy, "The Algebra of Infinite Justice," *Progressive*, December 2001.

8. Michael Scheuer, *Imperial Hubris*, Brassey's, Inc., Washington, D.C., 2004, p. 240. Richard Falk, *The Great Terror War*, Olive Branch Press, New York, 2003, p. 19.

9. Statement of Senator Ted Kennedy, Committee for a Democratic Majority, September 10, 2004.

10. Cited by Bob Herbert, "35 Years Later," *New York Times*, April 24, 2006, p. A-23.

11. Amy Goodman, radio interview with Cornel West, *Democracy Now*, September 7, 2004. Rashid Khalidi, *Resurrecting Empire*, Beacon Press, Boston, 2004, p. x. Maureen Dowd, *Bushworld*, G. P. Putnam, New York, 2004, p. 15. Bob Herbert, *Promises Betrayed*, Times Books, New York, 2005, p. 253.

12. George Soros, *The Bubble of American Supremacy*, Public Affairs, New York, 2004, p. 62. Stanley Hoffman, "Out of Iraq," *New York Review of Books*, October 21, 2004. Herbert, *Promises Betrayed*, p. 247.

13. Gore Vidal, *Imperial America*, Nation Books, New York, 2004, p. 165. Edward Said, "Thoughts About America," *Al-Ahram*, February 26–March 6, 2002.

14.   Arthur Schlesinger Jr., "Disgrace at Guantánamo," *New York Review of Books*, April 8, 2004. Paisley Dodds, "Amnesty Takes Aim at 'Gulag' in Guantánamo," Associated Press, London, May 25, 2005, aol.com.

15.   Mark Danner, "We Are All Torturers Now," *New York Times*, January 6, 2005.

16.   Wendy Kaminer, "Patriotic Dissent," *American Prospect*, online edition, November 5, 2001. Anthony Lewis, "Bush and the Lesser Evil," *New York Review of Books*, May 27, 2004.

17.   Falk, *The Great Terror War*, p. xxvi. Edward Said, *From Oslo to Iraq*, Pantheon, New York, 2004, p. 111. Benjamin Barber, *Jihad vs. McWorld*, Ballantine Books, New York, 1996, pp. 9, 213.

18.   Nicholas Kristof, "Iraq in the Rear-View Mirror," *New York Times*, November 15, 2005. Robert Scheer, "U.S. Occupation Is Worse Than Hussein," huffingtonpost.com, November 30, 2005.

19.   James Carroll, *Crusade*, Metropolitan Books, New York, 2004, p. 20. Robert Reich, *Reason*, Alfred Knopf, New York, 2004, p. 49. Soros, *The Bubble of American Supremacy*, p. 18.

20.   Christopher Hitchens, *Love, Poverty, and War*, Nation Books, New York, 2004, p. 413.

21.   Jonathan Franzen, "Alice's Wonderland," *New York Times Book Review*, November 14, 2004, p. 16. Bill Moyers, keynote address to the Environmental Grantmakers Association, Brainerd, Minnesota, October 16, 2001, commondreams.org. Stanley Greenberg, *The Two Americas*, Thomas Dunne Books, New York, 2005, p. 5.

22.   James Wolcott, "The Counter-Life," *The Nation*, November 22, 2004, p. 23. Jonathan Chait, "Mad About Me," *The New Republic*, December 13, 2004, p. 50. Pauline Jelinek, "Dean Defends Criticism of Republican Party," AP, June 8, 2005, aol.com.

23.   Josh Gerstein, "Audience Gasps as Judge Likens Election of Bush to Rise of Il Duce," *New York Sun*, June 21, 2004.

24.   Thomas Frank, *What's the Matter with Kansas?* Metropolitan Books, New York, 2004.

25.   Molly Ivins, "Pickup Driving Liberal," *Progressive*, July 2005, p. 50. Morris Fiorina, Samuel Abrams, and Jeremy Pope, *Culture War?* Pearson Longman, New York, 2005.

26.   "Beyond Red vs. Blue," Pew Research Center, Washington, D.C., 2005. "Voters Liked Campaign 2004, but Too Much Mud-Slinging," Pew Research Center, Washington, D.C., November 11, 2004.

27. See, e.g., Katharine Seelye, "Moral Values Cited as a Defining Issue of the Election," *New York Times*, November 4, 2004. John Green, Corwin Smidt, James Guth, and Lyman Kellstedt, "The American Religious Landscape and the 2004 Presidential Vote," pewforum.org; see also the Fourth National Survey of Religion and Politics, Bliss Institute, University of Akron, 2004.

28. "Beyond Red vs. Blue."

THREE

1. Salman Rushdie, *Imaginary Homelands*, Viking, New York, 1991, p. 170.

2. Bernard Lewis, *From Babel to Dragomans*, Oxford University Press, N.Y., 2004, pp. 34–35.

3. Ed Koch, "World War IV," *Commentary*, December 2004, p. 7.

4. Patrick Buchanan, "Creating a Nation Out of Paper," *American Conservative*, September 12, 2005, p. 6.

5. Edward Said, *Orientalism*, Vintage, New York, 1978.

6. Joseph Ellis, "Contain Ourself," *The New Republic*, July 4, 2005, p. 5.

7. Bernard Lewis, *What Went Wrong?* Oxford University Press, N.Y., 2002, pp. 3, 6.

8. Albert Hourani, *A History of the Arab Peoples*, Harvard University Press, Cambridge, 1991.

9. George Bush, news conference, White House, October 11, 2001, www.whitehouse.gov.

10. Dan Eggan and Scott Wilson, "Suicide Bombs Potent Tools of Terrorists," *Washington Post*, July 17, 2005.

11. Ziad Jarrah in Christian Caryl, "Why They Do It," *New York Review of Books*, September 22, 2005, p. 30. "London Bomber Video: Full Statement," London *Times*, September 3, 2005, www.timesonline.co.uk. Nasra Hassan, "An Arsenal of Believers," *The New Yorker*, November 19, 2001, pp. 37–41.

12. Elaine Sciolino, *Persian Mirrors*, Simon & Schuster, New York, 2000, p. 172. Gregory Crouch, "Van Gogh Defendant Confesses to Murder," *International Herald Tribune*, July 13, 2005, p. 3.

13. "Open Letter to America," Hamas, printed in *Al-Risala*, September 13, 2001, cited by memri.org, Special Dispatch Series No. 268. Al-Sarraj in David Remnick, "A Reporter at Large," *The New Yorker*, February 7, 2005, p. 67.

14.   See, e.g., Richard Dawkins, "Religion's Guided Missiles," *Guardian*, September 15, 2001.

15.   James Carroll, *Crusade*, Metropolitan Books, New York, 2004, pp. 2, 5.

16.   Cited by Bernard Lewis, *The Muslim Discovery of Europe*, W. W. Norton, New York, 1982, p. 18.

17.   Edward Said, *Culture and Imperialism*, Alfred Knopf, New York, 1993, p. 22.

18.   Rashid Khalidi, *Resurrecting Empire*, Beacon Press, Boston, 2004, p. 34.

19.   Lewis, *The Muslim Discovery of Europe*, pp. 30–31.

20.   Bernard Lewis, *The Crisis of Islam*, Modern Library, New York, 2003, p. 16.

21.   Cited by Daniel Pipes, *Militant Islam Reaches America*, W. W. Norton, New York, 2003, p. 97 and footnote.

22.   Bernard Lewis, *The Multiple Identities of the Middle East*, Schocken Books, New York, 1998, p. 27. *Islam in History*, Open Court Press, Chicago, 1993, p. 6.

23.   "London Bomber Video: Full Statement." Crouch, "Van Gogh Defendant Confesses to Murder."

24.   Samuel Huntington, *The Clash of Civilizations and the Remaking of World Order*, Simon & Schuster, New York, 1996, p. 209.

25.   See, e.g., Kenneth Woodward, "How Should We Think About Islam?" *Newsweek*, December 31, 2001, p. 102. Malise Ruthven, *Fundamentalism*, Oxford University Press, New York, 2004, p. 47.

26.   Sam Harris, *The End of Faith*, W. W. Norton, New York, 2005, p. 130. Remarks by Steven Weinberg on accepting his award as Humanist of the Year, reprinted in *Humanist*, September-October 2002. Dawkins, "Religion's Misguided Missiles."

27.   This point is made by Faisal Devji, *Landscapes of the Jihad*, Cornell University Press, Ithaca, New York, 2005, p. 162.

28.   Thomas Friedman, *Longitudes and Attitudes*, Anchor Books, New York, 2003, pp. 57, 78.

29.   John Anderson, "Public Floggings Used as Tool Against Reform," *Washington Post*, August 16, 2001. Reuters, "Public Floggings Fuel Iran Row," *Gulf News*, United Arab Emirates, August 16, 2001.

30.   See, e.g., Akbar Ahmed, *Islam Today*, I. B. Tauris Publishers, New York, 2002, p. 10. Seyyed Hossein Nasr, *The Heart of Islam*, HarperSanFrancisco, 2004, p. 22.

31.   Seyyed Hossein Nasr, *Islam*, HarperSanFrancisco, 2003, p. xxiii.

FOUR

1. "Turkish Delight," *Newsweek*, August 29, 2005. Ron Nachmann, "Can't Stop the Sling Shot: Hip-Hop Arises, in Palestine," *Tikkun* 20, no. 3, p. 79. Edward Wong, "On the Air, on Their Own: Iraqi Women Find a Forum," *New York Times*, September 4, 2005. Elaine Sciolino, *Persian Mirrors*, Simon & Schuster, New York, 2000, p. 44.

2. "A Year After the Iraq War," Pew Research Center, Washington, D.C., 2004. Ismail cited by Michael Scheuer, *Through Our Enemies' Eyes*, Brassey's, Washington, D.C., 2003, p. 262.

3. Jim Brunner, "Ad Watch," *Seattle Times*, September 4, 2004.

4. This point is corroborated by former CIA analyst Michael Scheuer: "According to his closest Muslim associates and many of the Westerners who have interviewed him, Osama Bin Laden appears to be a genuinely pious Muslim; a devoted family man; a talented, focused and patient insurgent commander; a frank and eloquent speaker; a successful businessman; and an individual of conviction, intellectual honesty, compassion, humility and physical bravery." Scheuer, *Through Our Enemies' Eyes*, p. 3. See also the testimony of bin Laden's bodyguard cited in Fawaz Gerges, *The Far Enemy*, Cambridge University Press, Cambridge, 2005, pp. 35–36, 182–83. Carmen bin Laden, the estranged wife of Osama bin Laden's half-brother Yeslam, wrote an exposé of Saudi male culture and of the bin Laden family but had virtually nothing negative to say about Osama bin Laden. She describes him as reserved yet charismatic, obstinate in his beliefs, and yet popular with his countrymen—"a Saudi hero." See Carmen bin Laden, *Inside the Kingdom*, Warner Books, New York, 2004.

5. Hamid Algar, *Roots of the Islamic Revolution in Iran*, Islamic Publications International, Oneonta, New York, 2001, p. 42.

6. "Jihad Against Jews and Crusaders," World Islamic Front Statement, February 23, 1998. "Interview: Osama Bin Laden," conducted by John Miller, PBS *Frontline*, May 1998. Neil MacFarquhar, "Bin Laden Denounces Muslim Infidels," *San Diego Union-Tribune*, November 4, 2001, p. A-3. Osama Bin Laden, "Among a Band of Knights," in Bruce Lawrence, ed., *Messages to the World*, Verso, New York, 2005, p. 188. Michael Slackman, "Bin Laden Says West Is Waging War Against Islam," *New York Times*, April 24, 2006, p. A-8.

7. "Full Text: Bin Laden's Letter to America," translated and reprinted in

Observer, November 24, 2002, observer.co.uk. "Interview with Osama Bin Laden," *Nida'ul Islam,* October 1996, reprinted in Barry Rubin and Judith Colp Rubin, *Anti-American Terrorism and the Middle East,* Oxford University Press, New York, 2002, p. 148. *The 9/11 Commission Report,* W. W. Norton, New York, 2004, p. 54.

8. Osama Bin Laden, "Depose the Tyrants," December 16, 2004, cited by Bruce Lawrence, ed., *Messages to the World,* Verso, New York, 2005, pp. 253, 255.

9. Atwan cited by Peter Bergen, "The Real Bin Laden," *Vanity Fair,* January 2006, p. 151. "Jihad Against Jews and Crusaders." Interview with Osama Bin Laden by Al-Jazeera, cited by Gilles Kepel, *The War for Muslim Minds,* Harvard University Press, Cambridge, 2004, p. 114.

10. "Bin Laden's Statement: The Sword Fell," *New York Times,* October 8, 2001, p. B-7. "Jihad Against Jews and Crusaders."

11. "Full Text: Bin Laden's Letter to America."

12. Text of al-Zarqawi message, January 24, 2004.

13. "Full Text: Bin Laden's Letter to America."

14. "Interview with Osama Bin Laden," *Nida'ul Islam,* October 1996, reprinted in Rubin and Rubin, *Anti-American Terrorism and the Middle East,* p. 147.

15. Peter Arnett interview with bin Laden, CNN, March 1997.

16. "Interview: Osama Bin Laden."

17. Cited by Michael Scheuer, *Imperial Hubris,* Brassey's Inc., Washington, D.C., 2004, p. 157, and in Peter Arnett interview with bin Laden, CNN, March 1997.

18. "Interview with Osama Bin Laden," *Nida'ul Islam,* October 1996, reprinted in Rubin and Rubin, *Anti-American Terrorism and the Middle East,* p. 147.

19. Victor Davis Hanson, *Carnage and Culture,* Doubleday, New York, 2001, pp. 97, 347–49.

20. "Full Text: Bin Laden's Letter to America." Osama Bin Laden broadcast, October 29, 2004, aljazeera.net.

21. David Bamber, "Bin Laden: Yes, I Did It," November 11, 2001, telegraph.co.uk. The estimate is by Al Qaeda spokesman Suleiman Abu Gheith, in his article "The Shadow of the Lances," posted on Islamic Web sites and reprinted in "Killing the Infidels," January 27, 2004, memri.org.

22. Ayman al-Zawahiri, *Knights Under the Prophet's Banner*, serialized in *Asharq al-Awsat*, December 2001.

23. *Arab Human Development Report*, United Nations Publications, New York, 2002.

24. Sayyid Qutb, *Social Justice in Islam*, Islamic Publications International, Oneonta, N.Y., 2000, pp. 35, 69.

25. Ibn Khaldun, *The Muqaddimah*, Princeton University Press, Princeton, 1967, pp. 24–25.

26. Qutb, *Social Justice in Islam*, pp. 175–77.

27. Ayatollah Khomeini, *Islam and Revolution*, Mizan Press, Berkeley, 1981, pp. 29–30.

28. Qutb, *Milestones*, Mother Mosque Foundation, Cedar Rapids, 2000, p. 118.

29. Charles Adams, "Mawdudi and the Islamic State," in John Esposito, ed., *Voices of Resurgent Islam*, Oxford University Press, New York, 1983.

30. For an introduction to Shariati's work, see Ali Shariati, *On the Sociology of Islam*, Mizan Press, Oneonta, N.Y., 1979.

31. Khomeini, speech at Feyziyeh Theological School, August 24, 1979. Khomeini, "On the Nature of the Islamic State," Tehran radio broadcast, September 8, 1979. Both are reprinted in Rubin and Rubin, *Anti-American Terrorism and the Middle East*, pp. 34–35.

32. Susan Sachs, "Shia Clerics' Ambitions Collide in an Iraqi Slum," *New York Times*, May 25, 2003.

33. "Interview with Umar Abd al-Rahman," in Rubin and Rubin, *Anti-American Terrorism and the Middle East*, p. 66.

34. Khomeini, *Islam and Revolution*, pp. 16, 31–32, 39.

35. Cited by Ibrahim Abu-Rabi, *Intellectual Origins of Islamic Resurgence in the Modern Arab World*, State University of New York Press, Albany, 1996, p. 129. John Esposito, *The Islamic Threat*, Oxford University Press, N.Y., 1999, p. 136. See also Gilles Kepel, *Muslim Extremism in Egypt*, Al-Saqi Books, London, 1985, p. 41.

36. Qutb, *Milestones*, p. 93.

37. Ibid., p. 98.

38. Excerpts from Sheikh Fahd Rahman Al-Abyan sermon, Al-Riyadh mosque, memri.org, Special Report No. 10, September 26, 2002. Excerpts from Sheikh Yusuf Qaradawi's program, Al-Jazeera, November 28, 2004, memri.org, TV Monitor Project, Clip No. 392.

39. Sayyid Qutb, *Islam and Universal Peace*, American Trust Publications, Indianapolis, 1977, pp. 510–11. Khomeini, *Islam and Revolution*, p. 195.

40. "The Islamic Revolution from the Shah to the Spice Girls," interview with Masoumeh Ebtekar, *New Perspectives Quarterly*, winter 2002. Anaraki cited by Yossef Bodansky, *Bin Laden*, Forum, Roseville, California, 2001, pp. xiii–xiv. Qutb, *Milestones*, p. 145. Shariati cited by Esposito, *The Islamic Threat*, p. 111.

41. Cited by Yvonne Haddad, "Sayyid Qutb: Ideologue of Islamic Revival," in Esposito, ed., *Voices of Resurgent Islam*, p. 85.

42. Cited by Abu-Rabi, *Intellectual Origins of Islamic Resurgence in the Modern Arab World*, p. 225.

FIVE

1. Patrick Buchanan, *The Death of the West*, Thomas Dunne Books, New York, 2002, p. 118.

2. Deepak Lal, *In Praise of Empires*, Palgrave Macmillan, New York, 2004, p. xviii.

3. Stephen Asma, "Lessons Taught, and Learned, in Phnom Penh," *Chronicle of Higher Education*, April 22, 2005, p. B-14.

4. "Views of a Changing World," Pew Research Center, Washington, D.C., June 2003. Afshin Molavi, *Persian Pilgrimages*, W. W. Norton, New York, 2002, p. 123.

5. Azar Nafisi, *Reading Lolita in Tehran*, Random House, New York, 2004, pp. 126–27, 133.

6. Elaine Sciolino, *Persian Mirrors*, Simon & Schuster, New York, 2000, pp. 95–97, 206.

7. See, e.g., Kevin Fagan, "Agents of Terror Leave Their Mark on Sin City," *San Francisco Chronicle*, October 4, 2001.

8. See, e.g., Ian Buruma, "Final Cut," *The New Yorker*, January 3, 2005.

9. Christopher Hitchens, "The Married State," March 3, 2004, opinion-journal.com.

10. Cited by Robert Knight, *The Age of Consent*, Spence Publishing, Dallas, 1998, p. 67.

11. *Primetime Thursday*, November 13, 2003.

12. Kelefa Sanneh, "A Rapper's Prison Time as a Resume Booster," *New York Times*, March 24, 2005, p. B-1.

13. For a study showing the ideological premises of the current generation of television shows, see Robert Lichter, Linda Lichter, and Stanley Rothman, *Prime Time: How TV Portrays American Culture*, Regnery, Washington, D.C., 1994.

14. Jami Bernard, "Gore's the Crime of Passion," *New York Daily News*, February 23, 2004. Jami Bernard, *Quentin Tarantino*, HarperCollins, New York, 1995.

15. Thomas Frank, *What's the Matter With Kansas?* Metropolitan Books, New York, 2004, p. 133.

16. Frank Rich, "The Greatest Dirty Joke Ever Told," *New York Times*, March 13, 2005; see also Frank Rich, "The Year of Living Indecently," *New York Times*, February 6, 2005.

17. Henry Louis Gates, "2 Live Crew Decoded," *New York Times*, June 19, 1990, p. A-23.

18. Miriam Horn, "The Mistress Cycle," *New York Times*, September 20, 2005. Martha Nussbaum, "Patriotism and Cosmopolitanism," *Boston Review*, 1994.

19. Bill Dedman, "TV Movie Led to Prostitute's Disclosures," *Washington Post*, August 27, 1989.

20. Pam Belluck, "To Avoid Divorce, Move to Massachusetts," *New York Times*, November 14, 2004.

21. Bill Carter, "Many Who Voted for Values Still Like Their Television Sin," *New York Times*, November 22, 2004.

22. Sean Mitchell, "With the Secrets Revealed, 'Housewives' Turns to New Mysteries," *New York Times*, September 24, 2005, p. A-15. Caryn James, "Partners Who Cheat but Tell the Truth," *New York Times*, December 8, 2004.

23. Calvin Tomkins, "Unzipped," *The New Yorker*, November 22, 2004.

24. Wendy Kaminer, foreword to Nadine Strossen, *Defending Pornography*, New York University Press, N.Y., 2000, p. xi. "Porn Again," *American Prospect*, July 1, 2002.

25. Jack Newfield, "An Interview with Frank Rich," *Tikkun*, May-June 1999.

26. Catharine MacKinnon, "Not a Moral Issue," in Drucilla Cornell, ed., *Feminism and Pornography*, Oxford University Press, N.Y., 2000, pp. 169, 171.

27. Elizabeth Wilson, *Bohemians*, Rutgers University Press, New Brunswick, 2000, p. 9.

28.   Charles Taylor, *The Ethics of Authenticity*, Harvard University Press, Cambridge, 1991, p. 27.

29.   Press Release, "ACLU Applauds Federal Government's Decision to Suspend Public Funding of Religion," August 22, 2005, aclu.org. Wendy Shalit, *A Return to Modesty*, Touchstone Books, New York, 2000, p. 189.

30.   See, e.g., "Human Sexuality: What Children Should Know and When They Should Know It," plannedparenthood.org.

SIX

1.   "Torture and Truth," interview of Mark Danner by Dave Gilson, *Mother Jones*, December 7, 2004. Anthony Lewis, "The Road to Abu Ghraib," *American Prospect*, October 1, 2004. Seymour Hersh, "The Gray Zone," *The New Yorker*, May 24, 2004.

2.   Schlesinger cited by Mark Danner, "Abu Ghraib: The Hidden Story," *New York Review of Books*, October 7, 2004. Bernard Goldberg, *100 People Who Are Screwing Up America*, HarperCollins, New York, 2005, p. 5. Remark by Limbaugh on his May 6, 2002 radio program. Tammy Bruce, "Why Abu Ghraib Matters," May 24, 2004, frontpagemagazine.com.

3.   Kate Zernike, "Behind Failed Abu Ghraib Plea, a Tale of Breakups and Betrayal," *New York Times*, May 10, 2005. James Polk, "Testimony: Abu Ghraib Photos Just for Fun," August 4, 2002, cnn.com.

4.   Anouar Abdel Malek, "After Abu Ghraib," *Al-Ahram*, June 3–June 9, 2004.

5.   Interview with Osama Bin Laden, Al Jazeera television, December 1998, reprinted in Barry Rubin and Judith Colp Rubin, eds., *Anti-American Terrorism and the Middle East*, Oxford University Press, N.Y., 2002, p. 156. "Iranian Leader Khamenei: Iran's Enemies Want to Destroy It with Miniskirts," memri.org, January 6, 2005, Clip No. 468. Al-Abyan cited by memri.org, Special Report No. 10, September 26, 2002.

6.   Sayyid Qutb, *Milestones*, Mother Mosque Foundation, Cedar Rapids, 2000, pp. 28–29, 97.

7.   Tariq Ramadan, *Western Muslims and the Future of Islam*, Oxford University Press, N.Y., 2004, p. 142.

8.   Seyyed Hossein Nasr, *The Heart of Islam*, HarperSanFrancisco, 2004, pp. 289–90. Seyyed Hossein Nasr, *Islam*, HarperSanFrancisco, 2003, p. 30.

9. Nicholas Kristof, "In India, One Woman's Stand Says Enough," *New York Times*, January 15, 2006. Ronald Inglehart and Pippa Norris, *Rising Tide*, Cambridge University Press, Cambridge, 2003, p. 9. Ellen Willis, "Bringing the Holy War Home," *Nation*, December 17, 2001.

10. As the chair of President Clinton's Interagency Council on Women, Hillary Clinton sought to redefine the term "sex trafficking" to outlaw only involuntary prostitution. The council sought to have consensual prostitution listed as a right with the same protections as other occupations. See Catherine Edwards, "Hillary Supports Sex Trafficking," the Gale Group, February 14, 2000.

11. Human Rights Watch, "Crime or Custom? Violence Against Women in Pakistan," October 1, 1999.

12. Inglehart and Norris, *Rising Tide*, pp. 42, 62. See also Ronald Inglehart and Pippa Norris, "The True Clash of Civilizations," *Foreign Policy*, March-April 2003.

13. Khalid Baig, "Beijing Plus 5," January 20, 2006, albalagh.net.

14. Cited by memri.org, Inquiry and Analysis Series No. 88, March 6, 2002.

15. Steven Weisman, "Saudi Women Depart from the Script," *New York Times*, September 28, 2005. Glenn Kessler, "Hughes Raises Driving Ban with Saudis," *Washington Post*, September 28, 2005.

16. Nasr, *Islam*, pp. 68, 102.

17. Strictly speaking, we are discussing polygyny, which is the term for one man taking multiple wives. Polygamy covers both polygyny and polyandry, which is the term for one woman taking multiple husbands. Polyandry is very rare historically and is not permitted in Islam.

18. "The Islamic Revolution: From the Shah to the Spice Girls," interview of Masoumeh Ebtekar by Nathan Gardels, *New Perspectives Quarterly*, spring 1998, p. 38. Elaine Sciolino, *Persian Mirrors*, Simon & Schuster, New York, 2000, pp. 111–12. Turabi cited in *Le Figaro*, April 15, 1995.

19. Camelia Fard, "Unveiled Threats," *Village Voice*, March 28–April 3, 2001; see also Elaine Sciolino, "Love Finds a Way in Iran: Temporary Marriage," *New York Times*, October 4, 2000.

20. "Honor Killing From an Islamic Perspective," June 17, islamonline.net.

21. Universal Declaration of Human Rights, United Nations, adopted by General Assembly Resolution 217 (A) on December 10, 1948.

22. Cited by Carrie Wickham, "The Problem with Coercive Democratization," *Muslim World Journal of Human Rights*, 2004.

23.   Stephanie Coontz, "The New Fragility of Marriage, for Better or
        Worse," *Chronicle Review*, May 6, 2005.

24.   Barbara Dafoe Whitehead, *The Divorce Culture*, Vintage, New York, 1996,
        p. 67.

25.   Kenji Yoshino, "The Pressure to Cover," *New York Times Magazine*, Jan-
        uary 15, 2006, p. 37.

26.   Gertrude Himmelfarb, *One Nation, Two Cultures*, Alfred Knopf, New
        York, 1999, p. 10. See Elizabeth Wilson, *Bohemians*, Rutgers University
        Press, New Brunswick, 2000, p. 105.

27.   Margaret Mead, *Coming of Age in Samoa*, William Morrow, New York,
        1961, pp. 83, 104–8.

28.   See, e.g., Derek Freeman, *Margaret Mead and Samoa*, Harvard University
        Press, Cambridge, 1983. Freeman calls Mead's work "the worst case of
        self-deception in the history of the behavioral sciences." A. O. Scott,
        "Where Many Were in Darkness, He Shone a Light," *New York Times*,
        November 12, 2004.

29.   Betty Friedan, *The Feminine Mystique*, W. W. Norton, New York, 2001,
        pp. 282, 305, 337. Germaine Greer, *The Female Eunuch*, Farrar, Straus
        and Giroux, New York, 2001, pp. 366–67.

30.   In a new introduction to her old classic, Greer stresses "the right to
        chastity, the right to defer physical intimacy until there is irrefutable ev-
        idence of commitment." Ibid., p. 10.

31.   Judith Wallerstein, Julia Lewis, and Sandra Blakeslee, *The Unexpected
        Legacy of Divorce*, Hyperion, New York, 2000, p. xxxi.

32.   Andrew Sullivan, ed., *Same Sex Marriage Pro and Con*, Vintage, New
        York, 1997, p. xxii.

33.   Tracy Jan, "Parents Rip School over Gay Storybook," *Boston Globe*, April
        20, 2006.

34.   Walzer, Editor's Page, *Dissent*, fall 2004, p. 3. Jonathan Rauch, "Family's
        Value," *The New Republic*, May 30, 2005, p. 15. "Statement of Senator
        Edward Kennedy on the Federal Marriage Amendment," July 13,
        2004, Committee for a Democratic Majority.

SEVEN

1.   "Mutual Incomprehension, Mutual Outrage," *Economist*, February 11,
        2006, p. 24.

2. Rajoub cited by David Remnick, "The Democracy Game," *The New Yorker*, February 27, 2006, p. 58. "Malaysia Warns of Islam, West Chasm," February 10, 2006, aljazeera.net.

3. Hamid Algar, *Roots of the Islamic Revolution in Iran*, IPI Press, Oneonta, N.Y., 2001, p. 140.

4. Ayatollah Khomeini, *Islam and Revolution*, Mizan Press, Berkeley, 1981, p. 75.

5. "Bin Laden's Statement: The Sword Fell," *New York Times*, October 8, 2001, p. B-7. Al-Rahman cited by Daniel Benjamin and Steven Simon, *The Age of Sacred Terror*, Random House, New York, 2003, pp. 17, 37.

6. Comment by William Styron in Steve MacDonogh, ed., *The Rushdie Letters*, University of Nebraska Press, Lincoln, 1993, p. 65. Gore cited by David Remnick, "The Wilderness Campaign," *The New Yorker*, September 13, 2004. Richard Dawkins, statement to the Freedom from Religion Foundation, Madison, Wisconsin, September 22, 2001. Madeleine Albright, *The Mighty and the Almighty*, HarperCollins, New York, 2006, p. 142. Jim Wallis, *God's Politics*, HarperSanFrancisco, 2005, pp. 67–68.

7. Broadcast by Osama bin Laden, Al Jazeera television, October 7, 2001, reprinted in Barry Rubin and Judith Colp Rubin, *Anti-American Terrorism and the Middle East*, Oxford University Press, N.Y., 2002, p. 250.

8. Comments by Sheikh Muhammad Tantawi after his meeting with the head of the Anglican Church of Scotland, cited by memri.org, Inquiry and Analysis Series No. 130, April 8, 2003. Comments by Sheikh Yusuf al-Qaradawi, cited by memri.org, Special Dispatch Series No. 858, February 4, 2005, and Special Dispatch Series No. 1017, November 3, 2005.

9. Michael Slackman, "Iranian Letter: Using Religion to Lecture Bush," *New York Times*, May 10, 2006, p. A-1. Sayyid Qutb, *Social Justice in Islam*, Islamic Publications International, Oneonta, N.Y., 2000, pp. 24, 273. Khurshid Ahmad, "The Nature of the Islamic Resurgence," in John Esposito, ed., *Voices of Resurgent Islam*, Oxford University Press, N.Y., 1983, p. 228.

10. Sermon by Sheikh Muhammad al-Qaysi, Abd Al-Qadir Mosque, Baghdad, March 28, 2003, memri.org, Special Report No. 13.

11. Rick Santorum, *It Takes a Family*, ISI Books, Wilmington, Delaware, 2005, p. 102. John Micklethwait and Adrian Woolridge, *The Right Nation*, Penguin, New York, 2004.

12. World Values Survey, "Strength of Religiosity Scale," 1981–2001, cited by Ronald Inglehart and Pippa Norris, *Rising Tide,* Cambridge University Press, Cambridge, 2003, p. 54. T. R. Reid, *The United States of Europe,* Penguin, New York, 2004, p. 215. Jason Horowitz, "Europe, Seeking Political Unity, Stumbles over Issue of Religion," *New York Times,* November 7, 2004.

13. Susan Jacoby, *Freethinkers,* Metropolitan Books, New York, 2004, p. 7.

14. Seyyed Hossein Nasr, *Islam,* HarperSanFrancisco, 2003, p. 179. Tariq Ramadan, *Western Muslims and the Future of Islam,* Oxford University Press, N.Y., 2004, p. 4.

15. Muhammad Qutb, introduction to Sayyid Qutb, *In the Shade of the Koran,* Islamic Book Service, New Delhi, 2001, p. xii.

16. Osama bin Laden, "Depose the Tyrants," in Bruce Lawrence, ed., *Messages to the World,* Verso, New York, p. 259.

17. Sayyid Qutb, *Milestones,* Mother Mosque Foundation, Cedar Rapids, 2000, p. 36.

18. Khomeini, *Islam and Revolution,* pp. 63, 79.

19. Bernard Lewis, *From Babel to Dragomans,* Oxford University Press, N.Y., 2004, p. 306.

20. Salman Rushdie, *Imaginary Homelands,* Viking, New York, 1991, p. 402.

21. Albert Hourani, *A History of the Arab Peoples,* Harvard University Press, Cambridge, 1991, p. 47.

22. Somini Sengupta, "Afghan Candidates Play Down Taliban Past," *International Herald Tribune,* September 17–18, 2005, p. 2.

23. Afshin Molavi, *Persian Pilgrimages,* W. W. Norton, New York, 2002, pp. 177–80.

24. Ramadan, *Western Muslims and the Future of Islam,* p. 146.

25. "Views of a Changing World," Pew Research Center, Washington, D.C., June 2003.

26. Khalid Baig, "UN Makes Big Strides in Campaign to Abrogate Sharia," January 20, 2006, albalagh.net. Bin Laden, "Depose the Tyrants," in Lawrence, ed., *Messages to the World,* pp. 214, 253.

27. See, e.g., Lewis, *From Babel to Dragomans,* p. 51.

28. Inglehart and Norris, *Rising Tide,* p. 49.

29. Salman Rushdie, "A War That Presents Us All with a Crisis of Faith," *Guardian,* November 3, 2001. Richard Rorty and Gianni Vattimo, *The Future of Religion,* Columbia University Press, New York, 2005, p. 72.

Editorial, "Election Results in Iraq," *New York Times*, January 21, 2006, p. A-28.

30.   Stanley Greenberg, *The Two Americas*, Thomas Dunne Books, New York, 2005, pp. 100, 129.

31.   Robert Bellah et al., *Habits of the Heart*, Perennial Library, New York, 1986, p. 221. Hillary Clinton, *It Takes a Village*, Touchstone Books, New York, 1996, p. 177. Press conference with Vice President Al Gore, December 22, 1997. *Planned Parenthood v. Casey*, 505 U.S. 833 (1992).

32.   Linda Greenhouse, "Justices Consider Religious Displays," *New York Times*, March 3, 2005, p. A-18.

33.   Sam Harris, *The End of Faith*, W. W. Norton, New York, 2005, pp. 26, 35. Robert Kuttner, "What Would Jefferson Do?" *American Prospect*, November 2004, p. 31.

34.   Henry Kamen, *The Spanish Inquisition*, Yale University Press, New Haven, 1999.

35.   Harris, *The End of Faith*, pp. 79, 101, 239, 259.

36.   Jacoby, *Freethinkers*, pp. 3–4; "Original Intent," *Mother Jones*, October 2005, p. 30.

37.   *Church of the Holy Trinity v. United States*, 143 U.S. 471 (1892).

38.   Diana Eck, *A New Religious America*, HarperSanFrancisco, 2001.

39.   Ramadan, *Western Muslims and the Future of Islam*, p. 100. "Belief by the Numbers," *Newsweek*, August 29–September 5, 2005, p. 54. Philip Jenkins, *The Next Christendom*, Oxford University Press, N.Y., 2002, pp. 103, 105.

40.   505 U.S. 577 (1992).

41.   Lewis Lapham, "Civil Obedience," *Harper's*, September 2005, p. 7. Boston cited in "John the Evangelist?" *Economist*, August 27, 2005, p. 25.

42.   George Marsden, *Understanding Fundamentalism and Evangelicalism*, William Eerdmans Publishing, Grand Rapids, 1991, p. 1.

43.   Robert Reich, *Reason*, Alfred Knopf, New York, 2004, p. 52.

44.   Karen Armstrong, *A History of God*, Ballantine Books, New York, 1993, p. 378.

EIGHT

1. Sayyid Qutb, *Milestones*, Mother Mosque Foundation, Cedar Rapids, 2000, pp. 9, 11.

2. Hamid Algar, *Roots of the Islamic Revolution in Iran*, Islamic Publications International, Oneonta, N.Y., 2001, p. 13.

3. Ayatollah Khomeini, *Islam and Revolution*, Mizan Press, Berkeley, 1981, pp. 75, 131.

4. Gary Sick, *All Fall Down*, Random House, New York, 1985.

5. Cited by Steven Hayward, *The Real Jimmy Carter*, Regnery, Washington, D.C., 2004, p. 110.

6. Sick, *All Fall Down*, p. 58. "The Khomeini Era Begins," *Time*, February 12, 1979.

7. Richard Falk, "Trusting Khomeini," *New York Times*, February 16, 1979.

8. Sick, *All Fall Down*, p. 85.

9. Mark Bowden, "Captivity Pageant," *Atlantic Monthly*, December 2005.

10. Ayman al-Zawahiri, "The Way to Jerusalem Passes Through Cairo," *Al-Mujahideen*, April 1995.

11. Montasser al-Zayyat, *The Road to Al Qaeda*, Pluto Press, London, 2004, p. 64.

12. Fawaz Gerges, *The Far Enemy*, Cambridge University Press, Cambridge, 2005, p. 25.

13. Ayman al-Zawahiri, *Knights Under the Prophet's Banner*, serialized in *Asharq al-Awsat*, December 2001.

14. "Full Text: Bin Laden's Letter to America," *Observer*, November 24, 2002, observer.co.uk. Statement by bin Laden on an Al Qaeda recruitment video, 2000, cited by Barry Rubin and Judith Colp Rubin, *Anti-American Terrorism and the Middle East*, Oxford University Press, N.Y., 2002, p. 181.

15. Edward Said, *Covering Islam*, Vintage, New York, 1997, pp. xx, xxxiv.

16. Bill Clinton, speech to the Washington Society of Associated Executives, October 2001, reported in *USA Today*, November 12, 2001. Richard Clarke, *Against All Enemies*, Free Press, New York, 2004, p. 204. Michael Scheuer, "How Not to Catch a Terrorist," *Atlantic Monthly*, December 2004, p. 52. Steve Coll, *Ghost Wars*, Penguin Books, New York, 2004, pp. 342, 376, 379–80. Bill Clinton, interview with Chris Wallace, Fox News Sunday, September 24, 2006.

17. Gore Vidal, *Imperial America*, Nation Books, New York, 2004, p. 15. Joe

Conason, *Big Lies*, Thomas Dunne Books, New York, 2003, p. 102. Lewis Lapham, "On Message," *Harper's*, October 2005, p. 7.

18. Ramsey Clark, "Why I'm Willing to Defend Hussein," *Los Angeles Times*, January 24, 2005. Larry Neumeister, "Left-Leaning Attorney Is Guilty of Aiding Terror," Associated Press, February 11, 2005; see also "The Week," *National Review*, March 14, 2005, p. 6.

19. Jim Krane, "Al Gore Decries Post 9-11 Treatment of Arabs," Associated Press Report, February 14, 2006. Kevin Johnson, "Rights Groups Detail Kafkaesque U.S. Detentions," *USA Today*, June 27, 2005, p. 4-A.

20. George Soros, *The Bubble of American Supremacy*, Public Affairs, New York, 2004, pp. ix, 16.

21. Laurence Tribe, "Liberty for All," *Boston Review*, December 2002–January 2003. Bob Herbert, "Our Battered Constitution," *New York Times*, February 4, 2005.

22. Ian Fisher, "Rights Group Lists 26 It Says U.S. Is Holding in Secret Abroad," *New York Times*, December 2, 2005, p. A-9.

23. Michelle Goldberg, "Bush's Impeachable Offense," December 22, 2005, salon.com. Eric Lichtblau and James Risen, "Defense Lawyers Plan Challenges over Spy Efforts," *New York Times*, December 28, 2005.

24. See, e.g., Anthony Lewis, "Making Torture Legal," *New York Review of Books*, July 15, 2004. Jonathan Schell, "What Is Wrong with Torture," January 24, 2005, commondreams.org. "Illegal, Immoral, and Pointless," *New York Times*, December 10, 2005, p. A-28.

25. Cited by Seymour Hersh, *Chain of Command*, HarperPerennial, New York, 2004, p. 71.

NINE

1. Osama bin Laden, "The Towers of Lebanon," October 29, 2004, reprinted in Bruce Lawrence, ed., *Messages to the World*, Verso, London, 2005, pp. 240–43.

2. See, e.g., Augustus Norton, "Pity the Region," *Nation*, February 6, 2006; this is a review of Robert Fisk's *The Great War for Civilization*. On Blum, see David Montgomery, "The Author Who Got a Big Boost from Bin Laden," *Washington Post*, January 21, 2006.

3. Montgomery, "The Author Who Got a Big Boost from Bin Laden." See

also Daniel Pipes, "Al Qaeda's Leftist Brigade," *New York Sun,* January 24, 2006.

4. David Gartenstein-Ross, "Bin Laden's Rhetorical Gambit," November 24, 2004, frontpagemagazine.com.

5. David Wallechinsky, "With Enemies Like George Bush, Who Needs Friends?" December 3, 2005, huffingtonpost.com. Fisk cited in "Bin Laden's Vote Is for George Bush," November 1, 2004, democracy now.com.

6. Daniel Benjamin and Steven Simon, "Al Qaeda's Big Boast," *New York Times,* January 25, 2006, p. A-23.

7. Interview with Noam Chomsky by Junaid Alam, December 7, 2004, Znet.com. Comment by Eric Hobsbawm, *Independent Review,* September 11, 2002. Noam Chomsky, *9–11,* Seven Stories Press, New York, 2002, p. 12.

8. William Blum, *Rogue State,* Common Courage Press, Monroe, Maine, 2005, p. 21. Pinter cited in *Granta,* London, March 2002. Jensen cited in James Bowman, "Towers of Intellect," *Wall Street Journal,* October 5, 2001. Mailer cited in "Notebook," *New Republic,* November 26, 2001.

9. Jean Baudrillard, *The Spirit of Terrorism and Requiem for the Twin Towers,* Verso, London, p. 5. Berthold cited in James Barron, "Professor Sorry for Pentagon Remark," *Daily Lobo,* New Mexico, September 24, 2001. De Genova cited by Tamar Lewin, "At Columbia, Call for Death of U.S. Forces Is Denounced," *New York Times,* March 29, 2003. Ward Churchill, *On the Justice of Roosting Chickens,* AK Press, Oakland, 2003, p. 14.

10. Glenda Gilmore, "Variations on Iraq," *Yale Daily News,* October 11, 2002. Joel Stein, "Warriors and Wusses," January 24, 2006, latimes.com. Churchill, *On the Justice of Roosting Chickens,* p. 21.

11. Hobsbawm, *The Independent Review,* September 11, 2002. Howard Zinn, "Our War on Terrorism," *The Progressive,* November 2004, p. 12. Robert Fisk, speech at Concordia University, Montreal, November 17, 2002, robert-fisk.com

12. Eric Foner remark, *London Review of Books,* October 4, 2001. Howard Zinn, "A Just Cause, Not a Just War," *The Progressive,* December 2001. Richard Falk, *The Great Terror War,* Olive Branch Press, New York, 2003, pp. 67, 92.

13. For the full list see www.nion.us.

14. Cited in *The New Republic,* December 27, 2004-January 10, 2005, p. 17.

15. Susan Watkins, "A Puppet for All Seasons," *Harper's*, December 2004, p. 20. Robert Jensen, "A Defeat for an Empire," *Fort Worth Star Telegram*, December 9, 2004. For Petty, see "Student Protest Stops CIA at NYU," April 4, 2005, antiwar.com. James Carroll, *Crusade*, Metropolitan Books, New York, 2004, p. 220. De Genova cited by Margaret Hunt Gram, "Professors Condemn War in Iraq at Teach-In," *Columbia Spectator*, March 26, 2003.

16. "Letter from al-Zawahiri to al-Zarqawi," October 11, 2005, Office of the Director of National Intelligence, www.dni.gov.

17. Editorial, "Democrats and the War," *The Nation*, November 28, 2005. Jeff Faux, "The Democrats' Opportunity," *Dissent*, winter 2006, p. 34. Al Franken, *Lies*, Plume Publishing, New York, 2004, p. 163. Joe Conason, *Big Lies*, Thomas Dunne Books, New York, 2003, p. 216. Cindy Sheehan, *Not One More Mother's Child*, Koa Books, Kihei, Hawaii, 2005, p. 116. Zbigniew Brzezinski, "The Dilemma of the Last Sovereign," *American Interest*, autumn 2005, p. 39.

18. Senator Barbara Boxer, speech at the Commonwealth Club, San Francisco, July 6, 2005. Bob Herbert, *Promises Betrayed*, Times Books, New York, 2005, p. 269.

19. Bill Clinton, statement at the Pentagon, February 17, 1998. Wesley Clark, "Bush Preemptive Strike Does Not Meet Test of Imminent Danger," *New Perspectives Quarterly*, spring 2003. Arthur Schlesinger, "The Immorality of Preemptive War," *New Perspectives Quarterly*, fall 2002.

20. Sheehan, *Not One More Mother's Child*, pp. 17, 26, 57, 67. Katha Pollitt, "Put Out No Flags," *The Nation*, October 28, 2001. Chalmers Johnson, *The Sorrows of Empire*, Henry Holt, New York, 2004, p. 229. Edward Said, *From Oslo to Iraq*, Pantheon, New York, 2004, p. 276. Arundhati Roy, *War Talk*, South End Press, Cambridge, Mass., 2003, p. 110. Michelle Goldberg, "The Peace Movement Prepares to Escalate," March 14, 2003, salon.com.

21. Steve Coll, *Ghost Wars*, Penguin, New York, 2004, p. 87.

22. Associated Press, "Gore Says America Betrayed by Bush," *USA Today*, February 8, 2004. Associated Press, "Kennedy Says Iraq War Case a Fraud," September 18, 2003.

23. Robert Tucker and David Hendrickson, "The Sources of American Legitimacy," *Foreign Affairs*, November-December 2004, p. 28.

24. Howard Zinn, "Dying for the Government," *Progressive*, June 2003; Howard Zinn, "Support Our Troops, Bring Them Home," *Miami Herald*,

January 22, 2005. Interview with Nancy Soderberg by Jon Stewart, *The Daily Show*, Comedy Central, March 1, 2005. Gary Kamiya, "Liberation Day," April 11, 2003, salon.com.

25.   Blum, *Rogue State*, pp.39–40. Fisk, *The Great War for Civilization*, p. 998.

26.   Arundhati Roy, *An Ordinary Person's Guide to Empire*, South End Press, Cambridge, 2004, p. 88. George Soros, *The Bubble of American Supremacy*, Public Affairs, New York, 2004, p. 22.

27.   For updated figures see iraqbodycount.net.

28.   Transcript of Peter Arnett interview on Iraqi TV, March 30, 2003, cnn.com.

29.   Gary Hart, "America the Vulnerable," *New York Review of Books*, October 20, 2005, p. 55. Soros, *The Bubble of American Supremacy*, p. 58.

30.   Maureen Dowd, *Bushworld*, G. P. Putnam, New York, 2004, p. 23. Tony Smith, "A Deal with the Devil," *Foreign Affairs*, November-December 2004, p. 130.

31.   Fouad Ajami, "The Way Forward," *US News and World Report*, May 30, 2005.

32.   Herbert, *Promises Betrayed*, p. 280. James Dobbins, "Iraq: Winning the Unwinnable War," *Foreign Affairs*, January-February 2005, p. 16. Robert Byrd, *Losing America*, W. W. Norton, New York, 2004, p. 212.

33.   Pete Yost, "Bush Warns Against U.S. Pullout from Iraq," December 18, 2005, aol.com. The data is summarized in "Iraq Index," Brookings Institution, Washington, D.C., May 18, 2006, brookings.edu.

34.   Bob Herbert, "Acts of Bravery," *New York Times*, January 31, 2005. Arianna Huffington, "Post Election Buzzkill," February 2, 2005, commondreams.org. Jonathan Steele, "The Cheers Were All Ours," *Guardian*, February 11, 2005. Robert Dreyfuss, "Civil War Elect," January 23, 2006, tompaine.com. Ivan Eland, "It's What We Do," *American Prospect*, January 2006, p. 38.

35.   Dowd, *Bushworld*, p. 443. Sam Zarifi, spokesman for Human Rights Watch, quoted in Paul Wiseman, "Afghanistan Marks Historic Yet Confusing Elections," *USA Today*, September 19, 2005, p. 1-A. Soros, *The Bubble of American Supremacy*, p. 45. Gilles Kepel, *The War for Muslim Minds*, Harvard University Press, Cambridge, 2004, p. 149. Senator Ted Kennedy, remarks at George Washington University, September 27, 2004.

36.   See previous note.

37.   Richard Clarke, *Against All Enemies*, Free Press, New York, 2004, p. xvii.

Jimmy Carter, *Our Endangered Values*, Simon & Schuster, New York, 2005, p. 158.

38. El Borai cited by Lawrence Kaplan, "Pressure Points," *The New Republic*, June 6-13, 2005, p. 23. Jumblatt cited in "Time for Syria to Go," *Economist*, February 6, 2005, p. 10.

39. Lawrence, ed., *Messages to the World*, p. 244.

40. "Full Text of Bin Laden Tape," January 19, 2006, newyorktimes.com.

TEN

1. "Seized Papers Said to Show Qaeda in Iraq Is Worried," *New York Times*, May 9, 2006, p. A-14.

2. Matthew Rothschild, "Why Zarqawi's Death Won't Solve the Iraq Crisis," June 8, 2006, progressive.org. Juan Cole, "Zarqawi Killed in Baquba," June 8, 2006, juancole.com. "The Death of Zarqawi," June 8, 2006, thenation.com.

3. "The Abu Ghraib Files," March 16, 2006, salon.com. Douglass Daniel, "Murtha: New Scandal Worse Than Abu Ghraib," AP Report, May 28, 2006; Editorial, "Why Haditha Matters," *The Nation*, June 19, 2006.

4. Mark Steyn, "Thumbs Up," *Washington Times*, December 19, 2005. David Horowitz, *Unholy Alliance*, Regnery, Washington, D.C., 2004.

5. Editorial, "A Threat to Iraqi Women," *New York Times*, March 24, 2005, p. A-22. Maureen Dowd, "Defining Victory Down," *New York Times*, January 9, 2005.

6. Sam Harris, *The End of Faith*, W. W. Norton, New York, 2005, p. 132. Joe Lockard, "Hegemonic Democracy in the Middle East," *Tikkun*, April-May 2005, p. 26.

7. Martha Nussbaum, *For Love of Country?* Beacon Press, Boston, 1996, p. 4. Richard Rorty, *Achieving Our Country*, Harvard University Press, Cambridge, 1998, p. 3.

8. "Morocco: Action Urged on Legal Code Reform," Human Rights Watch, March 20, 2001, Washington, D.C., hrw.org.

9. Sean Wilentz, "The Worst President in History?" *Rolling Stone*, May 4, 2006. Hobsbawm cited by Horowitz, *Unholy Alliance*, p. 61. "Saddam and Me: Interview with George Galloway," *Guardian*, September 16, 2002.

10. Paul Starr, "The Liberal Project Now," *American Prospect*, June 2005, p. 21.

11.   Ellen Willis, "The Pernicious Concept of Balance," *Chronicle of Higher Education*, September 9, 2005, p. B-11. John Nicholas, "Bill Moyers' Presidential Address," June 9, 2003, thenation.com.

12.   See, e.g., Felix Rohatyn, "Dead to the World," *New York Times*, January 26, 2006.

13.   Tony Judt, *Postwar*, Penguin, New York, 2005, p. 800.

14.   T. R. Reid, *The United States of Europe*, Penguin, New York, 2004, pp. 15, 154. Jeremy Rifkin, *The European Dream*, Penguin, New York, 2004, p. 3.

15.   Hillary Clinton, *It Takes a Village*, Touchstone Books, New York, 1996, pp. 221–22.

16.   George Soros, *The Bubble of American Supremacy*, Public Affairs, New York, 2004, p. 63.

17.   Rifkin, *The European Dream*, p. 304. Isobel Coleman, "Women, Islam and the New Iraq," *Foreign Affairs*, January-February 2006, pp. 37–38.

18.   Posting on April 1, 2004, dailykos.com.

19.   "Dean: U.S. Won't Win in Iraq," WOAI Radio, San Antonio, December 6, 2005, woai.com. Senator Patrick Leahy, statement on the Senate floor on the Iraq War, October 25, 2005. Zbigniew Brzezinski, "The Real Choice in Iraq," *Washington Post*, January 8, 2006.

20.   David Allyn, *Make Love, Not War*, Routledge, New York, 2001.

21.   Osama bin Laden, "To the People of Iraq," February 11, 2003, reprinted in Bruce Lawrence, ed., *Messages to the World*, Verso, London, 2005, p. 184.

ELEVEN

1.   Reuel Marc Gerecht, "Don't Fear the Shiites," *American Enterprise*, April-May 2005, p. 40.

2.   Pew Research Center, "Views of a Changing World," Washington, D.C., June 2003. Ronald Inglehart and Pippa Norris, "The True Clash of Civilizations," *Foreign Policy*, March-April 2003.

3.   Mustafa Akyol, "Show Us More of the Other America," *American Enterprise*, December 2004, taemag.com.

4.   Hamid Algar, *Roots of the Islamic Revolution in Iran*, Islamic Publications International, Oneonta, N.Y., 2001, p. 39. Khaled Abou El Fadl, *Islam*

and the Challenge of Democracy, Princeton University Press, Princeton, N.J., 2004, p. 30.

5.   Noah Feldman, *After Jihad*, Farrar, Straus and Giroux, New York, 2003, pp. 54, 60. Charles Taylor, *Modern Social Imaginaries*, Duke University Press, Durham, 2004.

6.   Seyyed Hossein Nasr, *The Heart of Islam*, HarperSanFrancisco, 2004, pp. 45, 184, 305. Mustafa Akyol, "Why Muslims Should Support Intelligent Design," September 14, 2004, islamonline.net. Akyol, "Show Us More of the Other America."

7.   Warren Hoge, "Rights Groups Fault U.S. Vote in U.N. on Gays," *New York Times*, January 27, 2006, p. A-6.

INDEX

ABOUT THE AUTHOR

Dinesh D'Souza, the Rishwain research scholar at the Hoover Institution at Stanford University, is the author of several bestselling books, including *Illiberal Education*, *The End of Racism*, and *What's So Great About America*. His Web site is dineshdsouza.com. He can be reached by email at dineshjdsouza@aol.com.